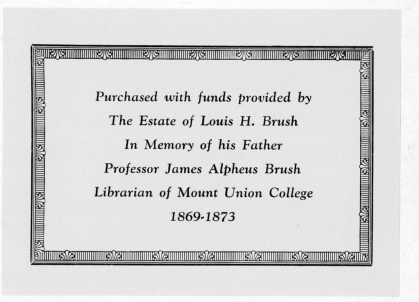

Excavation of Olive Mount

Samuel Smiles

THE LIVES OF
GEORGE AND ROBERT
STEPHENSON

Introduction by Eric de Maré

Bid Harbours open, Public Ways extend;
Bid Temples, worthier of God, ascend;
Bid the broad Arch the dang'rous flood contain,
The Mole projected break the roaring main,
Back to his bounds their subject sea command,
And roll obedient rivers through the land.
These honours, Peace to happy Britain brings;
These are imperial works, and worthy kings.

POPE

London
THE FOLIO SOCIETY
1975

The text of this edition is that of the author's last revision of 1874.
The cuts are taken from the edition of 1862.

PRINTED IN GREAT BRITAIN
by Richard Clay (The Chaucer Press) Ltd, Bungay, Suffolk

CONTENTS

PLATES

The publishers would like to thank the owners noted above for permission to reproduce the illustrations and John Bethal for providing photographs.

WOODCUTS

INTRODUCTION

THE LIFE of George Stephenson was published by John Murray in June 1857. It was Smiles's first popular work and it was so well received that his future as a writer was secure. Even the literati liked it, and George Eliot declared that she had read it with 'real profit and pleasure'. It was twice reprinted within the year and thereafter edition after edition appeared – an American one in 1858, an abridged English version in 1859, another edition with an added memoir by Robert Stephenson in 1864, and a centenary issue in 1881. By 1864 eighteen thousand copies had already been sold.

In 1861 and 1862 Smiles produced his famous panegyric, *The Lives of the Engineers*, in three volumes, the third volume being a revised and handsome version of his biography of George Stephenson with additional matter on his distinguished son Robert. It contained portraits of the two men engraved on steel and numerous wood engravings by Leitch and Skelton. The text reprinted here in full is that of the author's last version of 1874 together with some of the original engravings from the 1862 edition, as well as a number of the splendid lithographs that were published in monumental folios when the early railways were being so proudly and vigorously constructed.

The time is ripe for this reprint because the work has lasting value as a classic of its kind and second-hand copies of earlier editions are hard to come by; moreover, a general interest has grown during the last decade in the artifacts and structures of early industry which are now being studied and systematized under the new discipline of Industrial Archaeology. The book remains of value on three counts: as an accurate piece of technical and social history of a pregnant period – as a well-carpentered and thumping success story which, unlike the once immensely popular rags-to-riches tales such as those by the American Horatio Alger, is based not on fiction but on fact – and as the expression of a view of life that raises deep issues in moral philosophy, and therefore in political economy, which are moot. Indeed, the work indirectly tells us as much about the nature of a writer who had considerable standing and a world-wide influence a century ago as it does about its two famous subjects.

The Lives of the Engineers is pure hagiography, and of all those enshrined in Smiles's canon of industrious saints, George Stephenson, Father of Railways, was clearly his favourite. George comes alive vividly in the flesh in the biography, whereas his equally meritorious and productive son, builder of bridges of unprecedented techniques on an heroic scale, remains a somewhat remote figure like a statesman carved in white marble. A reason for this may be that the son, having had some formal education, became a rich bourgeois gentleman and so was to Smiles a less dramatic, interesting model of success than his father, the prototype of the working man who was entirely self-made as a result of character, thrift, perseverance, early rising, self-instruction, unremitting effort, and the continence that keeps him off women and drink. (Smiles rarely mentions women at all except as dim, domestic appendages to men; being no doubt wary of the Monstrous Regiment, one wonders how he reacted to Mill's *Subjection of Women* when it was published in 1869.)

The life of Samuel Smiles can be briefly told. One of eleven children of a paper-maker and merchant, he was born in 1812 (the year of the retreat from Moscow and the start of the war with America) at Haddington near Edinburgh, which significantly was also the birthplace of John Knox. He thus came into the world in the second year of the Regency and lived his long life right through Victoria's reign and into Edwardian years. Educated at the local grammar school and later at Edinburgh University, he qualified as a medical doctor in 1832, the year his father died of cholera. He began practising as a GP in his home town, supplementing his limited income by lecturing and journalism, but he failed to persevere in medicine and in 1838 departed on a tour of the Continent. On his return he became editor of the *Leeds Times*, being a supporter of the advanced liberal cause but an opponent of such radicalism as that of the Chartists. In 1840 at the opening of the North Midland Railway running between Leeds and Derby he met George Stephenson for the first time. Four years later he resigned his editorship to devote himself for some months to freelance lecturing and literary hackwork. Then in 1845 he took the post of assistant secretary of the projected Leeds and Thirsk Railway, and for the next twenty-one years he was closely connected with railway enterprise. In 1854 he left Leeds for London on his appointment as secretary to the South Eastern Railway, a post he held for the next twelve years. During this period he wrote his two most famous works, *The Lives of the Engineers* and *Self Help*. The latter appeared in 1859, a fertile year in Victorian publishing which conceived Darwin's *Origin*, Mill's *On Liberty*, Tennyson's *Idylls of the King*, Dickens's *A Tale of Two Cities*, George Eliot's *Adam Bede*, and, by way of philosophical contrast to Smiles's hopeful, dutiful *Self Help*, Fitzgerald's sensual, despairing, fatalistic *Omar Khayyám*. *The Rubáiyát* sold poorly while *Self Help*, that compendium of 'anecdotal illustration of life and character' was a momentous and lasting success. By 1905, a year after the author's death, it had sold no less than a quarter of a million copies, it had been translated into many languages and extracts from it had even been displayed on the walls of the khedive's palace in Egypt. It is still available as a paper-back. None of Smiles's other books – *Thrift, Duty, Life and Labour, The Huguenots, Boulton and Watt, Iron Workers and Tool Makers*, to mention the more important ones – were so successful for they tended to become repetitious on the theme that obsessed their author: biographical facts and entertaining anecdotes to illustrate and enliven an endless sermon on the Gospel of Toil.

In 1866 Smiles left the South Eastern Railway to become President of the National Provident Institution, but in 1871 he suffered a stroke, due no doubt to over-addiction to his creed. It disabled him for a year, but he recovered well to live for another thirty-two years. During those years he travelled a good deal in France, collecting information on the Huguenots and on the barber-poet of Agen, Jacques Jasmin (1798–1864), on whom he published a monograph in 1891. He spent his last years, before senility set in, on his autobiography which was not published until after he had died in his Kensington home in 1904 and been buried in Brompton Cemetery. He had married in Leeds in 1843 and his wife bore three daughters and two sons.

In his original Preface to his biography of the Stephensons, Smiles explained how the relations between father and son, notably in the improvement of locomotion and the building of the first passenger railways, were so intimately connected that it is impossible to dissociate the story of the one engineer from that of the other, and he tells how the work came to be written. The idea of writing George Stephenson's biography was suggested to Smiles soon after the engineer's death in 1848 by James Kitson, a locomotive manu-facturer and Mayor of Leeds, who considered that Smiles's con-nection with railways, his personal knowledge of the man, and his other qualifications fitted him well for the task. In 1851, the Crystal Palace year, Smiles called on Robert Stephenson at his office in Great George Street, Westminster, to broach the project. Robert was not particularly enthusiastic, believing the theme unlikely 'to attract the attention of literary men of eminence'; nor was he 'sanguine as to its popular interest, though his view on this point afterwards underwent a change'. Smiles decided that, in any case, a satisfactory biography could only be prepared after a period of residence in the district where George Stephenson had lived. He therefore abandoned the idea.

Three years later in 1854, however, his railway job took him by luck to Newcastle-upon-Tyne and there he was at last able to make his local researches in his leisure time. 'Thus, helped by the recollections of the engineer's former associates, his life was traced from boyhood to manhood, from the cradle almost to the grave.' All who had known George Stephenson in his early years were proud to speak of him, Smiles records, and to communicate what they remembered of his history. 'Though he had risen so much above them, there did not seem to mingle an atom of jealousy or envy in their recollections of him. They begrudged him neither his prosperity nor his fame. They spoke of "George" as if he had been of their own kin, a member of their own family, and were as proud of his career as if it had been their own.' A number of meetings with his son Robert supplied Smiles with further information. Being based on first-hand, eye-witness accounts, the work is therefore as near factual authenticity as any biography can hope to be, and this is one of its merits.

Smiles was a competent journalist and, in spite of the nagging insistence of his moralizing, he could hold the attention of his readers for he would always tell a good story and, with a rare skill, he could explain technical matters in a clear, simple way without jargon. He was the type of canny, obsessional, meticulous, and somewhat humourless Scot reared by a hard country in the Puritan tradition of Calvin and Knox. No doubt he felt an affinity with his hero, or as we now say, he could readily identify himself with the man whose grandparents, according to tradition, had crossed the border on the loss of considerable property in Scotland. George Stephenson, if we are to believe all the eulogies, does appear to have personified every mid-Victorian virtue as a paragon of self-help, thrift, duty, continence, perseverance, initiative, and tireless application – the all-conquering Super Ego incarnate of muscular Christianity. He kept his iron constitution going by an austere diet and plenty of manly exercise, and Smiles tells the lively anecdote of how he would still enjoy a wrestle in his advancing years with a friend at his son's London premises when nothing else was stirring. As Robert recalled, 'The two wrestled together so often and had so many "falls" (sometimes I thought they would bring the house down between them), that they broke half the chairs in my outer office. I remember once sending my father in a joiner's bill of about £2.10s. for mending broken chairs.'

Even if we make allowance for Smiles's righteous motive, the two engineers we discern through his words were clearly men of remarkable talents and character, not least in their tenacity and courage. Perhaps only the opportunities and incentives combined with the social-economic and moral situation of the early Victorian era could have produced men of such outstanding initiative and invention. Giants like them cannot be bred today.

The two Stephensons were by universal consent the chief progenitors of the Railway Age, an age that changed the life and face not only of Britain but of the whole world, and impelled the Industrial Revolution on to ever-growing momentum in a century which, in spite of the exploitation and degradation of the machine-minding urban masses, in spite of the shock to fundamentalism produced by *The Origin of Species*, in spite of the increasing doubts as the century advanced of the sanctity of uncontrolled *laissez-*

faire remained, nevertheless, more optimistic and confident than
our own has become.

To have risen from a farm boy, a picker of stones from coal heaps
and a colliery fireman to inventing and making a workable locomotive and organizing a number of magnificent new railway lines
with their great cuttings, embankments, tunnels, viaducts, and
termini, as George Stephenson did, must continue to inspire un-
stinted admiration. It was, of course, George's invention of the
steam blast combined with the multi-tubular boiler to locomotives
that ensured the general adoption and phenomenal success of the
railways. Two appendices, mainly written by Robert Stephenson,
that were printed at the end of the third volume of *The Lives of
the Engineers* have been omitted here. Suffice it to say that they
explain the improvements George Stephenson brought both to
permanent ways and to the steam locomotive; the second appendix
establishes the father's right to claim the invention of the steam
blast by which combustion and therefore power were so greatly
increased by sending the exuded waste steam up the chimney to
increase the draught.

In spite of aggressive, concerted opposition by the vested
interests against the construction of railways – by owners of land,
canals, carriages, stage-coaches, inns, and horse studs, as well as by
aesthetes like John Ruskin, the development of railways throughout the United Kingdom after the opening of the Stockton and
Darlington line in 1825 was a national undertaking on a gigantic
scale. It was accomplished at an incredible speed stimulated
eventually by speculation that reached a manic phase. Nothing so
vast in construction had ever before been achieved in human
history. The astounding growth of the iron network is revealed at
the end of Smiles's *Life of George Stephenson* published in 1857,
where an address on *The Railway System and its Results* was
printed which had been delivered by Robert Stephenson to the
Institute of Civil Engineers on his election as President in
January 1856.

By the end of 1854 about 18,000 miles of line had been laid –
nearly sufficient to girdle the globe – the work of only some twenty-
five years. To finance it £286 millions had been raised, about a
quarter of which had been expended on the purchase of land and its
conveyancing. In 1854 the number of passengers carried had
reached over three millions in the year – treble the number carried
ten years previously in 1845. Apart from passengers the railways
were also carrying mail and tremendous quantities of goods, not

least of coal – a traffic which the canals could not have accomplished on their own, however far extended, owing to the limits of water supplies to fill them. By 1854 seventy miles of tunnel had been constructed, often against immense difficulties caused by flooding; eleven miles of viaduct had been built in London and its suburbs alone, while no less than 25,000 railway bridges had been erected throughout the country, which is far more than the total number that had existed before. Five hundred and fifty million cubic yards of earth had been shifted by the muscles and barrows of formidable gangs of navvies which represented a mountain half a mile in diameter at its base towering a mile and a half into the clouds. All these lines required the working of at least 5,000 locomotive engines, while the vehicles of every kind needed would compose a train stretching 500 miles, that is from London to Aberdeen. (The railways, of course, made possible the gargantuan growth of cities in the nineteenth century. John Kellet notes in *The Impact of Railways on Victorian Cities* (1969) that 'in London, something of the order of eight hundred acres of central land was taken for railway uses in the course of the nineteenth century; an area sufficient for a fair sized town in itself'.)

Robert Stephenson, no doubt thinking of his own early years and of his 'late revered father' who had handed over to him all his railway appointments in 1840 when he retired at the age of sixty to a country retreat and who had died in his sixty-seventh year eight years previously in 1848, thus concluded his address: 'Our business, from a craft, has become a profession.' It could be a most remunerative profession, for Robert Stephenson became the first of the engineering millionaires.

Industrial development depends essentially on improvements in transport and communications, and it was the early engineers who provided them along the new roads, canals, and railways – men such as Heav'n-taught Brindley, Macadam, Telford, Rennie, Brunel, and the Stephensons. Until the Turnpike Acts improved the appalling roads that existed in the country and the brief, picturesque period of the stage-coach arrived, most transport had been by lumbering waggon or by pack-horse. When, in fact, did the Industrial Revolution begin? Some might say when a primitive man first lifted up a stone to hurl it at his prey, others that it was born in the inquiring minds of the Renaissance, others still that its true start came with the invention of new instruments of navigation in the seventeenth century. But if the Revolution can be said

to have had any clear and definite start it was surely when Coal,
Steam, and Iron were concatenated. And where could this so
readily have occurred as in England? Steam power, first through
the inventions of Newcomen and then of Watt, enabled deep
mines to be pumped clear of water, while the marriage of coal and
iron was consummated first by the new canals and then by the
railways which the canals to their own eventual disadvantage as
carriers made possible. Developments in the production of iron,
and later of steel, provided impetus and so did the revelation of
unsuspected ironstone beds when earth was being excavated for
the railways. On the psychological and social side of the situation
tremendous energy was released with the rapid rise, inaugurated
by the first Reform Act, of the new middle classes, with their
individualistic Puritan outlook and dedication to work, competitive struggle, and gain. They slowly undermined the old feudal
power and patronage of the landed aristocracy who regarded the
enjoyment of good, and therefore leisurely, living as their natural
birthright. Hence the whirring, smoky squalor of the Satanic mills,
the fogs of Victorian England, and ultimately the melancholy
twentieth-century words of Ambrose Silk in Evelyn Waugh's *Put
Out More Flags*: 'We had a foggy habit of life, and a rich, obscure,
choking literature. The great catch in the throat of English lyric
poetry is just *fog*, my dear, on the vocal chords. And out of that
fog we could rule the world; we were a voice of Sinai smiling
through the clouds. . . . *Then* some busybody invents electricity or
oil fuel or whatever it is they use nowadays. The fog lifts, the
world sees us as we are, and worse still, we see ourselves as we are.'

The impact of Protestant religion, particularly in its evangelical
guise, and in the industrial districts the abiding influence of
Wesley, was immense, not least in its faith that *laborare est orare*.
As Professor Tawney wrote in his notable *Religion and the Rise of
Capitalism*, 'The transition from the anabaptist to the company
promoter was less abrupt than might at first sight be supposed. It
had been prepared, however unintentionally, by Puritan moralists.
In their emphasis on the normal duty of untiring activity, on work
as an end in itself, on the evils of luxury and extravagance, on
foresight and thrift, on moderation and self-discipline and rational
calculation, they had created an ideal of Christian conduct which
canonized as an ethical principle the efficiency which economic
theorists were preaching as a specific for social disorders. . . . The
magnificent energy which changed in a century the face of material
civilization was to draw nourishment from that temper. The wor-

ship of production and ever greater production – the slavish drudgery of the millionaire and his unhappy servants – was to be hallowed by the precepts of the same compelling creed.'

Part of that creed lies in the reliance on personal character rather than on mutual aid and social organization. As Smiles firmly believed, 'National progress is the sum of individual industry, energy, and uprightness as national decay is of individual idleness, selfishness, and vice.' He would hardly have sympathized with Tawney's comment that 'a society which reverences the attainment of riches as the supreme felicity will naturally be disposed to regard the poor as damned in the next world, if only to justify itself for making their life a hell in this'.

Smiles had a host of eager listeners who aspired to middle-class status. His *Self Help* was, in fact, first presented in the mid-forties as a lecture to an audience of young workmen in Leeds who had set up a school for mutual improvement and wished to get on. As a liberal in the line of the Benthamite Felicitarians, he was not a fanatical supporter of *laissez-faire* and he saw sense in the social provision at least of schools, libraries, and drains. Yet in his advocacy of self-help and his faith that its rewards were available to any man, however humble his origins might be, he was clearly turning a blind eye on the egregious horrors of uncontrolled industrialism and its appalling poverty. He was misleading himself and his million readers. From the struggling, impoverished, exploited, and degenerating masses of Victorian England, only a handful of exceptional men like George Stephenson could possibly have emerged, and such inevitably came from healthy rural stock. As the century advanced opportunities of self-improvement grew ever less possible even for those of outstanding gifts and intelligence. How could a man with little or no education who, with a family to support, was compelled to toil all hours to gain £1 a week escape from his thraldom? He was worse off than a chattel slave for he had no security and a spell of unemployment resulting from a cyclical financial crisis which was not of his making, however hard he might be willing to work, could bring him and his family down either to utter degradation or to the dreaded workhouse, which could in some ways be worse than prison.

Smiles was presenting a dream. The best that can be said of it is that its homilies did less physical harm as dope than the chief solace of Victorian England – gin. And how could the average working man be thrifty if he and his family were not to go hungry and cold? Though shrewd enough, Smiles was no thinker and his

views were narrow. Intellectually he cheated, and he obviously
had no understanding of the monetary system with its built-in
mechanism of debt which can never be liquidated, and which, with
the support of the Bank Charter Act of 1844, was to gain ever-
increasing control of industry and governments as the nineteenth
century advanced. He naïvely assumed, as many still do, that
industry itself in some mystical way creates the purchasing power
by means of which its products can all be distributed. As for thrift,
how could industry flourish and its goods all be sold if men saved
large parts of their incomes for re-investment and thus curtailed
the available purchasing power which could not then cover the full
costs of production? Here lies paradox: you grow rich by im-
posing needless poverty on yourself. The paradox still prevails.

By the end of the nineteenth century the circumstances that had
allowed the rise of a few rare spirits like George Stephenson had
long since vanished. The philistine advice of Smiles and his kind
was seen at last to be if not entirely irrational at least ana-
chronistic. Some time before he died his popularity had waned,
and his final manuscript called *Conduct* was rejected by his pub-
lisher in 1898. Smiles praised Herschel for making his own reflecting telescope because he could not afford to buy one, but even a
Herschel might be daunted today by the thought of knocking up a
Jodrell Bank by himself in his backyard.

Of course virtue is always virtue but the circumstances must
exist as the soil from which it can grow. Yet to his credit Smiles
was no snob and believed that a true and natural Gentleman could
be found in any class of society. Although he stressed the value of
self-education, Smiles mentions Dr Arnold of Rugby with approval
a number of times in *Self Help*. He would hardly have approved of
the cynic who remarked that the Gentleman was merely the invention of the aristocracy designed to keep the middle classes in
order.

Having the outlook of a bourgeois provincial, Smiles was
against theory, imagination, and the classical, humanist tradition
of the aristocracy with its power to connect ideas. He preferred
deeds to words as a lover of mechanical do-it-yourself practicality
and the piling up of atomized bits and pieces of knowledge. His
aim, like others of his kind, was the reconciliation of the working
and middle classes through the universal acceptance of the liberal,
let-me-be-buried-with-the-men kind of stand. This complacent
teaching pervaded and weakened the whole labour movement, and
perhaps it played its part, as the building of the railways certainly

did, in preventing revolution in these islands by dangling an unattainable carrot before the donkey's nose.

Chained as we still are today by Puritan tradition, we are at last beginning to realize, if in a confused way, that the retention of the ethic of unremitting toil imposed on everyone for ever, together with the unworkable monetary system it has generated and the fortress wall it has erected between the concepts of Work and Leisure, does not make sense in the situation of the Second Industrial Revolution which is now upon us.

In spite of all this, perhaps in a way because of it, Smiles's major books remain historical documents which are revealing, informative, and highly entertaining. Among them *The Lives of the Stephensons* is the most readable. It would have been difficult to write a dull book about two such people; as Emerson remarked of the father, it had been worth crossing the Atlantic merely to meet him. Now we can here read all about both father and son in the way George Eliot did over a century ago – with 'real profit and pleasure'.

ERIC DE MARÉ

THE LIVES OF

GEORGE AND ROBERT STEPHENSON

CHAPTER I — NEWCASTLE AND THE GREAT NORTHERN COAL-FIELD

IN no quarter of England have greater changes been wrought by the successive advances made in the practical science of engineering than in the extensive colliery districts of the North, of which Newcastle-upon-Tyne is the centre and the capital.

In ancient times the Romans planted a colony at Newcastle, throwing a bridge across the Tyne near the site of the low-level bridge and erecting a strong fortification above it on the high ground now occupied by the Central Railway Station. North and north-west lay a wild country, abounding in moors, mountains, and morasses, but occupied to a certain extent by fierce and barbarous tribes. To defend the young colony against their ravages, a strong wall was built by the Romans, extending from Wallsend on the north bank of the Tyne, a few miles below Newcastle, across the country to Burgh-upon-Sands on the Solway Firth. The remains of the wall are still to be traced in the less populous hill-districts of Northumberland. In the neighbourhood of Newcastle they have been gradually effaced by the works of succeeding generations, though the 'Wallsend' coal consumed in our household fires still serves to remind us of the great Roman work.

After the withdrawal of the Romans, Northumbria became planted by immigrant Saxons from North Germany and Norsemen from Scandinavia, whose Eorls or Earls made Newcastle their principal seat. Then came the Normans, from whose *New* Castle, built some eight hundred years since, the town derived its present name. The keep of this venerable structure, black with age and smoke, still stands entire at the northern end of the noble high-level bridge – the utilitarian work of modern times thus confronting the warlike relic of the older civilization.

The nearness of Newcastle to the Scotch Border was a great hindrance to its security and progress in the middle ages of English history. Indeed, the district between it and Berwick continued to be ravaged by moss-troopers long after the union of the Crowns. The gentry lived in their strong Peel castles; even the larger farm-houses were fortified; and bloodhounds were trained for the purpose of tracking the cattle-reavers to their retreats in the hills. The Judges of Assize rode from Carlisle to Newcastle guarded by an escort armed to the teeth. A tribute called 'dagger and protection money' was annually paid by the Sheriff of Newcastle for the purpose of providing daggers and other weapons for the escort; and, though the need of such protection has long since ceased, the tribute continues to be paid in broad gold pieces of the time of Charles the First.

Until about the middle of last century the roads across Northumberland were little better than horse-tracks, and not many years since the primitive agricultural cart with solid wooden wheels was almost as common in the western parts of the county as it is in Spain now. The tract of the old Roman road continued to be the most practicable route between Newcastle and Carlisle, the traffic between the two towns having been carried along it upon pack-horses until a comparatively recent period.

Since that time great changes have taken place on the Tyne. When wood for firing became scarce and dear, and the forests of the South of England were found inadequate to supply the increasing demand for fuel, attention was turned to the rich stores of coal lying underground in the neighbourhood of Newcastle and Durham. It then became an article of increasing export, and 'seacoal' fires gradually supplanted those of wood. Hence an old writer described Newcastle as 'the Eye of the North, and the Hearth that warmeth the South parts of this kingdom with Fire'. Fuel has become the staple product of the district, the quantity exported increasing from year to year, until the coal raised from these northern mines amounts to upwards of sixteen millions of tons a year, of which not less than nine millions are annually conveyed away by sea.

Newcastle has in the meantime spread in all directions far beyond its ancient boundaries. From a walled medieval town of monks and merchants, it has been converted into a busy centre of commerce and manufactures inhabited by nearly 100,000 people. It is no longer a Border fortress – a 'shield and defence against the invasions and frequent insults of the Scots', as described in ancient charters – but a busy centre of peaceful industry, and the outlet for a vast amount of steam-power, which is exported in the form of coal to all parts of the world. Newcastle is in many respects a town of singular and curious interest, especially in its older parts, which are full of crooked lanes and narrow streets, wynds, and chares,* formed by tall, antique houses, rising tier above tier along the steep northern bank of the Tyne, as the similarly precipitous streets of Gateshead crowd the opposite shore.

All over the coal region, which extends from the Coquet to the Tees, about fifty miles from north to south, the surface of the soil exhibits the signs of extensive underground workings. As you pass through the country at night, the earth looks as if it were bursting with fire at many points; the blaze of coke-ovens, iron-furnaces, and coal-heaps reddening the sky to such a distance that the horizon seems to be a glowing belt of fire.

From the necessity which existed for facilitating the transport of coals from the pits to the shipping places, it is easy to understand how the railway and the locomotive should have first found their home in such a district as we have thus briefly described. At an early period the coal was carried to the boats in panniers, or in sacks upon horses' backs. Then carts were used, to facilitate the progress of which tramways of flag-stone were laid down. This led to the enlargement of the vehicle, which became known as a waggon, and it was mounted on four wheels instead of two. A local writer about the middle of the seventeenth century says, 'Many thousand people are engaged in this trade of coals; many live by working of them in the pits; and many live by conveying them in waggons and wains to the river Tyne.'

Still further to facilitate the haulage of the waggons, pieces of planking were laid parallel upon wooden sleepers, or imbedded in

---

* In the Newcastle dialect, a chare is a narrow street or lane. At the local assizes some years since, one of the witnesses in a criminal trial swore that 'he saw three men come out of the foot of a chare'. The judge cautioned the jury not to pay any regard to the man's evidence, as he must be insane. A little explanation by the foreman, however, satisfied his lordship that the original statement was correct.

the ordinary track, by which friction was still further diminished. It is said that these wooden rails were first employed by one Beaumont, about 1630; and on a road thus laid, a single horse was capable of drawing a large loaded waggon from the coal-pit to the shipping staith. Roger North, in 1676, found the practice had become extensively adopted, and he speaks of the large sums then paid for way-leaves; that is, the permission granted by the owners of lands lying between the coal-pit and the river-side to lay down a tramway between the one and the other. A century later, Arthur Young observed that not only had these roads become greatly multiplied, but important works had been constructed to carry them along upon the same level. 'The coal-waggon roads from the pits to the water,' he says, 'are great works, carried over all sorts of inequalities of ground, so far as the distance of nine or ten miles. The tracks of the wheels are marked with pieces of wood let into the road for the wheels of the waggons to run on, by which one horse is enabled to draw, and that with ease, fifty or sixty bushels of coals.'*

Similar waggon-roads were laid down in the coal district of Wales, Cumberland, and Scotland. At the time of the Scotch rebellion in 1745, a tramroad existed between the Tranent coal-pits and the small harbour of Cockenzie in East Lothian; and a portion of the line was selected by General Cope as a position for his cannon at the battle of Prestonpans.

In these rude wooden tracks we find the germ of the modern rail-road. Improvements were gradually made in them. Thus, at some collieries, thin plates of iron were nailed upon their upper surface, for the purpose of protecting the parts most exposed to friction. Cast-iron rails were also tried, the wooden rails having been found liable to rot. The first rails of this kind are supposed to have been used at Whitehaven as early as 1738. This cast-iron road was denominated a 'plate-way', from the plate-like form in which the rails were cast. In 1767, as appears from the books of the Coal-brookdale Iron Works, in Shropshire, five or six tons of rails were cast, as an experiment, on the suggestion of Mr Reynolds, one of the partners; and they were shortly after laid down to form a road.

In 1776, a cast-iron tramway, nailed to wooden sleepers, was laid down at the Duke of Norfolk's colliery near Sheffield. The person who designed and constructed this coal line was Mr John Curr, whose son has erroneously claimed for him the invention of

*Six Months' Tour, vol. iii.9.

the cast-iron railway. He certainly adopted it early, and thereby met the fate of men before their age; for his plan was opposed by the labouring people of the colliery, who got up a riot in which they tore up the road and burnt the coal-staith, while Mr Curr fled into a neighbouring wood for concealment, and lay there *perdu* for three days and nights, to escape the fury of the populace. The plates of these early tramways had a ledge cast on their edge to guide the wheel along the road.

In 1789, Mr William Jessop constructed a railway at Loughborough, in Leicestershire, and there introduced the cast-iron edge-rail, with flanches cast upon the tire of the waggon-wheels to keep them on the track, instead of having the margin or flanch cast upon the rail itself; and this plan was shortly after adopted in other places. In 1800, Mr Benjamin Outram, of Little Eaton, in Derbyshire (father of the distinguished General Outram), used stone props instead of timber for supporting the ends or joinings of the rails. Thus the use of railroads, in various forms, gradually extended, until they were found in general use all over the mining districts.

Such was the growth of the railway, which, it will be observed, originated in necessity, and was modified according to experience; progress in this, as in all departments of mechanics, having been effected by the exertions of many men, one generation entering upon the labours of that which preceded it, and carrying them onward to further stages of improvement. We shall afterwards find that the invention of the locomotive was made by like successive steps. It was not the invention of one man, but of a succession of men, each working at the proper hour, and according to the needs of that hour; one inventor interpreting only the first word of the problem which his successors were to solve after long and laborious efforts and experiments. 'The locomotive is not the invention of one man,' said Robert Stephenson at Newcastle, 'but of a nation of mechanical engineers.'

The same circumstances which led to the rapid extension of railways in the coal districts of the north tended to direct the attention of the mining engineers to the early development of the powers of the steam-engine as a useful instrument of motive power. The necessity which existed for a more effective method of hauling the coals from the pits to the shipping-places was constantly present to many minds; and the daily pursuits of a large class of mechanics occupied in the management of steam power, by which the coal was raised from the pits, and the mines were pumped clear of water, had the effect of directing their attention to the same agency as the best means for accomplishing that object.

Among the upper-ground workmen employed at the coal-pits, the principal are the firemen, enginemen, and brakesmen, who fire and work the engines, and superintend the machinery by means of which the collieries are worked. Previous to the introduction of the steam-engine the usual machine employed for the purpose was what is called a 'gin'. The gin consists of a large drum placed horizontally, round which ropes attached to buckets and corves are wound, which are thus drawn up or sent down the shafts by a horse travelling in a circular track or 'gin race'. This method was employed for drawing up both coals and water, and it is still used for the same purpose in small collieries; but where the quantity of water to be raised is great, pumps worked by steam power are called into requisition.

Newcomen's atmospheric engine was first made use of to work the pumps; and it continued to be so employed long after the more powerful and economical condensing engine of Watt had been invented. In the Newcomen or 'fire engine', as it was called, the power is produced by the pressure of the atmosphere forcing down the piston in the cylinder, on a vacuum being produced within it by condensation of the contained steam by means of cold-water injection. The piston-rod is attached to one end of a lever, while the pump-rod works in connection with the other – the hydraulic action employed to raise the water being exactly similar to that of a common sucking-pump.

The working of a Newcomen engine was a clumsy and apparently a very painful process, accompanied by an extraordinary amount of wheezing, sighing, creaking, and bumping. When the pump descended, there was heard a plunge, a heavy sigh, and a loud bump: then, as it rose, and the sucker began to act, there was heard a creak, a wheeze, another bump, and then a strong rush of water as it was lifted and poured out. Where engines of a more powerful and improved description are used, the quantity of water raised is enormous – as much as a million and a half gallons in the twenty-four hours.

The pitmen, or 'the lads belaw', who work out the coal below ground, are a peculiar class, quite distinct from the workmen on the surface. They are a people with peculiar habits, manners, and character, as much as fishermen and sailors, to whom, indeed, they bear, in some respects, a considerable resemblance. Some fifty years since they were a much rougher and worse educated class than they are now; hard workers, but very wild and uncouth; much given to 'steeks', or strikes; and distinguished, in their hours of leisure and on pay-nights, for their love of cock-fighting, dog-fighting, hard drinking, and cuddy races. The pay-night was a fortnightly saturnalia, in which the pitman's character was fully brought out, especially when the 'yel' was good. Though earning much higher wages than the ordinary labouring population of the upper soil, the latter did not mix nor intermarry with them; so that they were left to form their own communities, and hence their marked peculiarities as a class. Indeed, a sort of traditional dis-repute seems long to have clung to the pitmen, arising perhaps from the nature of their employment, and from the circumstance that the colliers were among the last classes enfranchized in England, as they were certainly the last in Scotland, where they continued bondmen down to the end of last century. The last thirty years, however, have worked a great improvement in the moral condition of the Northumbrian pitmen; the abolition of the twelve months' bond to the mine, and the substitution of a month's notice previous to leaving, having given them greater freedom and opportunity for obtaining employment; and day-schools and Sunday Schools, together with the important influences of rail-ways, have brought them fully up to a level with the other classes of the labouring population.

The coals, when raised from the pits, are emptied into the waggons placed alongside, from whence they are sent along the rails to the staiths erected by the riverside, the waggons sometimes descending by their own gravity along inclined planes, the waggoner standing behind to check the speed by means of a convoy or wooden brake bearing upon the rims of the wheels. Arrived at the staiths, the waggons are emptied at once into the ships waiting alongside for cargo. Anyone who has sailed down the Tyne from Newcastle Bridge cannot but have been struck with the appearance of the immense staiths, constructed of timber, which are erected at short distances from each other on both sides of the river.

But a great deal of the coal shipped from the Tyne comes from above-bridge, where seagoing craft cannot reach, and is floated down the river in 'keels', in which the coals are sometimes piled up according to convenience when large, or, when the coal is small or tender, it is conveyed in tubs to prevent breakage. These keels are of a very ancient model – perhaps the oldest extant in England: they are even said to be of the same build as those in which the Norsemen navigated the Tyne centuries ago. The keel is a tubby, grimy-looking craft, rounded fore and aft, with a single large square sail, which the keel-bullies, as the Tyne watermen are called, manage with great dexterity; the vessel being guided by the aid of the 'swape', or great oar, which is used as a kind of rudder at the stern of the vessel. These keelmen are an exceedingly hardy class of workmen, not by any means so quarrelsome as their designation of 'bully' would imply — the word being merely derived from the obsolete term 'boolie', or beloved, an appellation still in familiar use among brother workers in the coal districts. One of the most curious sights upon the Tyne is the fleet of hundreds of these black-sailed, black-hulled keels, bringing down at each tide their black cargoes for the ships at anchor in the deep water at Shields and other parts of the river below Newcastle.

These preliminary observations will perhaps be sufficient to explain the meaning of many of the occupations alluded to, and the phrases employed, in the course of the following narrative, some of which might otherwise have been comparatively unintelligible to the general reader.

CHAPTER II — WYLAM AND DEWLEY BURN — GEORGE STEPHENSON'S EARLY YEARS

THE colliery village of Wylam is situated on the north bank of the Tyne, about eight miles west of Newcastle. The Newcastle and Carlisle railway runs along the opposite bank; and the traveller by that line sees the usual signs of a colliery in the unsightly pumping-engines surrounded by heaps of ashes, coal-dust, and slag; while a neighbouring iron-furnace, in full blast throws out dense smoke and loud jets of steam by day and lurid flames at night. These works form the nucleus of the village, which is almost entirely occupied by coal-miners and iron-furnacemen. The place is remarkable for its large population, but not for its cleanness or neatness as a village; the houses, as in most colliery villages, being the property of the owners or lessees, who employ them in temporarily accommodating the workpeople, against whose earnings there is a weekly set-off for house and coals. About the end of last century the estate of which Wylam forms part, belonged to Mr Blackett, a gentleman of considerable celebrity in coal-mining, then more generally known as the proprietor of the *Globe* newspaper.

There is nothing to interest one in the village itself. But a few

hundred yards from its eastern extremity stands a humble detached dwelling, which will be interesting to many as the birthplace of one of the most remarkable men of our times – George
Stephenson, the Railway Engineer. It is a common two-storeyed,
red-tiled, rubble house, portioned off into four labourers' apart-
ments. It is known by the name of High Street House, and was
originally so called because it stands by the side of what used to
be the old riding post road or street between Newcastle and
Hexham, along which the post was carried on horseback within
the memory of persons living.

The lower room in the west end of this house was the home of
the Stephenson family; and there George Stephenson was born, the
second of a family of six children, on 9 June 1781. The apartment
is now, what it was then, an ordinary labourer's dwelling – its walls
are unplastered, its floor is of clay, and the bare rafters are
exposed overhead.

Robert Stephenson, or 'Old Bob', as the neighbours familiarly
called him, and his wife Mabel, were a respectable couple, careful
and hard-working. It is said that Robert Stephenson's father was a
Scotchman, and came into England as a gentleman's servant.
Mabel, his wife, was the daughter of Robert Carr, a dyer at
Ovingham. When first married, they lived at Walbottle, a village
situated between Wylam and Newcastle, afterwards removing to
Wylam, where Robert was employed as fireman of the old pumping-engine at that colliery.

An old Wylam collier, who remembered George Stephenson's
father, thus described him: 'Geordie's fayther war like a peer o'
deals nailed thegither, an' a bit o' flesh i' th'inside; he war as queer
as Dick's hatband – went thrice aboot, an' wudn't tie. His wife
Mabel war a delicat' boddie, an' varry flighty. Thay war an honest
family, but sair hadden doon i' th' world.' Indeed, the earnings of
old Robert did not amount to more than twelve shillings a week;
and, as there were six children to maintain, the family, during their
stay at Wylam, were necessarily in very straitened circumstances.
The father's wages being barely sufficient, even with the most rigid
economy, for the sustenance of the household, there was little to
spare for clothing, and nothing for education, so none of the
children were sent to school.

Old Robert was a general favourite in the village, especially
among the children, whom he was accustomed to draw about him
while tending the engine-fire, and feast their young imaginations
with tales of Sinbad the Sailor and Robinson Crusoe, besides others

of his own invention; so that 'Bob's engine-fire' came to be the most popular resort in the village. Another feature in his character, by which he was long remembered, was his affection for birds and animals; and he had many tame favourites of both sorts, which were as fond of resorting to his engine-fire as the boys and girls themselves. In the winter time he had usually a flock of tame robins about him; and they would come hopping familiarly to his feet to pick up the crumbs which he had saved for them out of his humble dinner. At his cottage he was rarely without one or more tame blackbirds, which flew about the house, or in and out at the door. In summer-time he would go a-birdnesting with his children; and one day he took his little son George to see a blackbird's nest for the first time. Holding him up in his arms, he let the wondering boy peep down, through the branches held aside for the purpose, into a nest full of young birds – a sight which the boy never forgot, but used to speak of with delight to his intimate friends when he himself had grown an old man.

The boy George led the ordinary life of working-people's children. He played about the doors; went birdnesting when he could; and ran errands to the village. He was also an eager listener, with the other children, to his father's curious tales; and he early imbibed from him that affection for birds and animals which continued throughout his life. In course of time he was promoted to the office of carrying his father's dinner to him while at work, and it was on such occasions his great delight to see the robins fed. At home he helped to nurse, and that with a careful hand, his younger brothers and sisters. One of his duties was to see that the other children were kept out of the way of the chaldron waggons, which were then dragged by horses along the wooden tramroad immediately in front of the cottage-door. This waggon-way was the first in the northern district on which the experiment of a locomotive engine was tried. But at the time of which we speak, the locomotive had scarcely been dreamt of in England as a practicable working power; horses only were used to haul the coal; and one of the first sights with which the boy was familiar was the coal-waggons dragged by them along the wooden railway at Wylam.

Thus eight years passed; after which, the coal having been worked out, the old engine, which had grown 'dismal to look at', as one of the workmen described it, was pulled down; and then Robert, having obtained employment as a fireman at the Dewley Burn Colliery, removed with his family to that place. Dewley

Burn, at this day, consists of a few old-fashioned low-roofed cottages standing on either side of a babbling little stream. They are connected by a rustic wooden bridge, which spans the rift in front of the doors. In the central one-roomed cottage of this group, on the right bank, Robert Stephenson lived for a time with his family; the pit at which he worked standing in the rear of the cottages.

Young though he was, George was now of an age to be able to contribute something towards the family maintenance; for in a poor man's house, every child is a burden until his little hands can be turned to profitable account. That the boy was shrewd and active, and possessed of a ready mother wit, will be evident enough from the following incident. One day his sister Nell went into Newcastle to buy a bonnet; and Geordie went with her 'for company'. At a draper's shop in the Bigg Market, Nell found a 'chip' quite to her mind, but on pricing it, alas! it was found to be fifteen pence beyond her means, and she left the shop very much disappointed. But Geordie said, 'Never heed, Nell; see if I canna win siller enough to buy the bonnet; stand ye there, till I come back.' Away ran the boy and disappeared amidst the throng of the market, leaving the girl to wait his return. Long and long she waited, until it grew dusk, and the market people had nearly all left. She had begun to despair, and fears crossed her mind that Geordie must have been run over and killed; when at last up he came running, almost breathless. 'I've gotten the siller for the bonnet, Nell!' cried he. 'Eh, Geordie!' she said, 'but hoo hae ye gotten it?' 'Haudin the gentlemen's horses!' was the exultant reply. The bonnet was forthwith bought, and the two returned to Dewley happy.

George's first regular employment was of a very humble sort. A widow, named Grace Ainslie, then occupied the neighbouring farmhouse of Dewley. She kept a number of cows, and had the privilege of grazing them along the waggon-road. She needed a boy to herd the cows, to keep them out of the way of the waggons, and prevent their straying or trespassing on the neighbours' 'liberties'; the boy's duty was also to bar the gates at night after all the waggons had passed. George petitioned for this post, and, to his great joy, he was appointed at the wage of twopence a day.

It was light employment, and he had plenty of spare time on his hands, which he spent in birdnesting, making whistles out of reeds and scrannel straws, and erecting Lilliputian mills in the little water-streams that ran into the Dewley bog. But his favourite amusement at this early age was erecting clay engines in conjunction with his chosen playmate, Bill Thirlwall. The place is still pointed out where the future engineers made their first essays in modelling. The boys found the clay for their engines in the adjoining bog, and the hemlocks which grew about supplied them with imaginary steam-pipes. They even proceeded to make a miniature winding-machine in connection with their engine, and the apparatus was erected upon a bench in front of the Thirlwalls' cottage. The corves were made out of hollowed corks; the ropes were supplied by twine; and a few bits of wood gleaned from the refuse of the carpenter's shop completed their materials. With this apparatus the boys made a show of sending the corves down the pit and drawing them up again, much to the marvel of the pitmen. But some mischievous person about the place seized the opportunity early one morning of smashing the fragile machinery, much to the grief of the young engineers.

As Stephenson grew older and abler to work, he was set to lead the horses when ploughing, though scarce big enough to stride across the furrows; and he used afterwards to say that he rode to his work in the mornings at an hour when most other children of his age were asleep in their beds. He was also employed to hoe turnips, and do similar farmwork, for which he was paid the advanced wage of fourpence a day. But his highest ambition was to be taken on at the colliery where his father worked; and he shortly joined his elder brother James there as a 'corf-bitter', or 'picker', to clear the coal of stones, bats, and dross. His wages were then advanced to sixpence a day, and afterwards to eightpence when he was set to drive the gin-horse.

Shortly after, George went to Black Callerton to drive the gin there; and as that colliery lies about two miles across the fields from Dewley Burn, he walked that distance early in the morning to his work, returning home late in the evening. One of the old residents at Black Callerton, who remembered him at that time, described him to the author as 'a grit growing lad, with bare legs an' feet'; adding that he was 'very quick-witted and full of fun and tricks: indeed, there was nothing under the sun but he tried to imitate'. He was usually foremost also in the sports and pastimes of youth.

Among his first strongly-developed tastes was the love of birds and animals, which he inherited from his father. Blackbirds were his special favourites. The hedges between Dewley and Black Callerton were capital birdnesting places; and there was not a nest there that he did not know of. When the young birds were old enough, he would bring them home with him, feed them, and teach them to fly about the cottage unconfined by cages. One of his blackbirds became so tame, that, after flying about the doors all day, and in and out of the cottage, it would take up its roost upon the bed-head at night. And most singular of all, the bird would disappear in the spring and summer months, when it was supposed to go into the woods to pair and rear its young, after which it would reappear at the cottage, and resume its social habits during the winter. This went on for several years. George had also a stock of tame rabbits, for which he built a little house behind the cottage, and for many years he continued to pride himself upon the superiority of his breed.

After he had driven the gin for some time at Dewley and Black Callerton, he was taken on as an assistant to his father in firing the engine at Dewley. This was a step of promotion which he had anxiously desired, his only fear being lest he should be found too young for the work. Indeed, he used afterwards to relate how he was wont to hide himself when the owner of the colliery went round, in case he should be thought too little a boy to earn the wages paid him. Since he had modelled his clay engines in the bog, his young ambition was to be an engineman; and to be an assistant fireman was the first step towards this position. Great therefore was his joy when, at about fourteen years of age, he was appointed assistant-fireman, at the wage of a shilling a day.

But the coal at Dewley Burn being at length worked out, the pit was ordered to be 'laid in', and old Robert and his family were again under the necessity of shifting their home; for, to use the common phrase, they must 'follow the wark'. They removed accordingly to a place called Jolly's Close, a few miles to the south, close behind the village of Newburn, where another coal-mine belonging to the Duke of Northumberland, called 'the Duke's Winnin', had recently been opened out.

One of the old persons in the neighbourhood, who knew the family well, describes the dwelling in which they lived as a poor cottage of only one room, in which the father, mother, four sons, and two daughters, lived and slept. It was crowded with three low-poled beds. The one apartment served for parlour, kitchen, sleeping-room, and all.

The children of the Stephenson family were now growing apace, and several of them were old enough to be able to earn money at various kinds of colliery work. James and George, the two eldest sons, worked as assistant-firemen; and the younger boys worked as wheelers or pickers on the bank-tops. The two girls helped their mother with the household work.

Other workings of the coal were opened out in the neighbourhood; and to one of these George was removed as fireman on his own account. This was called the 'Mid Mill Winnin', where he had for his mate a young man named Coe. They worked together there for about two years, by twelve-hour shifts, George firing the engine at the wage of a shilling a day. He was now fifteen years old. His ambition was as yet limited to attaining the standing of a full workman, at a man's wages; and with that view he endeavoured to attain such a knowledge of his engine as would eventually lead to his employment as an engineman, with its accompanying advantage of higher pay. He was a steady, sober, hard-working young man, but nothing more in the estimation of his fellow-workmen.

One of his favourite pastimes in by-hours was trying feats of strength with his companions. Although in frame he was not particularly robust, yet he was big and bony, and considered very strong for his age. At throwing the hammer George had no compeer. At lifting heavy weights off the ground from between his feet, by means of a bar of iron passed through them – placing the bar against his knees as a fulcrum, and then straightening his spine and lifting them sheer up – he was also very successful. On one occasion he lifted as much as sixty stones weight – a striking indication of his strength of bone and muscle.

When the pit at Mid Mill was closed, George and his companion Coe were sent to work another pumping-engine erected near Throckley Bridge, where they continued for some months. It was while working at this place that his wages were raised to 12s. a week – an event to him of great importance. On coming out of the foreman's office that Saturday evening on which he received the advance, he announced the fact to his fellow-workmen, adding triumphantly, 'I am now a made man for life!'

The pit opened at Newburn, at which old Robert Stephenson worked, proving a failure, it was closed; and a new pit was sunk at Water Row, on a strip of land lying between the Wylam waggon-way and the river Tyne, about half a mile west of Newburn Church. A pumping-engine was erected there by Robert Hawthorn, the Duke's engineer; and old Stephenson went to work it as fireman, his son George acting as the engineman or plugman. At that time he was about seventeen years old – a very youthful age at which to fill so responsible a post. He had thus already got

ahead of his father in his station as a workman; for the plugman
holds a higher grade than the fireman, requiring more practical
knowledge and skill, and usually receiving higher wages.

George's duty as plugman was to watch the engine, to see that
it kept well in work, and that the pumps were efficient in drawing
the water. When the water-level in the pit was lowered, and the
suction became incomplete through the exposure of the suction-
holes, it was then his duty to proceed to the bottom of the shaft
and plug the tube so that the pump should draw: hence the
designation of 'plugman'. If a stoppage in the engine took place
through any defect which he was incapable of remedying, it was
for him to call in the aid of the chief engineer to set it to rights.

But from the time when George Stephenson was appointed fireman, and more particularly afterwards as engineman, he applied
himself so assiduously and so successfully to the study of the
engine and its gearing – taking the machine to pieces in his leisure
hours for the purpose of cleaning and understanding its various
parts – that he soon acquired a thorough practical knowledge of its
construction and mode of working, and very rarely needed to call
the engineer of the colliery to his aid. His engine became a sort of
pet with him, and he was never wearied of watching and inspecting
it with admiration.

Though eighteen years old, like many of his fellow-workmen,
Stephenson had not yet learnt to read. All that he could do was to
get someone to read for him by his engine fire, out of any book or
stray newspaper which found its way into the neighbourhood.
Bonaparte was then overrunning Italy, and astounding Europe by
his brilliant succession of victories; and there was no more eager
auditor of his exploits, as read from the newspaper accounts, than
the young engineman at the Water Row Pit.

There were also numerous stray bits of information and intelligence contained in these papers, which excited Stephenson's
interest. One of these related to the Egyptian method of hatching
birds' eggs by means of artificial heat. Curious about everything
relating to birds, he determined to test it by experiment. It was
spring-time, and he forthwith went a birdnesting in the adjoining
woods and hedges. He gathered a collection of eggs of various sorts,
set them in flour in a warm place in the engine-house, covering the
whole with wool, and then waited the issue. The heat was kept as
steady as possible, and the eggs were carefully turned every twelve
hours, but though they chipped, and some of them exhibited well-
grown chicks, they never hatched. The experiment failed, but the

incident shows that the inquiring mind of the youth was fairly at work.

Modelling of engines in clay continued to be another of his favourite occupations. He made models of engines which he had seen, and of others which were described to him. These attempts were an improvement upon his first trials at Dewley Burn bog, when occupied there as a herd-boy. He was, however, anxious to know something of the wonderful engines of Boulton and Watt, and was told that they were to be found fully described in books, which he must search for information as to their construction, action, and uses. But, alas! Stephenson could not read; he had not yet learnt even his letters.

Thus he shortly found, when gazing wistfully in the direction of knowledge, that to advance further as a skilled workman, he must master this wonderful art of reading – the key to so many other arts. Only thus could he gain an access to books, the depositories of the wisdom and experience of the past. Although a grown man, and doing the work of a man, he was not ashamed to confess his ignorance, and go to school, big as he was, to learn his letters. Perhaps, too, he foresaw that, in laying out a little of his spare earnings for this purpose, he was investing money judiciously, and that, in every hour he spent at school, he was really working for better wages.

His first schoolmaster was Robin Cowens, a poor teacher in the village of Walbottle. He kept a night-school, which was attended by a few of the colliers' and labourers' sons in the neighbourhood. George took lessons in spelling and reading three nights in the week. Robin Cowens' teaching cost threepence a week; and though it was not very good, yet George, being hungry for knowledge and eager to acquire it, soon learnt to read. He also practised 'pothooks', and at the age of nineteen he was proud to be able to write his own name.

A Scotch dominie, named Andrew Robertson, set up a night-school in the village of Newburn, in the winter of 1799. It was more convenient for George to attend this school, as it was nearer to his work, and only a few minutes' walk from Jolly's Close. Besides, Andrew had the reputation of being a skilled arithmetician; and this branch of knowledge Stephenson was very desirous of acquiring. He accordingly began taking lessons from him, paying fourpence a week. Robert Gray, the junior fireman at the Water Row Pit, began arithmetic at the same time; and Gray afterwards told the author that George learnt 'figuring' so much faster than he did, that he could not make out how it was – 'he took to figures so wonderful'. Although the two started together from the same point, at the end of the winter George had mastered 'reduction', while Robert Gray was still struggling with the difficulties of simple division. But George's secret was his perseverance. He worked out the sums in his bye-hours, improving every minute of his spare time by the engine-fire, and studying there the arithmetical problems set for him upon his slate by the master. In the evenings he took to Robertson the sums which he had 'worked', and new ones were 'set' for him to study out the following day. Thus his progress was rapid, and, with a willing heart and mind, he soon became well advanced in arithmetic. Indeed, Andrew Robertson became very proud of his scholar; and shortly after, when the Water Row Pit was closed, and George removed to Black Callerton to work there, the poor schoolmaster, not having a very extensive connection in Newburn, went with his pupils, and set up his night-school at Black Callerton, where he continued his lessons.

George still found time to attend to his favourite animals while working at the Water Row Pit. Like his father, he used to tempt the robin-redbreasts to hop and fly about him at the engine-fire, by the bait of breadcrumbs saved from his dinner. But his chief favourite was his dog – so sagacious that he almost daily carried George's dinner to him at the pit. The tin containing the meal was suspended from the dog's neck, and, thus laden, he proceeded faithfully from Jolly's Close to Water Row Pit, quite through the village of Newburn. He turned neither to left nor right, nor heeded the barking of curs at his heels. But his course was not unattended with perils. One day the big strange dog of a passing butcher espying the engineman's messenger with the tin-can about his neck, ran after and fell upon him. There was a terrible tussle and worrying, which lasted for a brief while, and, shortly after, the dog's master, anxious for his dinner, saw his faithful servant approaching, bleeding but triumphant. The tin-can was still round his neck, but the dinner had been spilt in the struggle. Though George went without his dinner that day, he was prouder of his dog than ever when the circumstances of the combat were related to him by the villagers who had seen it.

It was while working at the Water Row Pit that Stephenson learnt the art of braking an engine. This being one of the higher departments of colliery labour, and among the best paid, George was very anxious to learn it. A small winding-engine having been put up for the purpose of drawing the coals from the pit, Bill Coe, his friend and fellow-workman, was appointed the brakesman. He frequently allowed George to try his hand at the machine, and instructed him how to proceed. Coe was, however, opposed in this by several of the other workmen – one of whom, a banksman named William Locke,* went so far as to stop the working of the pit because Stephenson had been called in to the brake. But one day as Mr Charles Nixon, the manager of the pit, was observed approaching, Coe adopted an expedient which put a stop to the opposition. He called upon Stephenson to 'come into the brake-house, and take hold of the machine'. Locke, as usual, sat down, and the working of the pit was stopped. When requested by the manager to give an explanation, he said that 'young Stephenson couldn't brake, and, what was more, never would learn, he was so clumsy'. Mr Nixon, however, ordered Locke to go on with the work, which he did; and Stephenson, after some further practice, acquired the art of braking.

After working at the Water Row Pit and at other engines near Newburn for about three years, George and Coe went to Black Callerton early in 1801. Though only twenty years of age, his employers thought so well of him that they appointed him to the responsible office of brakesman at the Dolly Pit. For convenience sake, he took lodgings at a small farmer's in the village, finding his own victuals, and paying so much a week for lodging and attendance. In the locality this was called 'picklin in his awn poke neuk'. It not unfrequently happens that the young workman about the collieries, when selecting a lodging, contrives to pitch his tent where the daughter of the house ultimately becomes his wife. This is often the real attraction that draws the youth from home, though a very different one may be pretended.

George Stephenson's duties as brakesman may be briefly described. The work was somewhat monotonous, and consisted in superintending the working of the engine and machinery by means of which the coals were drawn out of the pit. Brakesmen are almost invariably selected from those who have had considerable experience as engine-firemen, and borne a good character for steadiness, punctuality, watchfulness, and 'mother wit'. In George Stephenson's day the coals were drawn out of the pit in corves, or large baskets made of hazel rods. The corves were placed together in a cage, between which and the pit-ropes there was usually from fifteen to twenty feet of chain. The approach of the corves towards

* Father of Mr Locke, M.P., the engineer. He afterwards removed to Barnsley, in Yorkshire.

the pit mouth was signalled by a bell, brought into action by a piece of mechanism worked from the shaft of the engine. When the bell sounded, the brakesman checked the speed, by taking hold of the hand-gear connected with the steam-valves, which were so arranged that by their means he could regulate the speed of the engine, and stop or set it in motion when required. Connected with the fly-wheel was a powerful wooden brake, acting by pressure against its rim, something like the brake of a railway-carriage against its wheels. On catching sight of the chain attached to the ascending corve-cage, the brakesman, by pressing his foot upon a foot-step near him, was enabled, with great precision, to stop the revolutions of the wheel, and arrest the ascent of the corves at the pit mouth, when they were forthwith landed on the 'settle board'. On the full corves being replaced by empty ones, it was then the duty of the brakesman to reverse the engine, and send the corves down the pit to be filled again.

The monotony of George Stephenson's occupation as a brakesman was somewhat varied by the change which he made, in his turn, from the day to the night-shift. His duty, on the latter occasions, consisted chiefly in sending men and materials into the mine, and in drawing other men and materials out. Most of the workmen enter the pit during the night-shift, and leave it in the latter part of the day, while coal-drawing is proceeding. The requirements of the work at night are such, that the brakesman has a good deal of spare time on his hands, which he is at liberty to employ in his own way. From an early period, George was accustomed to employ those vacant night hours in working the sums set for him by Andrew Robertson upon his slate, practising writing in his copy-book, and mending the shoes of his fellow-workmen. His wages while working at the Dolly Pit amounted to from £1 15s. to £2 in the fortnight; but he gradually added to them as he became more expert at shoe-mending, and afterwards at shoe-making.

Probably he was stimulated to take in hand this extra work by the attachment he had by this time formed for a young woman named Fanny Henderson, who officiated as servant in the small farmer's house in which he lodged. We have been informed that the personal attractions of Fanny, though these were considerable, were the least of her charms. Mr William Fairbairn, who afterwards saw her in her home at Willington Quay, describes her as a very comely woman. But her temper was one of the sweetest; and those who knew her were accustomed to speak of the charming modesty of her demeanour, her kindness of disposition, and withal her sound good sense.

Among his various mendings of old shoes at Callerton, George was on one occasion favoured with the shoes of his sweetheart to sole. One can imagine the pleasure with which he would linger over such a piece of work, and the pride with which he would execute it. A friend of his, still living, relates that, after he had finished the shoes, he carried them about with him in his pocket on the Sunday afternoon, and that from time to time he would pull them out and hold them up, exclaiming, 'what a capital job he had made of them!'

Out of his earnings by shoe-mending at Callerton, George contrived to save his first guinea. The first guinea saved by a working man is no trivial thing. If, as in Stephenson's case, it has been the result of prudent self-denial, of extra labour at bye-hours, and of the honest resolution to save and economize for worthy purposes, the first guinea saved is an earnest of better things. When Stephenson had saved this guinea he was not a little elated at the achievement, and expressed the opinion to a friend, who many years after reminded him of it, that he was 'now a rich man'.

Not long after he began to work at Black Callerton as brakesman, he had a quarrel with a pitman named Ned Nelson, a roistering bully, who was the terror of the village. Nelson was a great fighter; and it was therefore considered dangerous to quarrel with him. Stephenson was so unfortunate as not to be able to please this pitman by the way in which he drew him out of the pit; and Nelson swore at him grossly because of the alleged clumsiness of his braking. George defended himself, and appealed to the testimony of the other workmen. But Nelson had not been accustomed to George's style of self-assertion; and, after a great deal of abuse, he threatened to kick the brakesman, who defied him to do so. Nelson ended by challenging Stephenson to a pitched battle; and the latter accepted the challenge, when a day was fixed on which the fight was to come off.

Great was the excitement at Black Callerton when it was known that George Stephenson had accepted Nelson's challenge. Everybody said he would be killed. The villagers, the young men, and especially the boys of the place, with whom George was a great favourite, all wished that he might beat Nelson, but they scarcely dared to say so. They came about him while he was at work in the engine-house to inquire if it was really true that he was 'goin to fight Nelson?' 'Ay; never fear for me; I'll fight him.' And fight him he did. For some days previous to the appointed day of battle, Nelson went entirely off work for the purpose of keeping himself fresh and strong, whereas Stephenson went on doing his daily work as usual, and appeared not in the least disconcerted by the prospect of the affair. So, on the evening appointed, after George had done his day's labour, he went into the Dolly Pit Field, where his already exulting rival was ready to meet him. George stripped, and 'went in' like a practised pugilist – though it was his first and last fight. After a few rounds, George's wiry muscles and practised strength enabled him severely to punish his adversary, and to secure an easy victory.

This circumstance is related in illustration of Stephenson's personal pluck and courage; and it was thoroughly characteristic of the man. He was no pugilist, and the very reverse of quarrelsome. But he would not be put down by the bully of the colliery, and he fought him. There his pugilism ended; they afterwards shook hands, and continued good friends. In after life, Stephenson's mettle was often as hardly tried, though in a different way; and he did not fail to exhibit the same resolute courage in contending with the bullies of the railway world, as he showed in his encounter with Ned Nelson, the fighting pitman of Callerton.

CHAPTER III — ENGINEMAN AT WILLINGTON QUAY AND KILLINGWORTH

GEORGE STEPHENSON had now acquired the character of an expert workman. He was diligent and observant while at work, and sober and studious when the day's work was over. His friend Coe described him to the author as 'a standing example of manly character'. On pay-Saturday afternoons, when the pitmen held their fortnightly holiday, occupying themselves chiefly in cock-fighting and dog-fighting in the adjoining fields, followed by adjournments to the 'yel-house', George was accustomed to take his engine to pieces, for the purpose of obtaining 'insight', and he cleaned all the parts and put the machine in thorough working order before leaving it.

In the evenings he improved himself in the arts of reading and writing, and occasionally took a turn at modelling. It was at Callerton, his son Robert informed us, that he began to try his hand at original invention; and for some time he applied his attention to a machine of the nature of an engine-brake, which reversed itself by its own action. But nothing came of the con-trivance, and it was eventually thrown aside as useless. Yet not altogether so; for even the highest skill must undergo the inevitable discipline of experiment, and submit to the wholesome correction of occasional failure.

After working at Callerton for about two years, he received an offer to take charge of the engine on Willington Ballast Hill at an advanced wage. He determined to accept it, and at the same time to marry Fanny Henderson, and begin housekeeping on his own account. Though he was only twenty-one years old, he had contrived, by thrift, steadiness, and industry, to save as much money as enabled him to take a cottage-dwelling at Willington Quay, and furnish it in a humble but comfortable style for the reception of his bride.

Willington Quay lies on the north bank of the Tyne, about six miles below Newcastle. It consists of a line of houses straggling along the riverside; and high behind it towers up the huge mound of ballast emptied out of the ships which resort to the quay for their cargoes of coal for the London market. The ballast is thrown out of the ships' holds into waggons laid alongside, which are run up to the summit of the Ballast Hill, and emptied out there. At the foot of the great mound of shot rubbish was the fixed engine of which George Stephenson acted as brakesman.

The cottage in which he took up his abode was a small two-storeyed dwelling, standing a little back from the quay with a bit of garden ground in front.* The Stephenson family occupied the upper room in the west end of the cottage. Close behind rose the Ballast Hill.

When the cottage dwelling had been made snug, and was ready for occupation, the marriage took place. It was celebrated in Newburn Church on 28 November 1802. After the ceremony, George, with his newly-wedded wife, proceeded to the house of his father at Jolly's Close. The old man was now becoming infirm, and, though he still worked as an engine-fireman, contrived with difficulty 'to keep his head above water'. When the visit had been paid, the bridal party set out for their new home at Willington Quay, whither they went in a manner quite common before travelling by railway came into use. Two farm horses, borrowed from a neighbouring farmer, were each provided with a saddle and pillion, and George having mounted one, his wife seated herself behind him, holding on by his waist. The bridesman and bridesmaid in like manner mounted the other horse; and in this wise the wedding

* The Stephenson Memorial Schools have since been erected on the site of the old cottage at Willington Quay represented in the engraving at the head of this chapter.

party rode across the country, passing through the old streets of
Newcastle, and then by Wallsend to Willington Quay – a ride of
about fifteen miles.

George Stephenson's daily life at Willington was that of a steady
workman. By the manner, however, in which he continued to
improve his spare hours in the evening, he was silently and surely
paving the way for being something more than a manual labourer.
He set himself to study diligently the principles of mechanics, and
to master the laws by which his engine worked. For a workman,
he was even at that time more than ordinarily speculative – often
taking up strange theories, and trying to sift out the truth that was
in them. While sitting by his wife's side in his cottage-dwelling in
the winter evenings, he was usually occupied in studying mechanical subjects, or in modelling experimental machines. Among his
various speculations while at Willington, he tried to discover a
means of Perpetual Motion. Although he failed, as so many others
had done before him, the very efforts he made tended to whet his
inventive faculties, and to call forth his dormant powers. He went
so far as to construct the model of a machine for the purpose. It
consisted of a wooden wheel, the periphery of which was furnished
with glass tubes filled with quicksilver: as the wheel rotated, the
quicksilver poured itself down into the lower tubes, and thus a sort
of self-acting motion was kept up in the apparatus, which, however, did not prove to be perpetual. Where he had first obtained
the idea of this machine – whether from conversation or reading, is
not known; but his son Robert was of opinion that he had heard
of the apparatus of this kind described in the *History of Inventions*.
As he had then no access to books, and indeed could barely read
with ease, it is probable that he had been told of the contrivance,
and set about testing its value according to his own methods.

Much of his spare time continued to be occupied by labour more
immediately profitable, regarded in a pecuniary point of view. In
the evenings, after his day's labour at his engine, he would occasionally employ himself for an hour or two in casting ballast out
of the collier ships, by which means he was enabled to earn a few
extra shillings weekly. Mr William Fairbairn of Manchester has
informed us that while Stephenson was employed at Willington,
he himself was working in the neighbourhood as an engine apprentice at the Percy Main Colliery. He was very fond of George, who
was a fine, hearty fellow, besides being a capital workman. In the
summer evenings young Fairbairn was accustomed to go down to
the Quay to see his friend, and on such occasions he would

frequently take charge of George's engine while he took a turn at heaving ballast out of the ships' holds. It is pleasant to think of the future President of the British Association thus helping the future Railway Engineer to earn a few extra shillings by overwork in the evenings, at a time when both occupied the rank of humble working men in an obscure northern village.

Mr Fairbairn was also a frequent visitor at George's cottage on the Quay, where, though there was no luxury, there was comfort, cleanliness, and a pervading spirit of industry. Even at home George was never for a moment idle. When there was no ballast to heave out at the Quay, he took in shoes to mend; and from mending he proceeded to making them, as well as shoe-lasts, in which he was admitted to be very expert.

But an accident occurred in Stephenson's household about this time, which had the effect of directing his industry into a new and still more profitable channel. The cottage chimney took fire one day in his absence, when the alarmed neighbours, rushing in, threw quantities of water upon the flames; and some, in their zeal, even mounted the ridge of the house, and poured buckets of water down the chimney. The fire was soon put out, but the house was thoroughly soaked. When George came home he found everything in disorder, and his new furniture covered with soot. The eight-day clock, which hung against the wall – one of the most highly-prized articles in the house – was much damaged by the steam with which the room had been filled; and its wheels were so clogged by the dust and soot that it was brought to a complete standstill. George was always ready to turn his hand to anything, and his ingenuity, never at fault, immediately set to work to repair the unfortunate clock. He was advised to send it to the clockmaker, but that would cost money; and he declared that he would repair it himself – at least he would try. The clock was accordingly taken to pieces and cleaned; the tools which he had been accumulating for the purpose of constructing his Perpetual Motion machine, enabled him to do this readily; and he succeeded so well that, shortly after, the neighbours sent him their clocks to clean, and he soon became one of the most famous clock-doctors in the neighbourhood.

It was while living at Willington Quay that George Stephenson's only son was born, on 16 October 1803. The child was a great favourite with his father, and added much to the happiness of his evening hours. George's 'philoprogenitiveness', as phrenologists call it, had been exercised hitherto upon birds, dogs, rabbits, and even the poor old gin-horses which he had driven at the Callerton

Pit; but in his boy he now found a much more genial object for the exercise of his affection.

The christening took place in the school-house at Wallsend, the old parish church being at the time in so dilapidated a condition from the 'creeping' or subsidence of the ground, consequent upon the excavation of the coal, that it was considered dangerous to enter it. On this occasion, Robert Gray and Anne Henderson, who had officiated as bridesman and bridesmaid at the wedding, came over again to Willington, and stood godfather and godmother to little Robert – so named after his grandfather.

After working for several years more as a brakesman at the Willington machine, George Stephenson was induced to leave his situation there for a similar one at the West Moor Colliery, Killingworth. It was not without considerable persuasion that he was induced to leave the Quay, as he knew that he should thereby give up the chance of earning extra money by casting ballast from the keels. At last, however, he consented, in the hope of making up the loss in some other way.

The village of Killingworth lies about seven miles north of Newcastle, and is one of the best-known collieries in that neighbourhood. The workings of the coal are of vast extent, and give employment to a large number of workpeople. To this place Stephenson first came as a brakesman about the beginning of 1805. He had not been long in his new place, ere his wife died (in 1806), shortly after giving birth to a daughter, who survived the mother only a few months. George deeply felt the loss of his wife, for they had been very happy together. Their lot had been sweetened by daily successful toil. The husband was sober and hard-working, and his wife made his hearth so bright and his home so snug, that no attraction could draw him from her side in the evening hours. But this domestic happiness was all to pass away; and George felt as one that had thenceforth to tread the journey of life alone.

Shortly after this event, while his grief was still fresh, he received an invitation from some gentlemen concerned in large spinning works near Montrose in Scotland, to proceed thither and superintend the working of one of Boulton and Watt's engines. He accepted the offer, and made arrangements to leave Killingworth for a time.

Having left his little boy in good keeping, he set out upon his long journey to Scotland on foot, with his kit upon his back. While working at Montrose he gave a striking proof of that practical ability in contrivance for which he was afterwards so distinguished.

It appears that the water required for the purposes of his engine, as well as for the use of the works, was pumped from a considerable depth, being supplied from the adjacent extensive sand strata. The pumps frequently got choked by the sand drawn in at the bottom of the well through the snore-holes, or apertures through which the water to be raised is admitted. The barrels soon became worn, and the bucket and clack leathers destroyed, so that it became necessary to devise a remedy; and with this object the engineman proceeded to adopt the following simple but original expedient. He had a wooden box or boot made, twelve feet high, which he placed in the sump or well, and into this he inserted the lower end of the pump. The result was, that the water flowed clear from the outer part of the well over into the boot, and being drawn up without any admixture of sand, the difficulty was thus conquered.*

Being paid good wages, Stephenson contrived, during the year he worked at Montrose, to save a sum of £28, which he took back with him to Killingworth. Longing to get back to his kindred, his heart yearning for the son whom he had left behind, our engineman took leave of his employers, and trudged back to Northumberland on foot as he had gone. While on his journey southward he arrived late one evening, footsore and wearied, at the door of a small farmer's cottage, at which he knocked, and requested shelter for the night. It was refused, and then he entreated that, being tired, and unable to proceed further, the farmer would permit him to lie down in the outhouse, for that a little clean straw would serve him. The farmer's wife appeared at the door, looked at the traveller, then retiring with her husband, the two confabulated a little apart, and finally they invited Stephenson into the cottage. Always full of conversation and anecdote, he soon made himself at home in the farmer's family, and spent with them a few pleasant hours. He was hospitably entertained for the night, and when he left the cottage in the morning, he pressed them to make some charge for his lodging, but they refused to accept any recompense. They only asked him to remember them kindly, and if he ever came that way, to be sure and call again. Many years after, when Stephenson had become a thriving man, he did not forget the humble pair who had

---

* This incident was related by Robert Stephenson during a voyage to the north of Scotland in 1857, when off Montrose, on board his yacht *Titania*; and the reminiscence was communicated to the author by the late Mr William Kell of Gateshead, who was present, at Mr Stephenson's request, as being worthy of insertion in his father's biography.

The Collier

succoured and entertained him on his way; he sought their cottage
again, when age had silvered their hair; and when he left the aged
couple, they may have been reminded of the old saying that we
may sometimes 'entertain angels unawares'.

Reaching home, Stephenson found that his father had met with
a serious accident at the Blucher Pit, which had reduced him to
great distress and poverty. While engaged in the inside of an
engine, making some repairs, a fellow-workman accidentally let in
the steam upon him. The blast struck him full in the face; he was
terribly scorched, and his eyesight was irretrievably lost. The help-
less and infirm man had struggled for a time with poverty; his
sons who were at home, poor as himself, were little able to help him,
while George was at a distance in Scotland. On his return, however, with his savings in his pocket, his first step was to pay off his
father's debts, amounting to about £15; and shortly after he
removed the aged pair from Jolly's Close to a comfortable cottage
adjoining the tramroad near the West Moor at Killingworth, where
the old man lived for many years, supported entirely by his son.

Stephenson was again taken on as a brakesman at the West
Moor Pit. He does not seem to have been very hopeful as to his
prospects in life about this time (1807–8). Indeed the condition of
the working class generally was very discouraging. England was
engaged in a great war, which pressed upon the industry, and
severely tried the resources of the country. There was a constant
demand for men to fill the army. The working people were also
liable to be pressed for the navy, or drawn for the militia; and
though they could not fail to be discontented under such circumstances, they scarcely dared even to mutter their discontent to
their neighbours.

Stephenson was drawn for the militia: he must therefore either
quit his work and go a-soldiering, or find a substitute. He adopted
the latter course, and borrowed £6, which, with the remainder of
his savings, enabled him to provide a militiaman to serve in his
stead. Thus the whole of his hard-won earnings were swept away
at a stroke. He was almost in despair, and contemplated the idea
of leaving the country, and emigrating to the United States.
Although a voyage thither was then a much more formidable
thing for a working man to accomplish than a voyage to Australia
is now, he seriously entertained the project, and had all but made
up his mind to go. His sister Ann, with her husband, emigrated
about that time, but George could not raise the requisite money,
and they departed without him. After all, it went sore against his

heart to leave his home and his kindred, the scenes of his youth
and the friends of his boyhood; and he struggled long with the
idea, brooding over it in sorrow. Speaking afterwards to a friend
of his thoughts at the time, he said: 'You know the road from my
house at the West Moor to Killingworth. I remember once when I
went along that road I wept bitterly, for I knew not where my lot
in life would be cast.'

In 1808, Stephenson, with two other brakesmen, took a small
contract under the colliery lessees for braking the engines at the
West Moor Pit. The brakesmen found the oil and tallow; they
divided the work among them, and were paid so much per score
for their labour. It was the interest of the brakesmen to economize
the working as much as possible, and George no sooner entered
upon the contract than he proceeded to devise ways and means of
making it 'pay'. He observed that the ropes which, at other pits
in the neighbourhood, lasted about three months, at the West
Moor Pit became worn out in about a month. He immediately set
about ascertaining the cause of the defect; and finding it to be
occasioned by excessive friction, he proceeded, with the sanction
of the head engine-wright and the colliery owners, to shift the
pulley-wheels and rearrange the gearing, which had the effect of
greatly diminishing the tear and wear, besides allowing the work
of the colliery to proceed without interruption.

About the same time he attempted an improvement in the
winding-engine which he worked, by placing a valve between the
air-pump and condenser. This expedient, although it led to no
practical result, showed that his mind was actively engaged in
studying new mechanical adaptations. It continued to be his
regular habit, on Saturdays, to take his engine to pieces, for the
purpose, at the same time, of familiarizing himself with its action,
and of placing it in a state of thorough working order. By master-
ing its details, he was enabled, as opportunity occurred, to turn to
practical account the knowledge he thus diligently and patiently
acquired.

Such an opportunity was not long in presenting itself. In the
year 1810, a new pit was sunk by the 'Grand Allies' (the lessees of
the mines) at the village of Killingworth, now known as the
Killingworth High Pit. An atmospheric or Newcomen engine,
made by Smeaton, was fixed there for the purpose of pumping out
the water from the shaft; but somehow it failed to clear the pit.
As one of the workmen has since described the circumstances –
'She couldn't keep her jack-head in water: all the enginemen in the

neighbourhood were tried, as well as Crowther of the Ouseburn, but they were clean bet.' The engine had been fruitlessly pumping for nearly twelve months, and began to be spoken of as a total failure. Stephenson had gone to look at it when in course of erection, and then observed to the over-man that he thought it was defective; he also gave it as his opinion that, if there were much water in the mine, the engine would never keep it under. Of course, as he was only a brakesman, his opinion was considered to be worth very little on such a point. He continued, however, to make frequent visits to the engine, to see 'how she was getting on'. From the bank-head where he worked his brake he could see the chimney smoking at the High Pit; and as the men were passing to and from their work, he would call out and inquire 'if they had gotten to the bottom yet?' And the reply was always to the same effect – the pumping made no progress, and the workmen were still 'drowned out'.

One Saturday afternoon he went over to the High Pit to examine the engine more carefully than he had yet done. He had been turning the subject over thoughtfully in his mind; and seemed to have satisfied himself as to the cause of the failure. Kit Heppel, one of the sinkers, asked him, 'Weel, George, what do you mak' o' her? Do you think you could do anything to improve her?' Said George, 'I could alter her, man, and make her draw: in a week's time I could send you to the bottom.'

Forthwith Heppel reported this conversation to Ralph Dodds, the head viewer, who, being now quite in despair, and hopeless of succeeding with the engine, determined to give George's skill a trial. At the worst he could only fail, as the rest had done. In the evening, Dodds went in search of Stephenson, and met him on the road, dressed in his Sunday's suit, on the way to 'the preaching' in the Methodist Chapel, which he attended. 'Well, George,' said Dodds, 'they tell me that you think you can put the engine at the High Pit to rights.' 'Yes, sir,' said George, 'I think I could.' 'If that's the case, I'll give you a fair trial, and you must set to work immediately. We are clean drowned out, and cannot get a step further. The engineers hereabouts are all bet; and if you really succeed in accomplishing what they cannot do, you may depend upon it I will make you a man for life.'

Stephenson began his operations early next morning. The only condition that he made, before setting to work, was that he should select his own workmen. There was, as he knew, a good deal of jealousy among the 'regular' men that a colliery brakesman should pretend to know more about their engine than they themselves did, and attempt to remedy defects which the most skilled men of their craft, including the engineer of the colliery, had failed to do. But George made the condition a *sine qua non.* 'The workmen,' said he, 'must either be all Whigs or all Tories.' There was no help for it, so Dodds ordered the old hands to stand aside. The men grumbled, but gave way; and then George and his party went in.

The engine was taken entirely to pieces. The cistern containing the injection water was raised ten feet; the injection cock, being too small, was enlarged to nearly double its former size, and it was so arranged that it should be shut off quickly at the beginning of the stroke. These and other alterations were necessarily performed in a rough way, but, as the result proved, on true principles. Stephenson also, finding that the boiler would bear a greater pressure than five pounds to the inch, determined to work it at a pressure of ten pounds, though this was contrary to the directions of both Newcomen and Smeaton. The necessary alterations were made in about three days, and many persons came to see the engine start, including the men who had put her up. The pit being nearly full of water, she had little to do on starting, and, to use George's words, 'came bounce into the house'. Dodds exclaimed, 'Why, she was better as she was; now, she will knock the house down.' After a short time, however, the engine got fairly to work, and by ten o'clock that night the water was lower in the pit than it had ever been before. It was kept pumping all Thursday, and by the Friday afternoon the pit was cleared of water, and the workmen were 'sent to the bottom', as Stephenson had promised. Thus the alterations effected in the pumping apparatus proved completely successful.

Dodds was particularly gratified with the manner in which the job had been done, and he made Stephenson a present of ten pounds, which, though very inadequate when compared with the value of the work performed, was accepted with gratitude. George was proud of the gift as the first marked recognition of his skill as a workman; and he used afterwards to say that it was the biggest sum of money he had up to that time earned in one lump. Ralph Dodds, however, did more than this. He released the brakesman from the handles of his engine at West Moor, and appointed him engineman at the High Pit, at good wages, during the time the pit was sinking – the job lasting for about a year; and he also kept him in mind for further advancement.

Stephenson's skill as an engine-doctor soon became noised

abroad, and he was called upon to prescribe remedies for all the old, wheezy, and ineffective pumping-machines in the neighbour-hood. In this capacity he soon left the 'regular' men far behind, though they in their turn were very much disposed to treat the Killingworth brakesman as no better than a quack. Nevertheless, his practice was really founded upon a close study of the principles of mechanics, and on an intimate practical acquaintance with the details of the pumping-engine.

Another of his smaller achievements in the same line is still told by the people of the district. At the corner of the road leading to Long Benton, there was a quarry from which a peculiar and scarce kind of ochre was taken. In the course of working it out, the water had collected in considerable quantities; and there being no means of draining it off, it accumulated to such an extent that the further working of the ochre was almost entirely stopped. Ordinary pumps were tried, and failed; and then a windmill was tried, and failed too. On this, George was asked what ought to be done to clear the quarry of the water. He said, 'he would set up for them an engine little bigger than a kail-pot, that would clear them out in a week'. And he did so. A little engine was speedily erected, by means of which the quarry was pumped dry in the course of a few days. Thus his skill as a pump-doctor soon became the marvel of the district.

In elastic muscular vigour, Stephenson was now in his prime, and he still continued to be zealous in measuring his strength and agility with his fellow workmen. The competitive element in his nature was always strong; and his success in these feats of rivalry was certainly remarkable. Few, if any, could lift such weights, throw the hammer and putt the stone so far, or cover so great a space at a standing or running leap. One day, between the engine hour and the rope-rolling hour, Kit Heppel challenged him to leap from one high wall to another, with a deep gap between. To Heppel's surprise and dismay, George took the standing leap, and cleared the eleven feet at a bound. Had his eye been less accurate, or his limbs less agile and sure, the feat must have cost him his life.

But so full of redundant muscular vigour was he, that leaping, putting, or throwing the hammer were not enough for him. He was also ambitious of riding on horseback, and, as he had not yet been promoted to an office enabling him to keep a horse of his own, he sometimes borrowed one of the gin-horses for a ride. On one of these occasions, he brought the animal back reeking; when Tommy Mitcheson, the bank horse-keeper, a rough-spoken fellow, ex-claimed to him: 'Set such fellows as you on horseback, and you'll soon ride to the De'il.' But Tommy Mitcheson lived to tell the joke, and to confess that, after all, there had been a better issue to George's horsemanship than that which he predicted.

Old Cree, the engine-wright at Killingworth High Pit, having been killed by an accident, George Stephenson was, in 1812, appointed engine-wright of the colliery at the salary of £100 a year. He was also allowed the use of a galloway to ride upon in his visits of inspection to the collieries leased by the 'Grand Allies' in that neighbourhood. The 'Grand Allies' were a company of gentlemen, consisting of Sir Thomas Liddell (afterwards Lord Ravensworth), the Earl of Strathmore, and Mr Stuart Wortley (afterwards Lord Wharncliffe), the lessees of the Killingworth collieries. Having been informed of the merits of Stephenson, of his indefatigable industry, and the skill which he had displayed in the repairs of the pumping-engines, they readily acceded to Mr Dodds's recommendation that he should be appointed the colliery engine-wright; and, as we shall afterwards find, they continued to honour him by distinguished marks of their approval.

CHAPTER IV — THE STEPHENSONS AT KILLING-WORTH — EDUCATION AND SELF-EDUCATION OF FATHER AND SON

GEORGE STEPHENSON had now been diligently employed for several years in the work of self-improvement, and he experienced the usual results in increasing mental strength, capability, and skill. Perhaps the secret of every man's best success is to be found in the alacrity and industry with which he takes advantage of the opportunities which present themselves for well-doing. Our engineman was an eminent illustration of the importance of cultivating this habit of life. Every spare moment was laid under contribution by him, either for the purpose of adding to his earnings, or to his knowledge. He missed no opportunity of extending his observations, especially in his own department of work, ever aiming at improvement, and trying to turn all that he did know to useful practical account.

He continued his attempts to solve the mystery of Perpetual Motion, and contrived several model machines with the object of embodying his ideas in a practical working shape. He afterwards used to lament the time he had lost in these futile efforts, and said that if he had enjoyed the opportunity which most young men now have, of learning from books what previous experimenters had accomplished, he would have been spared much labour and mortification. Not being acquainted with what other mechanics had done, he groped his way in pursuit of some idea originated by his own independent thinking and observation; and, when he had brought it into some definite form, lo! he found that his supposed invention had long been known and recorded in scientific books. Often he thought he had hit upon discoveries, which he subsequently found were but old and exploded fallacies. Yet his very struggle to overcome the difficulties which lay in his way, was of itself an education of the best sort. By wrestling with them, he strengthened his judgement and sharpened his skill, stimulating and cultivating his inventiveness and mechanical ingenuity. Being very much in earnest, he was compelled to consider the subject of his special inquiry in all its relations; and thus he gradually acquired practical ability even through his very efforts after the impracticable.

Many of his evenings were now spent in the society of John Wigham, whose father occupied the Glebe Farm at Benton, close at hand. John was a fair penman and a sound arithmetician, and Stephenson sought his society chiefly for the purpose of improving himself in writing and 'figures'. Under Andrew Robertson, he had never quite mastered the Rule of Three, and it was only when Wigham took him in hand that he made much progress in the higher branches of arithmetic. He generally took his slate with him to the Wigham's cottage, when he had his sums set, that he might work them out while tending his engine on the following day. When too busy to be able to call upon Wigham, he sent the slate to have the former sums corrected and new ones set. Sometimes also, at leisure moments, he was enabled to do a little 'figuring' with chalk upon the sides of coal-waggons. So much patient perseverance could not but eventually succeed; and by dint of practice and study, Stephenson was enabled to master successively the various rules of arithmetic.

John Wigham was of great use to his pupil in many ways. He was a good talker, fond of argument, an extensive reader as country reading went in those days, and a very suggestive thinker. Though his store of information might be comparatively small when measured with that of more highly-cultivated minds, much of it was entirely new to Stephenson, who regarded him as a very clever and ingenious person.

Wigham taught him to draw plans and sections; though in this branch Stephenson proved so apt that he soon surpassed his master. A volume of *Ferguson's Lectures on Mechanics*, which fell into their hands, was a great treasure to both the students. One who remembers their evening occupations says he used to wonder what they meant by weighing the air and water in so odd a way. They were trying the specific gravities of objects; and the devices which they employed, the mechanical shifts to which they were put, were often of the rudest kind. In these evening entertainments, the mechanical contrivances were supplied by Stephenson, while Wigham found the scientific rationale. The opportunity thus afforded to the former of cultivating his mind by contact with one wiser than himself proved of great value, and in after-life Stephenson gratefully remembered the assistance which, when a humble workman, he had derived from John Wigham, the farmer's son.

His leisure moments thus carefully improved, it will be inferred that Stephenson continued a sober man. Though his notions were never extreme on this point, he was systematically temperate. It appears that on the invitation of his master, he had, on one or two occasions, been induced to join him in a forenoon glass of ale in the public-house of the village. But one day, about noon, when Dodds had got him as far as the public-house door, on his invitation to 'come in and take a glass o' yel', Stephenson made a dead stop, and said, firmly, 'No, sir, you must excuse me; I have made a resolution to drink no more at this time of day.' And he went back. He desired to retain the character of a steady workman; and the instances of men about him who had made shipwreck of their character through intemperance, were then, as now, unhappily but too frequent.

But another consideration besides his own self-improvement had already begun to exercise an important influence on his life. This was the training and education of his son Robert, now growing up an active, intelligent boy, as full of fun and tricks as his father had been. When a little fellow, scarcely able to reach so high as to put a clock-head on when placed upon the table, his father would make him mount a chair for the purpose; and to 'help father' was the proudest work which the boy then, and ever after, could take part in. When the little engine was set up at the Ochre Quarry to pump it dry, Robert was scarcely absent for an hour. He watched the machine very eagerly when it was to set work; and he was very much annoyed at the fire burning away the grates. The man who fired the engine was a sort of wag, and thinking to get a laugh at the boy, he said, 'Those bars are getting varra bad, Robert; I think we maun cut up some of that hard wood, and put it in instead.' 'What would be the use of that, you fool?' said the boy quickly. 'You would no sooner have put them in than they would be burnt out again!'

So soon as Robert was of proper age, his father sent him over to the road-side school at Long Benton, kept by Rutter, the parish clerk. But the education which Rutter could give was of a very limited kind, scarcely extending beyond the primer and pothooks. While working as a brakesman on the pit-head at Killingworth, the father had often bethought him of the obstructions he had himself encountered in life through his want of schooling; and he formed the noble determination that no labour, nor pains, nor self-denial on his part should be spared to furnish his son with the best education that it was in his power to bestow.

It is true his earnings were comparatively small at that time. He was still maintaining his infirm parents; and the cost of living continued excessive. But he fell back upon his old expedient of working up his spare time in the evenings at home, or during the night-shifts when it was his turn to tend the engine, in mending and making shoes, cleaning clocks and watches, making shoe-lasts for the shoemakers of the neighbourhood, and cutting out the pit-men's clothes for their wives; and we have been told that to this day there are clothes worn at Killingworth made after 'Geordy Steevie's cut'. To give his own words: 'In the earlier period of my career,' said he, 'when Robert was a little boy, I saw how deficient I was in education, and I made up my mind that he should not labour under the same defect, but that I would put him to a good school, and give him a liberal training. I was, however, a poor man; and how do you think I managed? I betook myself to mending my neighbours' clocks and watches at nights, after my daily labour was done, and thus I procured the means of educating my son.'*

Carrying out the resolution as to his boy's education, Robert was sent to Mr Bruce's school in Percy Street, Newcastle, at Midsummer, 1815, when he was about twelve years old. His father bought for him a donkey, on which he rode into Newcastle and back daily; and there are many still living who remember the little boy, dressed in his suit of homely grey stuff, cut out by his father, cantering along to school upon the 'cuddy', with his wallet of pro-visions for the day and his bag of books slung over his shoulder.

When Robert went to Mr Bruce's school, he was a shy, un-

* Speech at Newcastle, on 18 June 1844, at the meeting held in celebration of the opening of the Newcastle and Darlington Railway.

polished country lad, speaking the broad dialect of the pitmen; and the other boys would occasionally tease him, for the purpose of provoking an outburst of his Killingworth Doric. As the shyness got rubbed off, his love of fun began to show itself, and he was found able enough to hold his own among the other boys. As a scholar he was steady and diligent, and his master was accustomed to hold him up to the laggards of the school as an example of good conduct and industry. But his progress, though satisfactory, was by no means extraordinary. He used in after-life to pride himself on his achievements in mensuration, though another boy, John Taylor, beat him at arithmetic. He also made considerable progress in mathematics; and in a letter written to the son of his teacher, many years after, he said, 'It was to Mr Bruce's tuition and methods of modelling the mind that I attribute much of my success as an engineer; for it was from him that I derived my taste for mathematical pursuits and the facility I possess of applying this kind of knowledge to practical purposes and modifying it according to circumstances.'

During the time Robert attended school at Newcastle, his father made the boy's education instrumental to his own. Robert was accustomed to spend some of his spare time at the rooms of the Literary and Philosophical Institute; and when he went home in the evening, he would recount to his father the results of his reading. Sometimes he was allowed to take with him to Killingworth a volume of the *Repertory of Arts and Sciences*, which father and son studied together. But many of the most valuable works belonging to the Newcastle Library were not lent out; these Robert was instructed to read and study, and bring away with him descriptions and sketches for his father's information. His father also practised him in reading plans and drawings without reference to the written descriptions. He used to observe that 'A good plan should always explain itself'; and, placing a drawing of an engine or machine before the youth, would say, 'There, now, describe that to me – the arrangement and the action.' Thus he taught him to read a drawing as easily as he would read a page of a book. Both father and son profited by this excellent practice, which enabled them to apprehend with the greatest facility the details of even the most difficult and complicated mechanical drawing.

While Robert went on with his lessons in the evenings, his father was usually occupied with his watch and clock cleaning; or in contriving models of pumping-engines; or endeavouring to embody in a tangible shape the mechanical inventions which he found described in the odd volumes on Mechanics which fell in his way. This daily and unceasing example of industry and application, in the person of a loving and beloved father, imprinted itself deeply upon the boy's heart in characters never to be effaced. A spirit of self-improvement was thus early and carefully planted and fostered in Robert's mind, which continued to influence him through life; and to the close of his career, he was proud to confess that if his professional success had been great, it was mainly to the example and training of his father that he owed it.

Robert was not, however, exclusively devoted to study, but, like most boys full of animal spirits, he was very fond of fun and play, and sometimes of mischief. Dr Bruce relates that an old Killingworth labourer, when asked by Robert, on one of his last visits to Newcastle, if he remembered him, replied with emotion, 'Ay, indeed! Haven't I paid your head many a time when you came with your father's bait, for you were always a sad hempy?'

The author had the pleasure, in the year 1854, of accompanying Robert Stephenson on a visit to his old home and haunts at Killingworth. He had so often travelled the road upon his donkey to and from school, that every foot of it was familiar to him; and each turn in it served to recall to mind some incident of his boyish days. His eyes glistened when he came in sight of Killingworth pit-head. Pointing to a humble red-tiled house by the roadside at Benton, he said, 'You see that house – that was Rutter's, where I learnt my A B C, and made a beginning of my school learning. And there,' pointing to a colliery chimney on the left, 'there is Long Benton, where my father put up his first pumping-engine; and a great success it was. And this humble clay-floored cottage you see here, is where my grandfather lived till the close of his life. Many a time have I ridden straight into the house, mounted on my cuddy, and called upon grandfather to admire his points. I remember the old man feeling the animal all over – he was then quite blind – after which he would dilate upon the shape of his ears, fetlocks, and quarters, and usually end by pronouncing him to be a "real blood". I was a great favourite with the old man, who continued very fond of animals, and cheerful to the last; and I believe nothing gave him greater pleasure than a visit from me and my cuddy.'

On the way from Benton to High Killingworth, Mr Stephenson pointed to a corner of the road where he had once played a boyish trick upon a Killingworth collier. 'Straker,' said he, 'was a great bully, a coarse, swearing fellow, and a perfect tyrant among the women and children. He would go tearing into old Nanny the huxter's shop in the village, and demand in a savage voice, "What's ye'r best ham the pund?" "What's floor the nunder?" "What d'ye ax for prime bacon?" – his questions often ending with the miserable order, accompanied with a tremendous oath, of "Gie's a penny rrow (roll) an' a baubee herrin!" The poor woman was usually set "all of a shake" by a visit from this fellow. He was also a great boaster, and used to crow over the robbers whom he had put to flight; mere men in buckram, as everybody knew. We boys,' he continued, 'believed him to be a great coward, and determined to play him a trick. Two other boys joined me in waylaying Straker one night at that corner,' pointing to it. 'We sprang out and called upon him, in as gruff voices as we could assume, to "stand and deliver!" He dropped down upon his knees in the dirt, declaring he was a poor man, with a sma' family, asking for "mercy", and imploring us, as "gentlemen, for God's sake, t' let him a-be!" We couldn't stand this any longer, and set up a shout of laughter. Recognizing our boys' voices, he sprang to his feet and rattled out a volley of oaths; on which we cut through the hedge, and heard him shortly after swearing his way along the road to the yel-house.'

On another occasion, Robert played a series of tricks of a somewhat different character. Like his father, he was very fond of reducing his scientific reading to practice; and after studying Franklin's description of the lightning experiment, he proceeded to expend his store of Saturday pennies in purchasing about half a mile of copper wire at a brazier's shop in Newcastle. Having prepared his kite, he sent it up in the field opposite his father's door, and bringing the wire, insulated by means of a few feet of silk cord, over the backs of some of Farmer Wigham's cows, he soon had them skipping about the field in all directions with their tails up. One day he had his kite flying at the cottage-door as his father's galloway was hanging by the bridle to the paling, waiting for the master to mount. Bringing the end of the wire just over the pony's crupper, so smart an electric shock was given it, that the brute was almost knocked down. At this juncture the father issued from the door, riding-whip in hand, and was witness to the scientific trick just played off upon his galloway. 'Ah! you mischievous scoundrel!' cried he to the boy, who ran off. He inwardly chuckled with pride, nevertheless, at Robert's successful experiment.*

* Robert Stephenson was, perhaps, prouder of this little boyish experiment than he was of many of his subsequent achievements. Not having been

At this time, and for many years after, Stephenson dwelt in a cottage standing by the side of the road leading from the West Moor colliery to Killingworth. The railway from the West Moor Pit crosses this road close by the east end of the cottage. The dwelling originally consisted of but one apartment on the ground-floor, with the garret overhead, to which access was obtained by means of a stepladder. But with his own hands Stephenson built an oven, and in the course of time he added rooms to the cottage, until it became a comfortable four-roomed dwelling, in which he lived as long as he remained at Killingworth.

He continued as fond of birds and animals as ever, and seemed to have the power of attaching them to him in a remarkable degree. He had a blackbird at Killingworth so fond of him that it would fly about the cottage, and on holding out his finger, would come and perch upon it. A cage was built for 'blackie' in the partition between the passage and the room, a square of glass forming its outer wall; and Robert used afterwards to take pleasure in describing the oddity of the bird, imitating the manner in which it would cock its head on his father's entering the house, and follow him with his eye into the inner apartment.

Neighbours were accustomed to call at the cottage and have their clocks and watches set to rights when they went wrong. One day, after looking at the works of a watch left by a pitman's wife, George handed it to his son: 'Put her in the oven, Robert,' said he, 'for a quarter of an hour or so.' It seemed an odd way of repairing a watch; nevertheless, the watch was put into the oven, and at the end of the appointed time it was taken out, going all right. The wheels had merely got clogged by the oil congealed by the cold; which at once explains the rationale of the remedy adopted.

There was a little garden attached to the cottage, in which, while a workman, Stephenson took a pride in growing gigantic leeks and astounding cabbages. There was great competition among the villagers in the growth of vegetables, all of whom he excelled, excepting one of his neighbours, whose cabbages some-times outshone his. In the protection of his garden-crops from the ravages of the birds, he invented a strange sort of 'fley-craw', which moved its arms with the wind; and he fastened his garden-

quite accurately stated in the first edition of this book, Mr Stephenson noted the correction for the second, and wrote the author (18 September 1857) as follows: 'In the kite experiment, will you say, that the copper-wire was insulated by a few feet of silk cord; without this, the experiment cannot be made.'

door by means of a piece of ingenious mechanism, so that no one but himself could enter it. His cottage was quite a curiosity-shop of models of engines, self-acting planes, and perpetual-motion machines. The last-named contrivances, however, were only unsuccessful attempts to solve a problem which had effectually baffled hundreds of preceding inventors. His odd and eccentric contrivances often excited great wonder among the Killingworth villagers. He won the women's admiration by connecting their cradles with the smoke-jack, and making them self-acting. Then he astonished the pitmen by attaching an alarm to the clock of the watchman whose duty it was to call them betimes in the morning. He also contrived a wonderful lamp which burned under water, with which he was afterwards wont to amuse the Brandling family at Gosforth – going into the fish-pond at night, lamp in hand, attracting and catching the fish, which rushed wildly towards the flame.

Dr Bruce tells of a competition which Stephenson had with the joiner at Killingworth, as to which of them could make the best shoe-last; and when the former had done his work, either for the humour of the thing, or to secure fair play from the appointed judge, he took it to the Morrisons in Newcastle, and got them to put their stamp upon it. So that it is possible the Killingworth brakesman, afterwards the inventor of the safety-lamp and the originator of the railway system, and John Morrison, the last-maker, afterwards the translator of the Scriptures into the Chinese language, may have confronted each other in solemn contemplation over the successful last, which won the verdict coveted by its maker.

Sometimes he would endeavour to impart to his fellow-workmen the results of his scientific reading. Everything that he learnt from books was so new and so wonderful to him, that he regarded the facts he drew from them in the light of discoveries, as if they had been made but yesterday. Once he tried to explain to some of the pitmen how the earth was round, and kept turning round. But his auditors flatly declared the thing to be impossible, as it was clear that 'at the bottom side they must fall off!' 'Ah!' said George, 'you don't quite understand it yet.' His son Robert also early endeavoured to communicate to others the information which he had gathered at school; and Dr Bruce has related that, when visiting Killingworth on one occasion, he found him engaged in teaching algebra to such of the pitmen's boys as would become his pupils.

While Robert was still at school, his father proposed to him during the holidays that he should construct a sundial, to be placed over their cottage-door at West Moor. 'I expostulated with him at first,' said Robert, 'that I had not learnt sufficient astronomy and mathematics to enable me to make the necessary calculations. But he would have no denial. "The thing is to be done," said he; "so just set about it at once." Well; we got a *Ferguson's Astronomy*, and studied the subject together. Many a sore head I had while making the necessary calculations to adapt the dial to the latitude of Killingworth. But at length it was fairly drawn out on paper, and then my father got a stone, and we hewed, and carved, and polished it, until we made a very respectable dial of it; and there it is, you see,' pointing to it over the cottage-door, 'still quietly numbering the hours when the sun is shining. I assure you, not a little was thought of that piece of work by the pitmen when it was put up, and began to tell its tale of time.' The date carved upon the dial is 'August 11th, MDCCCXVI'. Both father and son were in after-life very proud of the joint production. Many years after, George took a party of savans, when attending the meeting of the British Association at Newcastle, over to Killingworth to see the pits, and he did not fail to direct their attention to the sundial; and Robert, on the last visit which he made to the place, a short time before his death, took a friend into the cottage, and pointed out to him the very desk, still there, at which he had sat while making his calculations of the latitude of Killingworth.

From the time of his appointment as engineer at the Killingworth Pit, George Stephenson was in a measure relieved from the daily routine of manual labour, having, as we have seen, advanced himself to the grade of a higher class workman. But he had not ceased to be a worker, though he employed his industry in a different way. It might, indeed, be inferred that he had now the command of greater leisure; but his spare hours were as much as ever given to work, either necessary or self-imposed. So far as regarded his social position, he had already reached the summit of his ambition; and when he had got his hundred a year, and his dun galloway to ride on, he said he never wanted to be any higher. When Robert Whetherly offered to give him an old gig, his travelling having so much increased of late, he accepted it with great reluctance, observing, that he should be ashamed to get into it, 'people would think him so proud'.

When the High Pit had been sunk, and the coal was ready for working, Stephenson erected his first windingengine to draw the coals out of the pit, and also a pumpingengine for Long Benton

Colliery, both of which proved quite successful. Among other works of this time, he projected and laid down a selfacting incline along the declivity which fell towards the coal-loading place near Willington, where he had officiated as brakesman; and he so arranged it, that the full waggons descending drew the empty waggons up the railroad. This was one of the first selfacting inclines laid down in the district.

Stephenson had now much better opportunities than hitherto for improving himself in mechanics. His familiar acquaintance with the steam-engine proved of great value to him. His shrewd insight, and his intimate practical acquaintance with its mechanism, enabled him to apprehend, as if by intuition, its most abstruse and difficult combinations. The practical study which he had given to it when a workman, and the patient manner in which he had groped his way through all the details of the machine, gave him the power of a master in dealing with it as applied to colliery purposes.

Sir Thomas Liddell was frequently about the works, and took pleasure in giving every encouragement to the enginewright in his efforts after improvement. The subject of the locomotive engine was already closely occupying Stephenson's attention; although it was still regarded as a curious and costly toy, of comparatively little real use. But he had at an early period detected its practical value, and formed an adequate conception of the might which as yet slumbered within it; and he now bent his entire faculties to the development of its extraordinary powers.

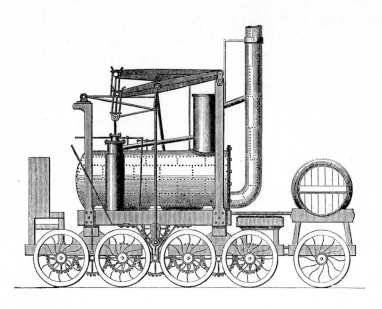

CHAPTER V — EARLY HISTORY OF THE LOCOMOTIVE — GEORGE STEPHENSON BEGINS ITS IMPROVEMENT

THE rapid increase in the coal trade of the Tyne about the beginning of the present century had the effect of stimulating the ingenuity of mechanics, and encouraging them to devise improved methods of transporting the coal from the pits to the shipping places. From our introductory chapter, it will have been observed that the improvements which had thus far been effected were confined almost entirely to the road. The railway waggons still continued to be drawn by horses. By improving and flattening the tramway, considerable economy in horse-power had indeed been secured; but unless some more effective method of mechanical traction could be devised, it was clear that railway improvements had almost reached its limits.

Many expedients had been tried with this object. One of the earliest was that of hoisting sails upon the waggons, and driving them along the waggon-way, as a ship is driven through the water by the wind. This method seems to have been employed by Sir Humphrey Mackworth, an ingenious coal-miner at Neath in Glamorganshire, about the end of the seventeenth century.

After having been lost sight of for more than a century, the same plan of impelling carriages was revived by Richard Lovell Edgworth, with the addition of a portable railway, since revived also, in Boydell's patent. But although Mr Edgworth devoted himself to the subject for many years, he failed in securing the adoption of his sailing carriage. It is indeed quite clear that a power so uncertain as wind could never be relied on for ordinary traffic, and Mr Edgworth's project was consequently left to repose in the limbo of the Patent Office, with thousands of other equally useless though ingenious contrivances.

A much more favourite scheme was the application of steam-power for the purpose of carriage traction. Savery, the inventor of the working steam-engine, was the first to propose its employment to propel vehicles along the common roads; and in 1759 Dr Robison, then a young man studying at Glasgow College, threw out the same idea to his friend James Watt; but the scheme was not matured.

The first locomotive steam-carriage was built at Paris by the French engineer Cugnot, a native of Lorraine. It is said to have been invented for the purpose of dragging cannon into the field independent of horses. The original model of this machine was made in 1763. Count Saxe was so much pleased with it, that on his recommendation a full-sized engine was constructed at the cost of the French monarch; and in 1769 it was tried in the presence of the Duc de Choiseul, Minister of War, General Gribeauval, and other officers. At one of the experiments it ran with such force as to knock down a wall in its way. But the new vehicle, loaded with four persons, could not travel faster than two and a half miles an hour. The boiler was insufficient in size, and it could only work for about fifteen minutes; after which it was necessary to wait until the steam had again risen to a sufficient pressure. To remedy this defect, Cugnot constructed a new machine in 1770, the working of which was more satisfactory. It was composed of two parts – the fore part consisting of a small steam-engine, formed of a round copper boiler, with a furnace inside, provided with two small chimneys and two single-acting brass steam cylinders, whose pistons acted alternately upon the single driving-wheel. The hinder part consisted merely of a rude carriage on two wheels to carry the load, furnished with a seat in front for the conductor. This engine was tried in the streets of Paris; but when passing near where the Madeleine now stands, it overbalanced itself on turning a corner, and fell over with a crash; after which, its employment being thought dangerous, it was locked up in the arsenal to prevent further mischief. The machine is, however, still to be seen in the collection of the Conservatoire des Arts et Métiers at Paris. It has very much the look of a long brewer's cart, with the addition of the circular boiler hung on at one end. Rough though it looks, it was a highly creditable piece of work, considering the period at which it was executed; and as the first actual machine constructed for the purpose of travelling on ordinary roads by the power of steam, it is certainly a most curious and interesting mechanical relic, well worthy of preservation.

But though Cugnot's road locomotive remained locked up from public sight, the subject was not dead; for we find inventors employing themselves from time to time in attempting to solve the problem of steam locomotion in places far remote from Paris. The idea had taken root in the minds of inventors, and was striving to grow into a reality. Thus Oliver Evans, the American, invented a steam-carriage in 1772 to travel on common roads; in 1787 he obtained from the State of Maryland an exclusive right to make and use steam-carriages, but his invention never came into use. Then, in 1784, William Symington, one of the early inventors of the steamboat, was similarly occupied in Scotland in endeavouring to develop the latent powers of the steam-carriage. He had a working model of one constructed, which he exhibited in 1786 to the professors of Edinburgh College; but the state of the Scotch roads was then so bad that he found it impracticable to proceed further with his scheme, which he shortly after abandoned in favour of steam navigation.

The same year in which Symington was occupied upon his steam-carriage, William Murdock, the friend and assistant of Watt, constructed his model of a locomotive at the opposite end of the island – at Redruth in Cornwall. His model was of small dimensions, standing little more than a foot high; and it was until recently in the possession of the son of the inventor, at whose house we saw it a few years ago.

It acted on the high-pressure principle, and, like Cugnot's engine, ran upon three wheels, the boiler being heated by a spirit-lamp. Small though the machine was, it went so fast on one occasion that it fairly outran its inventor. It seems that one night after returning from his duties at the Redruth mine, Murdock determined to try the working of his model locomotive. For this purpose he had recourse to the walk leading to the church, about a mile from the town. It was rather narrow, and was bounded on each side by high hedges. The night was dark, and Murdock set out alone to try his experiment. Having lit his lamp, the water boiled speedily, and off started the engine with the inventor after it. He soon heard distant shouts of terror. It was too dark to perceive objects; but he found, on following up the machine, that the cries proceeded from the worthy pastor of the parish, who, going towards the town, was met on this lonely road by the hissing and fiery little monster, which he subsequently declared he had taken to be the Evil One *in propriâ personâ*. No further steps were, however, taken by Murdock to embody his idea of a locomotive carriage in a more practical form.

The idea was next taken up by Murdock's pupil, Richard Trevithick, who resolved on building a steam-carriage adapted for common roads as well as railways. He took out a patent to secure the right of his invention in 1802. Andrew Vivian, his cousin, joined with him in the patent – Vivian finding the money, and Trevithick the brains. The steam-carriage built on this patent presented the appearance of an ordinary stage-coach on four wheels. The engine had one horizontal cylinder, which, together with the boiler and the furnace-box, was placed in the rear of the hind axle. The motion of the piston was transmitted to a separate crank-axle, from which, through the medium of spur-gear, the axle of the driving-wheel (which was mounted with a fly-wheel) derived its motion. The steam-cocks and the force-pump, as also the bellows used for the purpose of quickening combustion in the furnace, were worked off the same crank-axle.

John Petherick, of Camborne, has related that he remembers this first English steam-coach passing along the principal street of his native town. Considerable difficulty was experienced in keeping up the pressure of steam; but when there was pressure enough, Trevithick would call upon the people to 'jump up', so as to create a load upon the engine. It was soon covered with men attracted by the novelty, nor did their number seem to make any difference in the speed of the engine so long as there was steam enough; but it was constantly running short, and the horizontal bellows failed to keep it up.

This road-locomotive of Trevithick's was one of the first high-pressure working engines constructed on the principle of moving a piston by the elasticity of steam against the pressure only of the atmosphere. Such an engine had been described by Leopold, though in his apparatus it was proposed that the pressure should act only on one side of the piston. In Trevithick's engine the piston was not only raised, but was also depressed by the action of the steam, being in this respect an entirely original invention, and of great merit. The steam was admitted from the boiler under the

piston moving in a cylinder, impelling it upward. When the motion
had reached its limit, the communication between the piston and
the under side was shut off, and the steam allowed to escape into
the atmosphere. A passage being then opened between the boiler
and the upper side of the piston, which was pressed downwards,
the steam was again allowed to escape as before. Thus the power of
the engine was equal to the difference between the pressure of the
atmosphere and the elasticity of the steam in the boiler.

This steam-carriage excited considerable interest in the remote
district near the Land's End where it had been erected. Being so
far removed from the great movements and enterprise of the commercial world, Trevithick and Vivian determined upon exhibiting
their machine in the metropolis. They accordingly set out with it
to Plymouth, whence it was conveyed by sea to London.

The carriage safely reached the metropolis, and excited much
public interest. It also attracted the notice of scientific men,
among others of Mr Davies Gilbert, President of the Royal
Society, and Sir Humphry Davy, both Cornishmen like Trevithick,
who went to see the private performances of the engine, and were
greatly pleased with it. Writing to a Cornish friend shortly after its
arrival in town, Sir Humphry said: 'I shall soon hope to hear that
the roads of England are the haunts of Captain Trevithick's
dragons – a characteristic name.' The machine was afterwards
publicly exhibited in an enclosed piece of ground near Euston
Square, where the London and North-Western Station now stands,
and it dragged behind it a wheel-carriage full of passengers. On the
second day of the performance, crowds flocked to see it; but
Trevithick, in one of his odd freaks, shut up the place, and shortly
after removed the engine. It is, however, probable that the inventor came to the conclusion that the state of the roads at that
time was such as to preclude its coming into general use for purposes of ordinary traffic.

While the steam-carriage was being exhibited, a gentleman was
laying heavy wagers as to the weight which could be hauled by a
single horse on the Wandsworth and Croydon iron tramway; and
the number and weight of waggons drawn by the horse were something surprising. Trevithick very probably put the two things together – the steam-horse and the iron-way – and kept the performance in mind when he proceeded to construct his second or railway
locomotive. The idea was not, however, entirely new to him; for,
although his first engine had been constructed with a view to its
employment upon common roads, the specification of his patent

distinctly alludes to the application of his engine to travelling on railroads. Having been employed at the iron-works of Pen-y-darran, in South Wales, to erect a forge engine for the Company, a convenient opportunity presented itself, on the completion of this work, for carrying out his design of a locomotive to haul the minerals along the Pen-y-darran tramway. Such an engine was erected by him in 1803, in the blacksmith's shop at the Company's works, and it was finished and ready for trial before the end of the year.

The boiler of this second engine was cylindrical in form, flat at the ends, and made of wrought iron. The furnace and flue were inside the boiler, within which the single cylinder, eight inches in diameter and four feet six inches stroke, was placed horizontally. As in the first engine, the motion of the wheels was produced by spur gear, to which was also added a fly-wheel on one side, to secure a rotatory motion in the crank at the end of each stroke of the piston in the single cylinder. The waste steam was thrown into the chimney through a tube inserted into it at right angles; but it will be obvious that this arrangement was not calculated to produce any result in the way of a steam-blast in the chimney. In fact, the waste steam seems to have been turned into the chimney in order to get rid of the nuisance caused by throwing the jet directly into the air. Trevithick was here hovering on the verge of a great discovery; but that he was not aware of the action of the blast in contributing to increase the draught and thus quicken combustion, is clear from the fact that he employed bellows for this special purpose; and at a much later date (1815) he took out a patent which included a method of urging the fire by means of fanners.*

At the first trial of this engine it succeeded in dragging after it

---

* Mr Zerah Colburn, in his excellent work on *Locomotive Engineering and the Mechanism of Railways*, points out that Mr Davies Gilbert noted the effect of the discharge of the waste steam up the chimney of Trevithick's engine in increasing the draught, and wrote a letter to *Nicholson's Journal* (September 1805) on the subject. Mr Nicholson himself proceeded to investigate the subject, and in 1806 he took out a patent for 'steam-blasting apparatus', applicable to fixed engines. Trevithick himself, however, could not have had much faith in the steam-blast for locomotive purposes, else he would not have taken out his patent for urging the fire by means of fanners in 1815. But the fact is, that while the speed of the locomotive was only four or five miles an hour, the blast was scarcely needed. It was only when high speeds were adopted that artificial methods of urging the fire became necessary, and that the full importance of the invention was recognized. Like many other inventions, stimulated if not originated by necessity, the steam-blast was certainly reinvented, if not invented, by George Stephenson.

several waggons, containing ten tons of bar-iron, at the rate of about five miles an hour. Rees Jones, who worked at the fitting of the engine, and remembers its performances, says, 'She was used for bringing down metal from the furnaces to the Old Forge. She worked very well; but frequently, from her weight, broke the tram-plates and the hooks between the trams. After working for some time in this way, she took a load of iron from Pen-y-darran down the Basin-road, upon which road she was intended to work. On the journey she broke a great many of the tram-plates, and before reaching the basin ran off the road, and had to be brought back to Pen-y-darran by horses. The engine was never after used as a locomotive.'*

It seems to have been felt that unless the road were entirely reconstructed so as to bear the heavy weight of the locomotive – so much greater than that of the tram-waggons, to carry which the original rails had been laid down – the regular employment of Trevithick's high-pressure tram-engine was altogether impracticable; and as the owners of the works were not prepared to incur so serious a cost, it was determined to take the locomotive off the road, and employ it as an engine for other purposes. It was accordingly dismounted, and used for some time after as a pumping-engine, for which purpose it was found well adapted. Trevithick himself seems from this time to have taken no further steps to bring the locomotive into general use. We find him, shortly after, engaged upon schemes of a more promising character, abandoning the engine to other mechanical inventors, though little improvement was made in it for several years. An imaginary difficulty seems to have tended, among other obstacles, to prevent its adoption; viz. the idea that, if a heavy weight were placed behind the engine, the 'grip' or 'bite' of its smooth wheels upon the equally smooth iron rail, must necessarily be so slight that they would whirl round upon it, and, consequently, that the machine would not make progress. Hence Trevithick, in his patent, provided that the periphery of the driving-wheels should be made rough by the projection of bolts or cross-grooves, so that the adhesion of the wheels to the road might be secured.

Following up the presumed necessity for a more effectual adhesion between the wheels and the rails, Mr Blenkinsop of Leeds, in 1811, took out a patent for a racked or tooth-rail laid along one side of the road, into which the toothed-wheel of his locomotive worked as pinions work into a rack. The boiler of his engine was

* *Mining Journal,* 9 September 1858.

supported by a carriage with four wheels without teeth, and rested immediately upon the axles. These wheels were entirely independent of the working parts of the engine, and therefore merely supported its weight upon the rails, the progress being effected by means of the cogged-wheel working into the cogged-rail. The engine had two cylinders, instead of one as in Trevithick's engine. The invention of the double cylinder was due to Matthew Murray, of Leeds, one of the best mechanical engineers of his time; Mr Blenkinsop, who was not a mechanic, having consulted him as to all the practical arrangements. The connecting-rods gave the motion to two pinions by cranks at right angles to each other; these pinions communicating the motion to the wheel which worked into the cogged-rail.

Mr Blenkinsop's engines began running on the railway from the Middleton Collieries to Leeds, about $3\frac{1}{2}$ miles, on 12 August 1812. They continued for many years to be one of the principal curiosities of the place, and were visited by strangers from all parts. In 1816, the Grand Duke Nicholas (afterwards Emperor) of Russia observed the working of Blenkinsop's locomotive with curious interest and admiration. An engine dragged as many as thirty coal-waggons at a speed of about $3\frac{1}{4}$ miles per hour. These engines continued for many years to be thus employed in the haulage of coal, and furnished the first instance of the regular employment of locomotive power for commercial purposes.

The Messrs. Chapman, of Newcastle, in 1812, endeavoured to overcome the same fictitious difficulty of the want of adhesion between the wheel and the rail, by patenting a locomotive to work along the road by means of a chain stretched from one end of it to the other. This chain was passed once round a grooved barrel-wheel under the centre of the engine: so that, when the wheel turned, the locomotive, as it were, dragged itself along the railway. An engine, constructed after this plan, was tried on the Heaton Railway, near Newcastle; but it was so clumsy in its action, there was so great a loss of power by friction, and it was found to be so expensive and difficult to keep in repair, that it was soon abandoned. Another remarkable expedient was adopted by Mr Brunton, of the Butterley Works, Derbyshire, who, in 1813, patented his Mechanical Traveller, to go *upon legs* working alternately like those of a horse.* But this engine never got beyond the experi-

* Other machines, with legs, were patented in the following year by Lewis Gompertz and by Thomas Tindall. In Tindall's specification it is provided that the power of the engine is to be assisted by a *horizontal windmill*; and

mental state, for, at its very first trial, the driver, to make sure of a good start, overloaded the safety-valve, when the boiler burst and killed a number of the bystanders, wounding many more. These, and other contrivances with the same object, projected about the same time, show that invention was actively at work, and that many minds were anxiously labouring to solve the important problem of locomotive traction upon railways.

But the difficulties contended with by these early inventors, and the step-by-step progress which they made, will probably be best illustrated by the experiments conducted by Mr Blackett, of Wylam, which are all the more worthy of notice, as the persevering efforts of this gentleman in a great measure paved the way for the labours of George Stephenson, who, shortly after, took up the question of steam locomotion, and brought it to a successful issue.

The Wylam waggon-way is one of the oldest in the north of England. Down to the year 1807 it was formed of wooden spars or rails, laid down between the colliery at Wylam – where old Robert Stephenson had worked – and the village of Lemington, some four miles down the Tyne, where the coals were loaded into keels or barges, and floated down past Newcastle, to be shipped for London. Each chaldron-waggon had a man in charge of it, and was originally drawn by one horse. The rate at which the waggons were hauled was so slow that only two journeys were performed by each man and horse in one day, and three on the day following. This primitive waggon-way passed, as before stated, close in front of the cottage in which George Stephenson was born; and one of the earliest sights which met his infant eyes was this wooden tramroad worked by horses.

Mr Blackett was the first colliery owner in the North who took an active interest in the locomotive. Having formed the acquaintance of Trevithick in London, and inspected the performances of his engine, he determined to repeat the Pen-y-darran experiment upon the Wylam waggon-way. He accordingly obtained from Trevithick, in October 1804, a plan of his engine, provided with 'friction-wheels', and employed Mr John Whinfield, of Pipewell-gate, Gateshead, to construct it at his foundry there. The engine was constructed under the superintendence of one John Steele, an ingenious mechanic who had been in Wales, and worked under Trevithick in fitting the engine at Pen-y-darran. When the Gates-

the four pushers, or legs, are to be caused to come successively in contact with the ground, and impel the carriage!

head locomotive was finished, a temporary way was laid down in
the works, on which it was run backwards and forwards many
times. For some reason, however – it is said because the engine was
deemed too light for drawing the coal-trains – it never left the
works, but was dismounted from the wheels, and set to blow the
cupola of the foundry, in which service it long continued to be
employed.

Several years elapsed before Mr Blackett took any further steps
to carry out his idea. The final abandonment of Trevithick's locomotive at Pen-y-darran perhaps contributed to deter him from
proceeding further; but he had the wooden tramway taken up in
1808, and a plate-way of cast iron laid down instead – a single line
furnished with sidings to enable the laden waggons to pass the
empty ones. The new iron road proved so much smoother than the
old wooden one, that a single horse, instead of drawing one, was
now enabled to draw two, or even three, laden waggons.

Encouraged by the success of Mr Blenkinsop's experiment at
Leeds, Mr Blackett determined to follow his example; and in 1812
he ordered a second engine, to work with a toothed driving-wheel
upon a rack-rail. This locomotive was constructed by Thomas
Waters, of Gateshead, under the superintendence of Jonathan
Foster, Mr Blackett's principal engine-wright. It was a combination
of Trevithick's and Blenkinsop's engines; but it was of a more
awkward construction than either. The boiler was of cast iron. The
engine was provided with a single cylinder six inches in diameter,
with a fly-wheel working at one side to carry the crank over the
dead points. Jonathan Foster described it to the author in 1854,
as 'a strange machine, with lots of pumps, cog-wheels, and plugs,
requiring constant attention while at work'. The weight of the
whole was about six tons.

When finished, it was conveyed to Wylam on a waggon, and
there mounted upon a wooden frame supported by four pairs of
wheels, which had been constructed for its reception. A barrel of
water, placed on another frame upon wheels, was attached to it
as a tender. After a great deal of labour, the cumbrous machine
was got upon the road. At first it would not move an inch. Its
maker, Tommy Waters, became impatient, and at length enraged,
and taking hold of the lever of the safety valve, declared in his
desperation, that 'either *she* or *he* should go'. At length the
machinery was set in motion, on which, as Jonathan Foster described to the author 'she flew all to pieces, and, it was the biggest
wonder i' the world that we were not all blewn up'. The

incompetent and useless engine was declared to be a failure; it was shortly after dismounted and sold; and Mr Blackett's praiseworthy efforts thus far proved in vain.

He was still, however, desirous of testing the practicability of employing locomotive power in working the coal down to Leming-ton, and he determined on another trial. He accordingly directed his engine-wright to proceed with the building of a third engine in the Wylam workshops. This new locomotive had a single 8-inch cylinder, was provided with a fly-wheel like its predecessor, and the driving-wheel was cogged on one side to enable it to travel in the rack-rail laid along the road. This engine proved more success-ful than the former one; and it was found capable of dragging eight or nine loaded waggons, though at the rate of little more than a mile an hour, from the colliery to the shipping-place. It sometimes took six hours to perform the journey of five miles. Its weight was found too great for the road, and the cast-iron plates were con-stantly breaking. It was also very apt to get off the rack-rail, and then it stood still. The driver was one day asked how he got on. 'Get on?' said he, 'we don't get on; we only get off!' On such occasions, horses had to be sent to drag the waggons as before, and others to haul the engine back to the workshops. It was constantly getting out of order; its plugs, pumps, or cranks, got wrong; it was under repair as often as at work; at length it became so cranky that the horses were usually sent out after it to drag it when it gave up; and the workmen generally declared it to be a 'perfect plague'. Mr Blackett did not obtain credit among his neighbours for these experiments. Many laughed at his machines, regarding them only in the light of crotchets – frequently quoting the pro-verb that 'a fool and his money are soon parted'. Others regarded them as absurd innovations on the established method of hauling coal; and pronounced that they would 'never answer'.

Notwithstanding, however, the comparative failure of this second locomotive, Mr Blackett persevered with his experiments. He was zealously assisted by Jonathan Foster the engine-wright, and William Hedley, the viewer of the colliery, a highly ingenious person, who proved of great use in carrying out the experiments to a successful issue. One of the chief causes of failure being the rack-rail, the idea occurred to Mr Hedley that it might be possible to secure adhesion enough between the wheel and the rail by the mere weight of the engine, and he proceeded to make a series of experiments for the purpose of determining this problem. He had a frame placed on four wheels, and fitted up with windlasses attached by gearing to the several wheels. The frame having been properly weighted, six men were set to work the windlasses; when it was found that the adhesion of the smooth wheels on the smooth rails was quite sufficient to enable them to propel the machine without slipping. Having found the proportion which the power bore to the weight, he demonstrated by successive experiments that the weight of the engine would of itself produce sufficient adhesion to enable it to draw upon a smooth railroad the requisite number of waggons in all kinds of weather. And thus was the fallacy which had heretofore prevailed on this subject completely exploded, and it was satisfactorily proved that rack-rails, toothed wheels, endless chains, and legs, were alike unnecessary for the efficient traction of loaded waggons upon a moderately level road.

From this time forward considerably less difficulty was experienced in working the coal trains upon the Wylam tramroad. At length the rack-rail was dispensed with. The road was laid with heavier rails; the working of the old engine was improved; and a new engine was shortly after built and placed upon the road, still on eight wheels, driven by seven rack-wheels working inside them – with a wrought-iron boiler through which the flue was returned so as largely to increase the heating surface, and thus give increased power to the engine.

As may readily be imagined, the jets of steam from the piston, blowing off into the air at high pressure while the engine was in motion, caused considerable annoyance to horses passing along the Wylam road, at that time a public highway. The nuisance was felt to be almost intolerable, and a neighbouring gentleman threatened to have it put down. To diminish the noise as much as possible, Mr Blackett gave orders that so soon as any horse, or horses, came in sight, the locomotive was to be stopped, and the frightful blast of the engine thus suspended until the passing animals had got out of hearing. Much interruption was thus caused to the working of the railway, and it excited considerable dissatisfaction among the workmen. The following plan was adopted to abate the nuisance: a reservoir was provided immediately behind the chimney (as shown in the cut on p. 66) into which the waste steam was thrown after it had performed its office in the cylinder; and from this reservoir, the steam gradually escaped into the atmosphere without noise.

While Mr Blackett was thus experimenting and building locomotives at Wylam, George Stephenson was anxiously studying the same subject at Killingworth. He was no sooner appointed engine-wright of the collieries than his attention was directed to the means of more economically hauling the coal from the pits to the river-side. We have seen that one of the first important improvements which he made, after being placed in charge of the colliery machinery, was to apply the surplus power of a pumping steam-engine, fixed underground, to drawing the coals out of the deeper workings of the Killingworth mines – by which he succeeded in effecting a large reduction in the expenditure on manual and horse labour.

The coals, when brought above ground, had next to be labori-ously dragged by horses to the shipping staiths on the Tyne, several miles distant. The adoption of a tramroad, it is true, had tended to facilitate their transit: nevertheless the haulage was both tedious and costly. With the view of economizing labour, Stephenson laid down inclined planes where the nature of the ground would admit of this expedient. Thus, a train of full waggons let down the incline by means of a rope running over wheels laid along the tramroad, the other end of which was attached to a train of empty waggons placed at the bottom of the parallel road on the same incline, dragged them up by the simple power of gravity. But this applied only to a comparatively small part of the road. An economical method of working the coal trains, instead of by horses – the keep of which was at that time very costly, from the high price of corn – was still a great desideratum; and the best practical minds in the collieries were actively engaged in the attempts to solve the problem.

In the first place Stephenson resolved to make himself thor-oughly acquainted with what had already been done. Mr Blackett's engines were working daily at Wylam, past the cottage where he had been born; and thither he frequently went to inspect the improvements made by Mr Blackett from time to time both in the locomotive and in the plateway along which it worked. Jonathan Foster informed us that, after one of these visits, Stephenson declared to him his conviction that a much more effective engine might be made, that should work more steadily and draw the load more effectively.

He had also the advantage, about the same time, of seeing one of Blenkinsop's Leeds engines, which was placed on the tramway leading from the collieries of Kenton and Coxlodge, on 2 Sept-ember 1813. This locomotive drew sixteen chaldron waggons con-taining an aggregate weight of seventy tons, at the rate of about three miles an hour. George Stephenson and several of the Killing-worth men were among the crowd of spectators that day; and after examining the engine and observing its performances, he observed to his companions, that 'he thought he could make a better engine than that, to go upon legs'. Probably he had heard of the invention of Brunton, whose patent had by this time been published, and proved the subject of much curious speculation in the colliery districts. Certain it is, that, shortly after the inspection of the Coxlodge engine, he contemplated the construction of a new locomotive, which was to surpass all that had preceded it. He observed that those engines which had been constructed up to this time, however ingenious in their arrangements, had proved practical failures. Mr Blackett's was as yet both clumsy and expensive. Chapman's had been removed from the Heaton tramway in 1812, and was regarded as a total failure. And the Blenkinsop engine at Coxlodge was found very unsteady and costly in its working; besides, it pulled the rails to pieces, the entire strain being upon the rack-rail on one side of the road. The boiler, however, having soon after blown up, there was an end of that engine; and the colliery owners did not feel encouraged to try any further experiment.

An efficient and economical working locomotive, therefore, still remained to be invented; and to accomplish this object Mr Stephenson now applied himself. Profiting by what his predecessors had done, warned by their failures and encouraged by their partial successes, he commenced his labours. There was still wanting the man who should accomplish for the locomotive what James Watt had done for the steam-engine, and combine in a complete form the best points in the separate plans of others, embodying with them such original inventions and adaptations of his own as to entitle him to the merit of inventing the working locomotive, in the same manner as James Watt is to be regarded as the inventor of the working condensing-engine. This was the great work upon which George Stephenson now entered, though probably without any adequate idea of the ultimate importance of his labours to society and civilization.

He proceeded to bring the subject of constructing a 'Travelling Engine', as he then denominated the locomotive, under the notice of the lessees of the Killingworth Colliery, in the year 1813. Lord Ravensworth, the principal partner, had already formed a very favourable opinion of the new engine-wright, from the improvements which he had effected in the colliery engines, both above and below ground; and, after considering the matter, and hearing Stephenson's explanations, he authorized him to proceed with the construction of a locomotive – though his lordship was, by some, called a fool for advancing money for such a purpose. 'The first locomotive that I made,' said Stephenson, many years after,* when speaking of his early career at a public meeting in Newcastle, 'was at Killingworth Colliery, and with Lord Ravensworth's money. Yes; Lord Ravensworth and partners were the first to entrust me, thirty-two years since, with money to make a locomotive engine. I said to my friends, there was no limit to the speed of such an engine, if the works could be made to stand.'

Our engine-wright had, however, many obstacles to encounter before he could get fairly to work with the erection of his locomotive. His chief difficulty was in finding workmen sufficiently skilled in mechanics, and in the use of tools, to follow his instructions and embody his designs in a practical shape. The tools then in use about the collieries were rude and clumsy; and there were no such facilities as now exist for turning out machinery of an entirely new character. Stephenson was under the necessity of working with such men and tools as were at his command; and he had in a great measure to train and instruct the workmen himself. The engine was built in the workshops at the West Moor, the leading mechanic employed being the colliery blacksmith, an excellent workman in his way, though quite new to the work now entrusted to him.

In this first locomotive constructed at Killingworth, Stephenson to some extent followed the plan of Blenkinsop's engine. The boiler was cylindrical, of wrought iron, 8 feet in length and 34 inches in diameter, with an internal flue-tube 20 inches wide passing through it. The engine had two vertical cylinders of 8 inches diameter, and 2 feet stroke, let into the boiler, working the propelling gear with cross heads and connecting rods. The power of the two cylinders was combined by means of spurwheels, which communicated the motive power to the wheels supporting the engine on the rail, instead of, as in Blenkinsop's engine, to cogwheels which acted on the cogged rail independent of the four supporting wheels. The engine thus worked upon what is termed the second motion. The chimney was of wrought iron, round which was a chamber extending back to the feed-pumps, for the purpose of heating the water previous to its injection into the boiler. The engine had no springs, and was mounted on a wooden frame supported on four wheels. In order to neutralize as much as possible the jolts and shocks which such an engine would necessarily encounter from the ob-

* Speech at the opening of the Newcastle and Darlington Railway, 18 June 1844.

John Lucas   William Holl

George Stephenson

stacles and inequalities of the then very imperfect plateway, the water-barrel which served for a tender was fixed to the end of a lever and weighted, the other end of the lever being connected with the frame of the locomotive carriage. By this means the weight of the two was more equally distributed, though the contrivance did not by any means compensate for the absence of springs.

The wheels of the locomotive were all smooth, Mr Stephenson having satisfied himself by experiment that the adhesion between the wheels of a loaded engine and the rail would be sufficient for the purpose of traction. Robert Stephenson informed us that his father caused a number of workmen to mount upon the wheels of a waggon moderately loaded, and throw their entire weight upon the spokes on one side, when he found that the waggon could thus be easily propelled forward without the wheels slipping. This, together with other experiments, satisfied him of the expediency of adopting smooth wheels on his engine, and it was so finished accordingly.

The engine was, after much labour and anxiety, and frequent alterations of parts, at length brought to completion, having been about ten months in hand. It was placed upon the Killingworth Railway on 25 July 1814; and its powers tried on the same day. On an ascending gradient of 1 in 450, the engine succeeded in drawing after it eight loaded carriages of thirty tons' weight at about four miles an hour; and for some time after it continued regularly at work.

Although a considerable advance upon previous locomotives, 'Blutcher' (as the engine was popularly called) was nevertheless a somewhat cumbrous and clumsy machine. The parts were huddled together. The boiler constituted the principal feature; and being the foundation of the other parts, it was made to do duty not only as a generator of steam, but also as a basis for the fixings of the machinery and for the bearings of the wheels and axles. The want of springs was seriously felt; and the progress of the engine was a succession of jolts, causing considerable derangement to the machinery. The mode of communicating the motive power to the wheels by means of the spur-gear also caused frequent jerks, each cylinder alternately propelling or becoming propelled by the other, as the pressure of the one upon the wheels became greater or less than the pressure of the other; and when the teeth of the cog-wheels became at all worn, a rattling noise was produced during the travelling of the engine.

As the principal test of the success of the locomotive was its

economy as compared with horse-power, careful calculations were
made with the view of ascertaining this important point. The result
was, that it was found the working of the engine was at first barely
economical; and at the end of the year the steam-power and the
horse-power were ascertained to be as nearly as possible upon a par
in point of cost. The fate of the locomotive in a great measure
depended on this very engine. Its speed was not beyond that of a
horse's walk, and the heating surface presented to the fire being
comparatively small, sufficient steam could not be raised to enable
it to accomplish more on an average than about four miles an hour.
The result was anything but decisive; and the locomotive might
have been condemned as useless, had not our engineer at this
juncture applied the steam-blast, and by its means carried his
experiment to a triumphant issue.

The steam, after performing its duty in the cylinders, was at first
allowed to escape into the open atmosphere with a hissing blast,
to the terror of horses and cattle. It was complained of as a
nuisance; and an action at law against the colliery lessees was
threatened unless it was stopped. Stephenson's attention had been
drawn to the much greater velocity with which the steam issued
from the exit pipe compared with that at which the smoke escaped
from the chimney. He conceived that, by conveying the eduction
steam into the chimney, by means of a small pipe, after it had performed its office in the cylinders, allowing it to escape in a vertical
direction, its velocity would be imparted to the smoke from the
fire, or to the ascending current of air in the chimney, thereby
increasing the draught, and consequently the intensity of combustion in the furnace.

The experiment was no sooner made than the power of the
engine was at once more than doubled; combustion was stimulated
by the blast; consequently the capability of the boiler to generate
steam was greatly increased, and the effective power of the engine
augmented in precisely the same proportion, without in any way
adding to its weight. This simple but beautiful expedient was really
fraught with the most important consequences to railway communication; and it is not too much to say that the success of the
locomotive has in a great measure been the result of its adoption.
Without the steam-blast, by means of which the intensity of combustion is maintained at its highest point, producing a correspond-
ingly rapid evolution of steam, high rates of speed could not have
been kept up; the advantages of the multitubular boiler (afterwards invented) could never have been fairly tested; and loco-

motives might still have been dragging themselves unwieldily along at little more than five or six miles an hour.

The steam-blast had scarcely been adopted, with so decided a success, when Stephenson, observing the numerous defects in his engine, and profiting by the experience which he had already acquired, determined to construct a second engine, in which to embody his improvements in their best form. Careful and cautious observation of the working of his locomotive had convinced him that the complication arising out of the action of the two cylinders being combined by spur-wheels would prevent its coming into practical use. He accordingly directed his attention to an entire change in the construction and mechanical arrangements of the machine; and in the following year, conjointly with Mr Dodds, who provided the necessary funds, he took out a patent, dated 28 February 1815, for an engine which combined in a remarkable degree the essential requisites of an economical locomotive; that is to say, few parts, simplicity in their action, and directness in the mode by which the power was communicated to the wheels supporting the engine.

This locomotive, like the first, had two vertical cylinders, which communicated *directly* with each pair of the four wheels that supported the engine, by means of a crosshead and a pair of connecting-rods. But in attempting to establish a direct communication between the cylinders and the wheels that rolled upon the rails, considerable difficulties presented themselves. The ordinary joints could not be employed to unite the parts of the engine, which was a rigid mass, with the wheels rolling upon the irregular surface of the rails; for it was evident that the two rails of the line of way – more especially in those early days of imperfect construction of the permanent road – could not always be maintained at the same level, that the wheel at one end of the axle might be depressed into one part of the line which had subsided, while the other wheel would be comparatively elevated; and in such a position of the axle and wheels, it was obvious that a rigid communication between the cross head and the wheels was impracticable. Hence it became necessary to form a joint at the top of the piston-rod where it united with the cross head, so as to permit the cross head to preserve complete parallelism with the axle of the wheels with which it was in communication.

In order to obtain that degree of flexibility combined with direct action, which was essential for ensuring power and avoiding needless friction and jars from irregularities in the road, Stephenson

made use of the 'ball and socket' joint for effecting a union between the ends of the cross heads where they united with the
connecting-rods, and between the ends of the connecting-rods
where they were united with the crank-pins attached to each
driving-wheel. By this arrangement the parallelism between the
cross head and the axle was at all times maintained and preserved, without producing any serious jar or friction on any part
of the machine. Another important point was, to combine each
pair of wheels by means of some simple mechanism instead of by
the cogwheels which had formerly been used. And, with this
object, Stephenson made cranks in each axle at right angles to
each other, with rods communicating horizontally between them.

A locomotive was constructed upon this plan in 1815, and was
found to answer extremely well. But at that period the mechanical
skill of the country was not equal to forging cranked axles of the
soundness and strength necessary to stand the jars incident to
locomotive work. Stephenson was accordingly compelled to fall
back upon a substitute, which, although less simple and efficient,
was within the mechanical capabilities of the workmen of that day,
in respect of construction as well as repair. He adopted a chain
which rolled over indented wheels placed on the centre of each
axle, and was so arranged that the two pairs of wheels were
effectually coupled and made to keep pace with each other. The
chain, however, after a few years' use, became stretched; and then
the engines were liable to irregularity in their working, especially
in changing from working back to working forward again. Eventually the chain was laid aside, and the front and hind wheels were
united by rods on the outside, instead of by rods and crank axles
inside, as specified in the original patent. This expedient completely answered the purpose required, without involving any
expensive or difficult workmanship.

Thus, in 1815, by dint of patient and persevering labour – by
careful observation of the works of others, and never neglecting to
avail himself of their suggestions – Stephenson succeeded in manufacturing an engine which included the following important
improvements on all previous attempts in the same direction,
viz. simple and direct communication between the cylinders and
the wheels rolling upon the rails; joint adhesion of all the wheels,
attained by the use of horizontal connecting-rods; and finally, a
beautiful method of exciting the combustion of the fuel by employing the waste steam, which had formerly been allowed to
escape uselessly into the air. Although many improvements in

detail were afterwards introduced in the locomotive by George Stephenson himself, as well as by his equally distinguished son, it is perhaps not too much to say that this engine, as a mechanical contrivance, contained the germ of all that has since been effected. It may in fact be regarded as the type of the present locomotive engine.

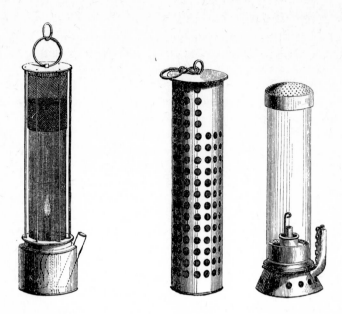

CHAPTER VI – INVENTION OF THE 'GEORDY' SAFETY-LAMP

EXPLOSIONS of fire-damp were unusually frequent in the coal-mines of Northumberland and Durham about the time when George Stephenson was engaged in the construction of his first locomotives. These explosions were often attended with fearful loss of life and dreadful suffering to the workpeople. Killingworth Colliery was not free from such deplorable calamities; and during the time that Stephenson was employed as a brakesman at the West Moor, several 'blasts' took place in the pit, by which many workmen were scorched and killed, and the owners of the colliery sustained heavy losses. One of the most serious of these accidents occurred in 1806, not long after he had been appointed brakesman, by which ten persons were killed. Stephenson was working at the mouth of the pit at the time, and the circumstances connected with the accident made a deep impression on his mind.

Another explosion took place in the same pit in 1809, by which twelve persons lost their lives. The blast did not reach the shaft as in the former case; the unfortunate persons in the pit having been suffocated by the after-damp. More calamitous still were the explosions which took place in the neighbouring collieries; one of the worst being that of 1812, in the Felling Pit, near Gateshead, by

which no fewer than ninety men and boys were suffocated or burnt
to death. And a similar accident occurred in the same pit in the
year following, by which twenty-two persons perished.

It was natural that George Stephenson should devote his attention to the causes of these deplorable accidents, and to the means
by which they might if possible be prevented. His daily occupation
led him to think much and deeply on the subject. As engine-wright
of a colliery so extensive as that of Killingworth, where there were
nearly 160 miles of gallery excavation, in which he personally
superintended the working of the inclined planes along which the
coals were sent to the pit entrance, he was necessarily very often
underground, and brought face to face with the dangers of fire-
damp. From fissures in the roofs of the galleries, carburetted
hydrogen gas was constantly flowing; in some of the more dangerous places it might be heard escaping from the crevices of the coal
with a hissing noise. Ventilation, firing, and all conceivable modes
of drawing out the foul air had been adopted, and the more
dangerous parts of the galleries were built up. Still the danger
could not be wholly prevented. The miners must necessarily guide
their steps through the extensive underground ways with lighted
lamps or candles, the naked flame of which, coming in contact with
the inflammable air, daily exposed them and their fellow-workers
in the pit to the risk of death in one of its most dreadful forms.

One day, in 1814, a workman hurried into Stephenson's cottage
with the startling information that the deepest main of the colliery
was on fire! He immediately hastened to the pit-head, about a
hundred yards off, whither the women and children of the colliery
were running, with wildness and terror depicted in every face. In a
commanding voice Stephenson ordered the engineman to lower
him down the shaft in the corve. There was peril, it might be
death, before him, but he must go.

He was soon at the bottom, and in the midst of the men, who
were paralysed by the danger which threatened the lives of all in
the pit. Leaping from the corve on its touching the ground, he
called out: 'Are there six men among you who have the courage to
follow me? If so, come, and we will put the fire out.' The Killingworth pitmen had the most perfect confidence in their engine-
wright, and they readily volunteered to follow him. Silence succeeded the frantic tumult of the previous minute, and the men set
to work with a will. In every mine, bricks, mortar, and tools
enough are at hand, and by Stephenson's direction the materials
were forthwith carried to the required spot, where, in a very short

time, a wall was raised at the entrance to the main, he himself
taking the most active part in the work. The atmospheric air was
by this means excluded, the fire was extinguished, the people were
saved from death, and the mine was preserved.

This anecdote of Stephenson was related to the writer, near the
pit-mouth, by one of the men who had been present and helped to
build up the brick wall by which the fire was stayed, though several
workmen were suffocated. He related that, when down the pit
some days after, seeking out the dead bodies, the cause of the
accident was the subject of conversation, and Stephenson was
asked, 'Can nothing be done to prevent such awful occurrences?'
His reply was that he thought something might be done. 'Then,'
said the other, 'the sooner you start the better; for the price of
coal-mining now is *pitmen's lives.*'

Fifty years since, many of the best pits were so full of the
inflammable gas given forth by the coal, that they could not be
worked without the greatest danger; and for this reason some were
altogether abandoned. The rudest possible methods were adopted
of producing light sufficient to enable the pitmen to work by. The
phosphorescence of decayed fish-skins was tried; but this, though
safe, was very inefficient. The most common method employed was
what was called a steel mill, the notched wheel of which, being
made to revolve against a flint, struck a succession of sparks,
which scarcely served to do more than make the darkness visible.
A boy carried the apparatus after the miner, working the wheel,
and by the imperfect light thus given forth he plied his dangerous
trade. Candles were only used in those parts of the pit where gas
was not abundant. Under this rude system not more than one-
third of the coal could be worked; and two-thirds were left.

What the workmen, not less than the coal-owners, eagerly
desired was a lamp that should give forth sufficient light, without
communicating flame to the inflammable gas which accumulated
in certain parts of the pit. Something had already been attempted
towards the invention of such a lamp by Dr Clanny, of Sunderland,
who, in 1813, contrived an apparatus to which he gave air from
the mine through water, by means of bellows. This lamp went out
of itself in inflammable gas. It was found, however, too unwieldy
to be used by the miners for the purposes of their work, and did
not come into general use. A committee of gentlemen was formed
to investigate the causes of the explosions, and to devise, if possible, some means of preventing them. At the invitation of that
Committee, Sir Humphry Davy, then in the full zenith of his

reputation, was requested to turn his attention to the subject. He accordingly visited the collieries near Newcastle on 24 August 1815; and on 9 November following, he read before the Royal Society of London his celebrated paper 'On the Fire-Damp of Coal Mines, and on Methods of lighting the Mine so as to prevent its explosion.'

But a humbler though not less diligent and original thinker had been at work before him, and had already practically solved the problem of the Safety-Lamp. Stephenson was, of course, well aware of the anxiety which prevailed in the colliery districts as to the invention of a lamp which should give light enough for the miners to work by without exploding the fire-damp. The painful incidents above described only served to quicken his eagerness to master the difficulty.

For several years he had been engaged, in his own rude way, in making experiments with the fire-damp in the Killingworth mine. The pitmen used to expostulate with him on these occasions, believing his experiments to be fraught with danger. One of the sinkers, observing him holding up lighted candles to the windward of the 'blower' or fissure from which the inflammable gas escaped, entreated him to desist; but Stephenson's answer was, that 'he was busy with a plan by which he hoped to make his experiments useful for preserving men's lives'. On these occasions the miners usually got out of the way before he lit the gas.

In 1815, although he was very much occupied with the business of the collieries and the improvement of his locomotive engine, he was also busily engaged in making experiments upon inflammable gas in the Killingworth pit. According to the explanation afterwards given by him, he imagined that if he could construct a lamp with a chimney so arranged as to cause a strong current, it would not fire at the top of the chimney; as the burnt air would ascend with such a velocity as to prevent the inflammable air of the pit from descending towards the flame; and such a lamp, he thought, might be taken into a dangerous atmosphere without risk of exploding.

Such was Stephenson's theory when he proceeded to embody his idea of a miner's safety-lamp in a practical form. In the month of August 1815, he requested his friend Nicholas Wood, the head viewer, to prepare a drawing of a lamp according to the description which he gave him. After several evenings' careful deliberations, the drawing was made, and shown to several of the head men about the works.

Stephenson proceeded to order a lamp to be made by a Newcastle

tinman, according to his plan; and at the same time he
directed a glass to be made for the lamp at the Northumberland
Glass House. Both were received by him from the makers on
21 October, and the lamp was taken to Killingworth for the
purpose of immediate experiment.

'I remember that evening so distinctly as if it had been but
yesterday,' said Robert Stephenson, describing the circumstances
to the author in 1857: 'Moodie came to our cottage about dusk,
and asked, "if father had got back yet with the lamp?" "No."
"Then I'll wait till he comes," said Moodie, "he can't be long now."
In about half an hour, in came my father, his face all radiant. He
had the lamp with him! It was at once uncovered, and shown to
Moodie. Then it was filled with oil, trimmed, and lighted. All was
ready, only the head viewer hadn't arrived. "Run over to Benton
for Nichol, Robert," said my father to me, "and ask him to come
directly; say we're going down the pit to try the lamp." By this
time it was quite dark; and off I ran to bring Nicholas Wood. His
house was at Benton, about a mile off. There was a short cut
through the Churchyard, but just as I was about to pass the
wicket, I saw what I thought was a white figure moving about
among the grave-stones. I took it for a ghost! My heart fluttered,
and I was in a great fright, but to Wood's house I must get, so I
made the circuit of the Churchyard; and when I got round to the
other side I looked, and lo! the figure was still there. But what do
you think it was? Only the grave-digger, plying his work at that
late hour by the light of his lantern set upon one of the grave-
stones! I found Wood at home, and in a few minutes he was
mounted and off to my father's. When I got back, I was told they
had just left – it was then about eleven – and gone down the shaft
to try the lamp in one of the most dangerous parts of the mine.'

Arrived at the bottom of the shaft with the lamp, the party
directed their steps towards one of the foulest galleries in the pit,
where the explosive gas was issuing through a blower in the roof
of the mine with a loud hissing noise. By erecting some deal board-
ing round that part of the gallery into which the gas was escaping,
the air was made more foul for the purpose of the experiment.
After waiting about an hour, Moodie, whose practical experience
of fire-damp in pits was greater than that of either Stephenson or
Wood, was requested to go into the place which had thus been
made foul; and, having done so, he returned, and told them that
the smell of the air was such, that if a lighted candle were now
introduced, an explosion must inevitably take place. He cautioned

Stephenson as to the danger both to themselves and to the pit, if the gas took fire. But Stephenson declared his confidence in the safety of his lamp, and, having lit the wick, he boldly proceeded with it towards the explosive air. The others, more timid and doubtful, hung back when they came within hearing of the blower; and apprehensive of the danger, they retired into a safe place, out of sight of the lamp, which gradually disappeared with its bearer in the recesses of the mine.*

* The Editor of the *Athenaeum* having (8 November 1862) characterized the author's account of this affair as 'perfectly untrue' and a 'fiction', it becomes necessary to say a few words in explanation of it. The Editor of the *Athenaeum* quotes in support of his statement a passage from Mr Nicholas Wood, who, however, does not say that the anecdote is 'perfectly untrue', but merely that 'the danger was *not quite so great* as is represented': he adds that 'at most an explosion might have burnt the hands of the operator, but would not extend a few feet from the blower'. However that may be, we were not without good authority for making the original statement. The facts were verbally communicated to the author in the first place by Robert Stephenson, to whom the chapter was afterwards read in MS., in the presence of Mr Sopwith, F.R.S. at Mr Stephenson's house in Gloucester Square, and received his entire approval. But at the time at which Mr Stephenson communicated the verbal information, he also handed a little book with his name written in it, still in the author's possession, saying, 'Read that, you will find it all there.' We have again referred to the little book which contains, among other things, a pamphlet, entitled *Report on the Claims of Mr George Stephenson relative to the Invention of his Safety Lamp. By the Committee appointed at a Meeting holden in Newcastle, on this 1st of November 1817. With an Appendix containing the Evidence.* Among the witnesses examined were George Stephenson, Nicholas Wood, and John Moodie, and their evidence is given in the pamphlet. We quote that of Stephenson and Moodie, which was not contradicted, but in all material points confirmed by Wood, and was published, we believe, with his sanction. George Stephenson said, that he tried the first lamp 'in a part of the mine where the air was highly explosive. Nicholas Wood and John Moodie were his companions when the trial was made. They became frightened when they came within hearing of the blower, and would not go any further. Mr Stephenson went alone with the lamp to the mouth of the blower,' etc. This evidence was confirmed by John Moodie, who said the air of the place where the experiment was about to be tried was such, that, if a lighted candle had been introduced, an explosion would have taken place that would have been 'extremely dangerous'. 'Told Stephenson it was foul, and hinted at the danger; nevertheless, Stephenson *would* try the lamp, confiding in its safety. Stephenson took the lamp and went with it into the place in which Moodie had been, and Moodie and Wood, apprehensive of the danger, retired to a greater distance,' etc. The other details of the statement made in the text, are fully borne out by the published evidence, the accuracy of which, so far as the author is aware, has never before been called in question.

Advancing to the place of danger, and entering within the fouled air, his lighted lamp in hand, Stephenson held it firmly out, in the full current of the blower, and within a few inches of its mouth! Thus exposed, the flame of the lamp at first increased, then flickered, and then went out; but there was no explosion of the gas. Returning to his companions, who were still at a distance, he told them what had occurred. Having now acquired somewhat more confidence, they advanced with him to a point from which they could observe him repeat his experiment, but still at a safe distance. They saw that when the lighted lamp was held within the explosive mixture, there was a great flame; the lamp became almost full of fire; and then it smothered out. Again returning to his companions, he relighted the lamp, and repeated the experiment several times with the same result. At length Wood and Moodie ventured to advance close to the fouled part of the pit; and, in making some of the later trials, Mr Wood himself held up the lighted lamp to the blower.

Before leaving the pit, Stephenson expressed his opinion that by an alteration of the lamp which he then contemplated, he could make it burn better; this was by a change in the slide through which the air was admitted into the lower part, under the flame. After making some experiments on the air collected at the blower, by bladders which were mounted with tubes of various diameters, he satisfied himself that, when the tube was reduced to a certain diameter, the foul air would not pass through; and he fashioned his slide accordingly, reducing the diameter of the tube, until he conceived it was quite safe. In about a fortnight the experiments were repeated, in a place purposely made foul as before; on this occasion a larger number of persons ventured to witness them, and they again proved successful. The lamp was not yet, however, so efficient as the inventor desired. It required, he observed, to be kept very steady when burning in the inflammable gas, otherwise it was liable to go out, in consequence, as he imagined, of the contact of the burnt air (as he then called it), or azotic gas, which lodged round the exterior of the flame. If the lamp was moved horizontally, the azote came in contact with the flame and extinguished it. 'It struck me,' said he, 'that if I put more tubes in, I should discharge the poisonous matter that hung round the flame, by admitting the air to its exterior part.' Although he had then no access to scientific books, nor intercourse with scientific men, nor anything that could assist him in his investigation, besides his own indefatigable spirit of inquiry, he contrived a rude apparatus by which he tested the explosive properties of the gas and the velocity of current (for this was the direction of his inquiries) necessary to enable the explosive gas to pass through tubes of different diameters. In making these experiments in his humble cottage at the West Moor, Nicholas Wood and George's son Robert usually acted as his assistants, and sometimes the gentlemen of the neighbourhood interested in coal-mining attended as spectators.

These experiments were not performed without risk, for on one occasion the experimenting party had nearly blown off the roof of the cottage. One of these 'blows up' was described by Stephenson himself before the Committee on Accidents in Coal Mines, in 1835: 'I made several experiments,' said he, 'as to the velocity required in tubes of different diameters, to prevent explosion from fire-damp. We made the mixtures in all proportions of light car-buretted hydrogen with atmospheric air in the receiver, and we found by the experiments that when a current of the most ex-plosive mixture that we could make was forced up a tube $\frac{4}{10}$ of an inch in diameter, the necessary current was 9 inches in a second to prevent its coming down that tube. These experiments were repeated several times. We had two or three blows up in making the experiments, by the flame getting down into the receiver, though we had a piece of very fine wire-gauze put at the bottom of the pipe, between the receiver and the pipe through which we were forcing the current. In one of these experiments I was watch-ing the flame in the tube, my son was taking the vibrations of the pendulum of the clock, and Mr Wood was attending to give me the column of water as I called for it, to keep the current up to a certain point. As I saw the flame descending in the tube I called for more water, and Wood unfortunately turned the cock the wrong way, the current ceased, the flame went down the tube, and all our implements were blown to pieces, which at the time we were not very able to replace.'

Stephenson followed up those experiments by others of a similar kind, with the view of ascertaining whether ordinary flame would pass through tubes of a small diameter and with this object he filed off the barrels of several small keys. Placing these together. he held them perpendicularly over a strong flame, and ascertained that it did not pass upward. This was a further proof to him of the soundness of the course he was pursuing.

In order to correct the defect of his first lamp he resolved to alter it so as to admit the air to the flame by several tubes of reduced diameter, instead of by a single tube. He inferred that a sufficient quantity of air would thus be introduced into the lamp for the purposes of combustion, while the smallness of the apertures would still prevent the explosive gas passing downwards, at the same time that the 'burnt air' (the cause, in his opinion, of the lamp going out) would be more effectually dislodged. He accordingly took the lamp to a tinman in Newcastle, and had it altered so that the air was admitted by three small tubes inserted in the bottom of the lamp, the openings of which were placed on the outside of the burner, instead of having (as in the original lamp) the one tube opening directly under the flame.

This second or altered lamp was tried in the Killingworth pit on 4 November, and was found to burn better than the first, and to be perfectly safe. But as it did not yet come quite up to the inventor's expectations, he proceeded to contrive a third lamp, in which he proposed to surround the oil vessel with a number of capillary tubes. Then it struck him, that if he cut off the middle of the tubes, or made holes in metal plates, placed at a distance from each other, equal to the length of the tubes, the air would get in better, and the effect in preventing explosion would be the same.

He was encouraged to persevere in the completion of his safety-lamp by the occurrence of several fatal accidents about this time in the Killingworth pit. On 9 November a boy was killed by a blast in the *A* pit, at the very place where Stephenson had made the experiments with his first lamp; and, when told of the accident, he observed that if the boy had been provided with his lamp, his life would have been saved. On 20 November he went over to Newcastle to order his third lamp from a plumber in that town. The plumber referred him to his clerk, whom Stephenson invited to join him at a neighbouring public-house, where they might quietly talk over the matter, and finally settle the plan of the new lamp. They adjourned to the 'Newcastle Arms', near the present High Level Bridge, where they had some ale, and a design of the lamp was drawn in pencil upon a half-sheet of foolscap, with a rough specification subjoined. The sketch, when shown to us by Robert Stephenson some years since, still bore the marks of the ale. It was a very rude design, but sufficient to work from. It was immediately placed in the hands of the workmen, finished in the course of a few days, and experimentally tested in the Killingworth pit like the previous lamps, on 30 November. At that time neither Stephenson nor Wood had heard of Sir Humphry Davy's experiments nor of the lamp which that gentleman proposed to construct.

An angry controversy afterwards took place as to the respective merits of George Stephenson and Sir Humphry Davy in respect of the invention of the safety-lamp. A committee was formed on both sides, and the facts were stated in various ways. It is perfectly clear, however, that Stephenson had ascertained *the fact* that flame will not pass through tubes of a certain diameter – the principle on which the safety-lamp is constructed – before Sir Humphry Davy had formed any definite idea on the subject, or invented the model lamp afterwards exhibited by him before the Royal Society. Stephenson had actually constructed a lamp on such a principle, and proved its safety, before Sir Humphry had communicated his views on the subject to any person; and by the time that the first public intimation had been given of his discovery, Stephenson's second lamp had been constructed and tested in like manner in the Killingworth pit. The *first* was tried on 21 October 1815; the *second* was tried on 4 November; but it was not until 9 November that Sir Humphry Davy presented his first lamp to the public. And by the 30th of the same month, as we have seen, Stephenson had constructed and tested his *third* safety-lamp.

Stephenson's theory of the 'burnt air' and the 'draught' was no doubt wrong; but his lamp was right, and that was the great fact which mainly concerned him. Torricelli did not know the rationale of his tube, nor Otto Gürike that of his air-pump; yet no one thinks of denying them the merit of their inventions on that account. The discoveries of Volta and Galvani were in like manner independent of theory; the greatest discoveries consisting in bringing to light certain grand facts, on which theories are afterwards framed. Our inventor had been pursuing the Baconian method, though he did not think of that, but of inventing a safe lamp, which he knew could only be done through the process of repeated experiment. He experimented upon the fire-damp at the blowers in the mine, and also by means of the apparatus which was blown up in his cottage, as above described by himself. By experiment he distinctly ascertained that the explosion of fire-damp could not pass through small tubes; and he also did what had not before been done by any inventor – he constructed a lamp on this principle, and repeatedly proved its safety at the risk of his life. At the same time, there is no doubt that it was to Sir Humphry Davy that the merit belonged of having pointed out the true law on which the safety-lamp is constructed.

The subject of this important invention excited so much interest in the northern mining districts, and Stephenson's numerous friends considered his lamp so completely successful – having stood the test of repeated experiments – that they urged him to bring his invention before the Philosophical and Literary Society of Newcastle, of whose apparatus he had availed himself in the course of his experiments on fire-damp. After much persuasion he consented, and a meeting was appointed for the purpose of receiving his explanations, on the evening of 5 December 1815. Stephenson was at that time so diffident in manner and unpractised in speech, that he took with him his friend Nicholas Wood, to act as his interpreter and expositor on the occasion. From eighty to a hundred of the most intelligent members of the society were present at the meeting, when Mr Wood stood forward to expound the principles on which the lamp had been formed, and to describe the details of its construction. Several questions were put, to which Mr Wood proceeded to give replies to the best of his knowledge. But Stephenson, who up to that time had stood behind Wood, screened from notice, observing that the explanations given were not quite correct, could no longer control his reserve, and, standing forward, he proceeded in his strong Northumbrian dialect, to describe the lamp, down to its minutest details. He then produced several bladders full of carburetted hydrogen, which he had collected from the blowers in the Killingworth mine, and proved the safety of his lamp by numerous experiments with the gas, repeated in various ways; his earnest and impressive manner exciting in the minds of his auditors the liveliest interest both in the inventor and his invention.

Shortly after, Sir Humphry Davy's model lamp was received and exhibited to the coal-miners at Newcastle, on which occasion the observation was made by several gentlemen, 'Why, it is the same as Stephenson's!'

Notwithstanding Stephenson's claim to be regarded as the first inventor of the Tube Safety-lamp, his merits do not seem to have been generally recognized; and Sir Humphry Davy carried off the larger share of the éclat which attached to the discovery. What chance had the unknown workman of Killingworth with so distinguished a competitor? The one was as yet but a colliery engine-wright, scarce raised above the manual-labour class, pursuing his experiments in obscurity, with a view only to usefulness; the other was the scientific prodigy of his day, the most brilliant of lecturers, and the most popular of philosophers.

No small indignation was expressed by the friends of Sir

Robert Stephenson

Humphry Davy at Stephenson's 'presumption' in laying claim to the invention of the safety-lamp. In 1831 Dr Paris, in his *Life of Sir Humphry Davy*, thus wrote: 'It will hereafter be scarcely believed that an invention so eminently scientific, and which could never have been derived but from the sterling treasury of science, should have been claimed on behalf of an engine-wright of Killingworth, of the name of Stephenson – a person not even possessing a knowledge of the elements of chemistry.'

But Stephenson was far above claiming for himself any invention not his own. He had already accomplished a far greater feat than the making of a safety-lamp – he had constructed a successful locomotive, which was to be seen in daily work on the Killingworth railway. By the improvements he had made in the engine, he might almost be said to have *invented* it; but no one – not even the philosophers – detected the significance of that wonderful machine. What railways were to become, rested in a great measure with that 'engine-wright of Killingworth, of the name of Stephenson', though he was scarcely known as yet beyond the bounds of his own district.

As to the value of the invention of the safety-lamp there could be no doubt; and the colliery owners of Durham and Northumberland, to testify their sense of its importance, determined to present a testimonial to its inventor. The friends of Sir Humphry Davy met in August 1816, to take steps for raising a subscription for the purpose. The advertised object of the meeting was to present him with a reward for 'the invention of *his* safety-lamp'. To this no objection could be taken; for though the principle on which the safety-lamps of Stephenson and Davy were constructed was the same; and although Stephenson's lamp was, unquestionably, the first successful lamp that had been constructed on such principle, and proved to be efficient – yet Sir Humphry Davy did invent a safety-lamp, no doubt quite independent of all that Stephenson had done; and having directed his careful attention to the subject, and elucidated the true theory of explosion of carburetted hydrogen, he was entitled to all praise and reward for his labours. But when the meeting of coal-owners proposed to raise a subscription for the purpose of presenting Sir Humphry Davy with a reward for 'his invention of *the* safety-lamp', the case was entirely altered; and Stephenson's friends then proceeded to assert his claims to be regarded as its first inventor.

Many meetings took place on the subject, and much discussion ensued, the result of which was that a sum of £2000 was presented to Sir Humphry Davy as 'the inventor of the safety-lamp'; but, at the same time, a purse of 100 guineas was voted to George Stephenson, in consideration of what he had done in the same direction. This result was, however, very unsatisfactory to Stephenson, as well as to his friends, and Mr Brandling, of Gosforth, suggested to him that, the subject being now fairly before the public, he should publish a statement of the facts on which his claim was founded.

This was not at all in George's line. He had never appeared in print; and it seemed to him a more formidable thing to write a letter for 'the papers' than to invent a safety-lamp or design a locomotive. However, he called to his aid his son Robert, set him down before a sheet of foolscap, and told him to 'put down there just what I tell you'. The composition of this letter, as we were informed by the writer of it, occupied more evenings than one; and when it was at length finished, after many corrections, and fairly copied out, the father and son set out – the latter dressed in his Sunday's round jacket – to lay the joint production before Mr Brandling, at Gosforth House. Glancing over the letter, Mr Brandling said, 'George, this will never do.' 'It is all true, sir,' was the reply. 'That may be; but it is badly written.' Robert blushed, for he thought the penmanship was called in question, and he had written his best. Mr Brandling, however, revised the letter, which was shortly after published in the local journals.

Stephenson's friends, fully satisfied of his claims to priority as the inventor of the safety-lamp used in the Killingworth and other collieries, held a public meeting for the purpose of presenting him with a reward 'for the valuable service he had thus rendered to mankind'. A subscription was immediately commenced with this object, and a committee was formed, consisting of the Earl of Strathmore, C. J. Brandling, and others. The subscriptions, when collected, amounted to £1,000. Part of the money was devoted to the purchase of a silver tankard, which was presented to the inventor, together with the balance of the subscription, at a public dinner given in the Assembly Rooms at Newcastle.* But what

* The tankard bore the following inscription: 'This piece of plate, purchased with a part of the sum of £1,000, a subscription raised for the remuneration of MR GEORGE STEPHENSON for having discovered the fact that inflamed fire-damp will not pass through tubes and apertures of small dimensions, and having been *the first* to apply that principle in the construction of a safety-lamp calculated for the preservation of human life in situations formerly of the greatest danger, was presented to him at a general meeting of the subscribers, Charles John Brandling, Esq., in the Chair. January 12th, 1818.'

gave Stephenson even greater pleasure than the silver tankard and purse of sovereigns was the gift of a silver watch, purchased by small subscriptions among the colliers themselves, and presented by them as a token of their personal esteem and regard for him, as well as of their gratitude for the perseverance and skill with which he had prosecuted his valuable and life-saving invention to a successful issue.

However great the merits of Stephenson in connection with the invention of the tube safety-lamp, they cannot be regarded as detracting from the reputation of Sir Humphry Davy. His inquiries into the explosive properties of carburetted hydrogen gas were quite original; and his discovery of the fact that explosion will not pass through tubes of a certain diameter was made independently of all that Stephenson had done in verification of the same fact. It even appears that Mr Smithson Tennant and Dr Wollaston had observed the same fact several years before, though neither Stephenson nor Davy knew it while they were prosecuting their experiments. Sir Humphry Davy's subsequent modification of the tube-lamp, by which, while diminishing the diameter, he in the same ratio shortened the tubes without danger, and in the form of wire-gauze enveloped the safety-lamp by a multiplicity of tubes, was a beautiful application of the true theory which he had formed upon the subject.   *171446*

The increased number of accidents which have occurred from explosions in coal-mines since the general introduction of the Davy lamp, have led to considerable doubts as to its safety, and to inquiries as to the means by which it may be further improved; for experience has shown that, under certain circumstances, the Davy lamp is *not* safe. Stephenson was himself of opinion that the modification of his own and Sir Humphry Davy's lamp, combining the glass cylinder with the wire-gauze, was the most secure; at the same time it must be admitted that the Davy and the Geordy lamps alike failed to stand the severe tests to which they were submitted by Dr Pereira, before the Committee on Accidents in Mines. Indeed, Dr Pereira did not hesitate to say, that when exposed to a current of explosive gas the Davy lamp is 'decidedly unsafe', and that the experiments by which its safety had been 'demonstrated' in the lecture-room had proved entirely 'fallacious'.

It is worthy of remark, that under circumstances in which the wire-gauze of the Davy lamp becomes red-hot from the high explosiveness of the gas, the Geordy lamp is extinguished; and we cannot but think that this fact testifies to the decidedly superior

safety of the Geordy. An accident occurred in the Oaks Colliery
Pit at Barnsley on 20 August 1857, which strikingly exemplified
the respective qualities of the lamps. A sudden outburst of gas
took place from the floor of the mine, along a distance of fifty
yards. Fortunately the men working in the pit at the time were all
supplied with safety-lamps – the hewers with Stephenson's, and
the hurriers with Davy's. Upon this occasion, the whole of the
Stephenson's lamps, over a space of five hundred yards, were extinguished almost instantaneously; whereas the Davy lamps were
filled with fire, and became red-hot – so much so, that several of
the men using them had their hands burnt by the gauze. Had a
strong current of air been blowing through the gallery at the time,
an explosion would most probably have taken place – an accident
which, it will be observed, could not, under such circumstances,
occur from the use of the Geordy, which is immediately extinguished as soon as the air becomes explosive.*

Nicholas Wood, a good judge, has said of the two inventions,
'Priority has been claimed for each of them – I believe the inventions to be parallel. By different roads they both arrived at the
same result. Stephenson's is the superior lamp. Davy's is safe –
Stephenson's is safer.'

When the question of priority was under discussion at the studio
of Mr Lough, the sculptor, in 1857, Sir Matthew White Ridley
asked Robert Stephenson, who was present, for his opinion on the
subject. His answer was, 'I am not exactly the person to give an
unbiased opinion; but, as you ask me frankly, I will as frankly
say, that if George Stephenson had never lived, Sir Humphry Davy
could and most probably would have invented the safety-lamp;
but again, if Sir Humphry Davy had never lived, George Stephenson certainly would have invented the safety-lamp, as I believe he
did, independent of all that Sir Humphry Davy had ever done in
the matter.'

* The accident above referred to was described in the *Barnsley Times*, a
copy of which, containing the account, Robert Stephenson forwarded to the
author, with the observation that 'it is evidently written by a practical
miner, and is, I think, worthy of record in my father's Life'.

CHAPTER VII – GEORGE STEPHENSON'S FURTHER IMPROVEMENTS IN THE LOCOMOTIVE – THE HETTON RAILWAY – ROBERT STEPHENSON AS VIEWER'S APPRENTICE AND STUDENT

STEPHENSON'S experiments on fire-damp, and his labours in connection with the invention of the safety-lamp, occupied but a small portion of his time, which was necessarily devoted for the most part to the ordinary business of the colliery. From the day of his appointment as engine-wright, one of the subjects which particularly occupied his attention was the best practical method of winning and raising the coal. He was one of the first to introduce steam machinery underground with the latter object. Indeed, the Killingworth mines came to be regarded as the models of the district; the working arrangements generally being conducted in a skilful and efficient manner, reflecting the highest credit on the colliery engineer.

Besides attending to the underground arrangements, the improved transit of the coals aboveground from the pithead to the shipping-place, demanded an increasing share of his attention. Every day's experience convinced him that the locomotive constructed by him after his patent of the year 1815, was far from perfect; though he continued to entertain confident hopes of its eventual success. He even went so far as to say that the locomotive would yet supersede every other traction-power for drawing heavy loads. Many still regarded his travelling engine as little better than a curious toy; and some, shaking their heads, predicted for it 'a terrible blow-up some day'. Nevertheless, it was daily performing its work with regularity, dragging the coal-waggons between the colliery and the staiths, and saving the labour of many men and horses. There was not, however, so marked a saving in haulage as to induce the colliery masters to adopt locomotive power generally as a substitute for horses. How it could be improved and rendered more efficient as well as economical, was constantly present to Stephenson's mind.

At an early period of his labours, or about the time when he had completed his second locomotive, he began to direct his particular attention to the state of the Road; as he perceived that the extended use of the locomotive must necessarily depend in a great measure upon the perfection, solidity, continuity, and smoothness of the way along which the engine travelled. Even at that early period, he was in the habit of regarding the road and the locomotive as one machine, speaking of the rail and the wheel as 'man and wife'.

All railways were at that time laid in a careless and loose manner, and great inequalities of level were allowed to occur without much attention being paid to repairs. The consequence was a great loss of power, as well as much tear and wear of the machinery, by the frequent jolts and blows of the wheels against the rails. His first object, therefore, was to remove the inequalities produced by the imperfect junction between rail and rail. At that time (in 1816) the rails were made of cast iron, each rail being about three feet long; and sufficient care was not taken to maintain the points of junction on the same level. The chairs, or cast-iron pedestals into which the rails were inserted, were flat at the bottom; so that, whenever any disturbance took place in the stone blocks or sleepers supporting them, the flat base of the chair upon which the rails rested being tilted by unequal subsidence, the end of one rail became depressed, while that of the other was elevated. Hence constant jolts and shocks, the reaction of which very often caused the fracture of the rails, and occasionally threw the engine off the road.

To remedy this imperfection Mr Stephenson devised a new chair, with an entirely new mode of fixing the rails therein. Instead of adopting the *butt joint* which had hitherto been used in all cast-iron rails, he adopted the *half-lap joint*, by which means the rails extended a certain distance over each other at the ends, like a scarf joint. These ends, instead of resting upon the flat chair, were made to rest upon the apex of a curve forming the bottom of the chair. The supports were also extended from three feet to three feet nine inches or four feet apart. These rails were accordingly substituted for the old cast-iron plates on the Killingworth Colliery Railway, and they were found to be a very great improvement upon the previous system, adding both to the efficiency of the horse-power, still employed in working the railway, and to the smooth action of the locomotive engine, but more particularly increasing the efficiency of the latter.

This improved form of rail and chair was embodied in a patent taken out in the joint names of Mr Losh, of Newcastle, iron-founder, and of Mr Stephenson, bearing date 30 September 1816. Mr Losh being a wealthy, enterprising iron-manufacturer, and having confidence in George Stephenson and his improvements, found the money for the purpose of taking out the patent, which, in those days, was a very costly as well as troublesome affair.

The specification of the same patent also described various important improvements in the locomotive itself. The wheels of the engine were improved, being altered from cast to malleable iron, in whole or in part, by which they were made lighter as well as more durable and safe. But the most ingenious and original contrivance embodied in this patent was the substitute for springs which Mr Stephenson invented. He contrived that the steam generated in the boiler should perform this important office. The method by which this was effected displayed such genuine mechanical genius, that we would particularly call attention to the device, which was the more remarkable, as it was contrived long before the possibility of steam locomotion had become an object of general inquiry or of public interest.

It has already been observed that up to, and indeed after, the period of which we speak, there was no such class of skilled mechanics, nor were there any such machines and tools in use, as are now available to inventors and manufacturers. Although skilled workmen were in course of gradual training in a few of the larger manufacturing towns, they did not, at the date of Stephenson's patent, exist in any considerable numbers, nor was there then any class of mechanics capable of constructing springs of sufficient strength and elasticity to support locomotive engines of ten tons weight.

In order to avoid the dangers arising from the inequalities of the road, Stephenson so arranged the boiler of his new patent locomotive that it was supported upon the frame of the engine by four

cylinders, which opened into the interior of the boiler. These
cylinders were occupied by pistons with rods, which passed downwards and pressed upon the upper side of the axles. The cylinders
opening into the interior of the boiler, allowed the pressure of
steam to be applied to the upper side of the piston; and the pressure
being nearly equivalent to one-fourth of the weight of the engine,
each axle, whatever might be its position, had at all times nearly
the same amount of weight to bear, and consequently the entire
weight was pretty equally distributed among the four wheels of
the locomotive. Thus the four floating pistons were ingeniously
made to serve the purpose of springs in equalizing the weight, and
in softening the jerks of the machine; the weight of which, it must
also be observed, had been increased, on a road originally calculated
to bear a considerably lighter description of carriage. This mode of
supporting the engine remained in use until the progress of spring-
making had so far advanced that steel springs could be manufactured of sufficient strength to bear the weight of locomotive
engines.

The result of the actual working of the new locomotive on the
improved road amply justified the promises held forth in the
specification. The traffic was conducted with greater regularity and
economy, and the superiority of the engine, as compared with
horse traction, became still more marked. It is a fact worthy of
notice, that the identical engines constructed in 1816 after the plan
above described are to this day to be seen in regular useful work
upon the Killingworth Railway, conveying heavy coal-trains at the
speed of between five and six miles an hour, probably as economically as any of the more perfect locomotives now in use.

Mr Stephenson's endeavours having been attended with such
marked success in the adaptation of locomotive power to railways,
his attention was called by many of his friends, about the year
1818, to the application of steam to travelling on common roads.
It was from this point that the locomotive started, Trevithick's
first engine having been constructed with this special object.
Stephenson's friends having observed how far behind he had left
the original projector of the locomotive in its application to railroads, perhaps naturally inferred that he would be equally successful in applying it to the purpose for which Trevithick and
Vivian had intended their first engine. But the accuracy with
which he estimated the resistance to which loads were exposed on
railways, arising from friction and gravity, led him at a very early
stage to reject the idea of ever applying steam power economically

to common-road travelling. In October 1818, he made a series of careful experiments in conjunction with Nicholas Wood, on the resistance to which carriages were exposed on railways, testing the results by means of a dynamometer of his own construction. The series of practical observations made by means of this instrument were interesting, as the first systematic attempt to determine the precise amount of resistance to carriages moving along railways. It was then for the first time ascertained by experiment that the friction was a constant quantity at all velocities. Although this theory had long before been developed by Vince and Coulomb, and was well known to scientific men as an established truth, yet, at the time when Stephenson made his experiments, the deductions of philosophers on the subject were neither believed in nor acted upon by practical engineers.

He ascertained that the resistances to traction were mainly three; the first being upon the axles of the carriages, the second, or rolling resistance, being between the circumference of the wheel and the surface of the rail, and the third being the resistance of gravity. The amount of friction and gravity he could accurately ascertain; but the rolling resistance was a matter of greater difficulty, being subject to much variation. He satisfied himself, however, that it was so great when the surface presented to the wheel was of a rough character, that the idea of working steam carriages economically on common roads was dismissed by him as entirely impracticable. Taking it as 10 lbs to a ton weight on a level railway, it became obvious to him that so small a rise as 1 in 100 would diminish the useful effort of a locomotive by upwards of 50 per cent. This was demonstrated by repeated experiments, and the important fact, thus rooted in his mind, was never lost sight of in the course of his future railway career.

It was owing in a great measure to these painstaking experiments that he early became convinced of the vital importance, in an economical point of view, of reducing the country through which a railway was intended to pass as nearly as possible to a level. Where, as in the first coal railways of Northumberland and Durham, the load was nearly all one way – that is, from the colliery to the shipping-place – it was an advantage to have an inclination in that direction. The strain on the powers of the locomotive was thus diminished, and it was easy for it to haul the empty waggons back to the colliery up even a pretty steep incline. But when the loads were both ways, he deemed it of great importance that the railroad should be constructed as nearly as possible on a level.

These views, thus early entertained, originated in Stephenson's mind the peculiar character of railroad works as distinguished from other roads; for, in railways, he early contended that large sums would be wisely expended in perforating barriers of hills with long tunnels, and in raising the lower levels with the excess cut down from the adjacent high ground. In proportion as these views forced themselves upon his mind and were corroborated by his daily experience, he became more and more convinced of the hopelessness of applying steam locomotion to common roads; for every argument in favour of a level railway was, in his view, an argument against the rough and hilly course of a common road.

Although Stephenson's locomotive engines were in daily use for many years on the Killingworth Railway, they excited comparatively little interest. They were no longer experimental, but had become an established tractive power. The experience of years had proved that they worked more steadily, drew heavier loads, and were, on the whole, considerably more economical than horses. Nevertheless eight years passed before another locomotive railway was constructed and opened for the purposes of coal or other traffic.

Stephenson had no means of bringing his important invention prominently under the notice of the public. He himself knew well its importance, and he already anticipated its eventual general adoption; but being an unlettered man, he could not give utterance to the thoughts which brooded within him on the subject. Killingworth Colliery lay far from London, the centre of scientific life in England. It was visited by no savans nor literary men, who might have succeeded in introducing to notice the wonderful machine of Stephenson. Even the local chroniclers seem to have taken no notice of the Killingworth Railway.

There seemed, indeed, to be so small a prospect of introducing the locomotive into general use, that Stephenson – perhaps feeling the capabilities within him – again recurred to his old idea of emigrating to the United States. Before joining Mr Burrel as partner in a small foundry at Forth Banks, Newcastle, he had thrown out to him the suggestion that it would be a good speculation for them to emigrate to North America, and introduce steamboats upon the great inland lakes there. The first steamers were then plying upon the Tyne before his eyes; and he saw in them the germ of a great revolution in navigation. It occurred to him that North America presented the finest field for trying their wonderful powers. He was an engineer, his partner was an iron-founder; and between them he thought they might strike out a path to fortune in the mighty West. Fortunately, this idea remained a mere speculation so far as Stephenson was concerned; and it was left to others to do what he had dreamt of achieving. After all his patient waiting, his skill, industry, and perseverance were at length about to bear fruit.

In 1819 the owners of the Hetton Colliery, in the county of Durham, determined to have their waggon-way altered to a locomotive railroad. The result of the working of the Killingworth Railway had been so satisfactory, that they resolved to adopt the same system. One reason why an experiment so long continued and so successful as that at Killingworth should have been so slow in producing results, perhaps was, that to lay down a railway and furnish it with locomotives, or fixed engines where necessary, required a very large capital, beyond the means of ordinary coal-owners; while the small amount of interest felt in railways by the general public, and the supposed impracticability of working them to a profit, as yet prevented ordinary capitalists from venturing their money in the promotion of such undertakings. The Hetton Coal Company were, however, possessed of adequate means; and the local reputation of the Killingworth engine-wright pointed him out as the man best calculated to lay out their line, and superintend their works. They accordingly invited him to act as the engineer of the proposed railway, which was to be the longest locomotive line that had, up to that time, been constructed. It extended from the Hetton Colliery, situated about two miles south of Houghton-le-Spring, in the county of Durham, to the shipping-places on the banks of the Wear, near Sunderland. Its length was about eight miles; and in its course it crossed Warden Law, one of the highest hills in the district. The character of the country forbade the construction of a flat line, or one of comparatively easy gradients, except by the expenditure of a much larger capital than was placed at the engineer's disposal. Heavy works could not be executed; it was therefore necessary to form the line with but little deviation from the natural conformation of the district which it traversed, and also to adapt the mechanical methods employed for its working to the character of the gradients, which in some places were necessarily heavy.

Although Stephenson had, with every step made towards its increased utility, become more and more identified with the success of the locomotive engine, he did not allow his enthusiasm to carry him away into costly mistakes. He carefully drew the line between

the cases in which the locomotive could be usefully employed, and
those in which stationary engines were calculated to be more
economical. This led him, as in the instance of the Hetton Railway,
to execute lines through and over rough countries, where gradients
within the powers of the locomotive engine of that day could not
be secured, employing in their stead stationary engines where locomotives were not practicable. In the present case, this course was
adopted by him most successfully. On the original Hetton line,
there were five self-acting inclines, the full waggons drawing the
empty ones up, and two inclines worked by fixed reciprocating
engines of 60 horse-power each. The locomotive travelling engine,
or 'the iron horse', as the people of the neighbourhood then styled
it, did the rest. On the day of the opening of the Hetton Railway,
18 November 1822, crowds of spectators assembled from all parts
to witness the first operations of this ingenious and powerful
machinery, which was entirely successful. On that day five of
Stephenson's locomotives were at work upon the railway, under
the direction of his brother Robert; and the first shipment of coal
was then made by the Hetton Company, at their new staiths on
the Wear. The speed at which the locomotives travelled was about
4 miles an hour, and each engine dragged after it a train of 17
waggons, weighing about 64 tons.

While thus advancing step by step, attending to the business of
the Killingworth Colliery, and laying out railways in the neighbourhood, he was carefully watching over the education of his son.
We have already seen that Robert was sent to Bruce's school at
Newcastle, where he remained about four years. He left it in the
summer of 1819, and was then put apprentice to Mr Nicholas
Wood, the head viewer at Killingworth, to learn the business of
the colliery. He served in that capacity for about three years,
during which time he became familiar with most departments of
underground work. The occupation was not unattended with peril,
as the following incident will show. Though the use of the Geordy
lamp had become general in the Killingworth pits, and the workmen were bound, under a penalty of half a crown, not to use a
naked candle, it was difficult to enforce the rule, and even the
masters themselves occasionally broke it. One day Nicholas Wood,
the head viewer, Moodie the under viewer, and Robert Stephenson, were proceeding along one of the galleries, Wood with a naked
candle in his hand, and Robert following him with a lamp. They
came to a place where a fall of stones from the roof had taken
place, on which Wood, who was first, proceeded to clamber over

the stones, holding high the naked candle. He had nearly reached the summit of the heap, when the fire-damp, which had accumulated in the hollow of the roof, exploded, and instantly the whole party were blown down, and the lights extinguished. They were a mile from the shaft, and quite in the dark. There was a rush of the workpeople from all quarters towards the shaft, for it was feared that the fire might extend to more dangerous parts of the pit, where, if the gas had exploded, every soul in the mine must inevitably have perished. Robert Stephenson and Moodie, on the first impulse, ran back at full speed along the dark gallery leading to the shaft, coming into collision, on their way, with the hindquarters of a horse stunned by the explosion. When they had gone halfway, Moodie halted, and bethought him of Nicholas Wood. 'Stop, laddie!' said he to Robert, 'stop; we maun gang back, and seek the maister.' So they retraced their steps. Happily, no further explosion had taken place. They found the master lying on the heap of stones, stunned and bruised, with his hands severely burnt. They led him to the bottom of the shaft; and he took care afterwards not to venture into the dangerous parts of the mine without the protection of a Geordy lamp.

The time that Robert spent at Killingworth as viewer's apprentice was of advantage both to his father and himself. The evenings were generally devoted to reading and study, the two from this time working together as friends and co-labourers. One who used to drop in at the cottage of an evening, well remembers the animated and eager discussions which on some occasions took place, more especially with reference to the growing powers of the locomotive engine. The son was even more enthusiastic than the father on this subject. Robert would suggest numerous alterations and improvements in details. His father, on the contrary, would offer every possible objection, defending the existing arrangements, proud, nevertheless of his son's suggestions, and often warmed and excited by his brilliant anticipations of the ultimate triumph of the locomotive.

These discussions probably had considerable influence in inducing Stephenson to take the next important step in the education of his son. Although Robert, who was only nineteen years of age, was doing well, and was certain at the expiration of his apprenticeship to rise to a higher position, his father was not satisfied with the amount of instruction which he had as yet given him. Remembering the disadvantages under which he had himself laboured through his ignorance of practical chemistry during his investigations connected with the safety-lamp, more especially with reference to the properties of gas, as well as in the course of his experiments with the object of improving the locomotive engine, he determined to furnish his son with as complete a scientific culture as his means would afford. He also believed that a proper training in technical science was indispensable to success in the higher walks of the engineer's profession; and he determined to give to his son that kind and degree of education which he so much desired for himself. He would thus, he knew, secure a hearty and generous co-worker in the elaboration of the great ideas now looming before him, and with their united practical and scientific knowledge he probably felt that they would be equal to any enterprise.

He accordingly took Robert from his labours as under-viewer in the West Moor Pit, and in October 1822, sent him to the Edinburgh University, there being then no college in England accessible to persons of moderate means, for purposes of scientific culture. Robert was furnished with letters of introduction to several men of literary eminence in Edinburgh; his father's reputation in connection with the safety-lamp being of service to him in this respect. He lodged in Drummond Street, in the immediate vicinity of the college, and attended the Chemical Lectures of Dr Hope, the Natural Philosophy Lectures of Sir John Leslie, and the Natural History Class of Professor Jameson. He also devoted several evenings in each week to the study of practical Chemistry under Dr John Murray, himself one of the numerous designers of a safety-lamp. He took careful notes of all the lectures, which he copied out at night before he went to bed; so that, when he returned to Killingworth, he might read them over to his father. He afterwards had the notes bound up, and placed in his library. Long years after, when conversing with Thomas Harrison, C.E., at his house in Gloucester Square, he rose from his seat and took down a volume from the shelves. Mr Harrison observed that the book was in MS., neatly written out. 'What have we here?' he asked. The answer was: 'When I went to college, I knew the difficulty my father had in collecting the funds to send me there. Before going I studied short-hand; while at Edinburgh, I took down verbatim every lecture; and in the evenings, before I went to bed, I transcribed those lectures word for word. You see the result in that range of books.'

One of the practical sciences in the study of which Robert Stephenson took special interest while at Edinburgh was that of geology. The situation of the city, in the midst of a district of highly interesting geological formation, easily accessible to pedestrians, is indeed most favourable to the pursuit of such a study; and it was the practice of Professor Jameson frequently to head a band of his pupils, armed with hammers, chisels, and clinometers, and take them with him on a long ramble into the country, for the purpose of teaching them habits of observation and reading to them from the open book of Nature itself. At the close of this session, the professor took with him a select body of his pupils on an excursion along the Great Glen of the Highlands, in the line of the Caledonian Canal, and Robert formed one of the party. They passed under the shadow of Ben Nevis, examined the famous old sea-margins known as the 'parallel roads of Glen Roy', and extended their journey as far as Inverness; the professor teaching the young men as they travelled how to observe in a mountain country. Not long before his death, Robert Stephenson spoke in glowing terms of the great pleasure and benefit which he had derived from that interesting excursion. 'I have travelled far, and enjoyed much,' he said; 'but that delightful botanical and geological journey I shall never forget, and I am just about to start in the *Titania* for a trip round the east coast of Scotland, returning south through the Caledonian Canal, to refresh myself with the recollection of that first and brightest tour of my life.'

Towards the end of the summer of 1822 the young student returned to Killingworth to re-enter upon the active business of life. The six month's study had cost his father £80; but he was amply repaid by the better scientific culture which his son had acquired, and the evidence of ability and industry which he was enabled to exhibit in a prize for mathematics which he had won at the University.

CHAPTER VIII – GEORGE STEPHENSON ENGINEER OF THE STOCKTON AND DARLINGTON RAILWAY

THE district west of Darlington, in Durham, is one of the richest mineral fields of the North. Vast stores of coal underlie the Bishop Auckland Valley; and from an early period new and good roads to market were felt to be exceedingly desirable. As yet it remained almost a closed field, the cost of transport of the coal in carts, or on horses' or donkeys' backs, greatly limiting the sale. Long ago, in the days of canal formations, Brindley was consulted about a canal; afterwards, in 1812, a tramroad was surveyed by Rennie; and eventually, in 1817, a railway was projected from Darlington to Stockton-on-Tees.

Of this railway Edward Pease was the projector. A thoughtful and sagacious man, ready in resources, possessed of indomitable energy and perseverance, he was eminently qualified to undertake what appeared to many the hopeless enterprise of obtaining an Act for a railway through such an unpromising district. One who knew him in 1818 said, 'he was a man who could see a hundred years ahead'. When the writer last saw him, in the autumn of 1854, Mr Pease was in his eighty-eighth year; yet he still possessed the hopefulness and mental vigour of a man in his prime. Hale and hearty, and full of reminiscences of the past, he continued to take an active interest in all measures calculated to render men happier and better. Still sound in health, his eye had not lost its brilliancy, nor his cheek its colour; and there was an elasticity in his step which younger men might have envied.*

In getting up a company for surveying and forming a railway, Mr Pease had great difficulties to encounter. The people of the neighbourhood spoke of it as a ridiculous undertaking, and predicted that it would be ruinous to all concerned. Even those most interested in the opening of new markets for their coal, were indifferent, if not actually hostile. The Stockton merchants and shipowners, whom it was calculated so greatly to benefit, gave the project no support; and not twenty shares were subscribed for in the whole town. Mr Pease nevertheless persevered; and he induced many of his friends and relations to subscribe the capital required.

The necessary preliminary steps were taken in 1818 to apply for an act to authorize the construction of a tramroad from Witton to Stockton. The measure was, however, strongly opposed by the Duke of Cleveland, because the proposed line passed close by one of his fox covers; and the bill was rejected. A new survey was then made, avoiding the Duke's cover; and in 1819 a renewed application was made to Parliament. The promoters were this time successful, and the royal assent was given to the first Stockton and Darlington Railway Act on 19 April 1821.

The projectors did not originally contemplate the employment of locomotives. The Act provided for the making and maintaining of tramroads for the passage 'of waggons and other carriages, *with men and horses* or otherwise', and a further clause made provision for damages done in course of traffic by the 'waggoners'. The public were to be free 'to use with horses, cattle, and carriages', the roads formed by the company, on payment of the authorized rates, 'between the hours of seven in the morning and six in the evening', during winter; 'between six in the morning and eight in the evening', in two of the spring and autumn months; and 'between five in the morning and ten in the evening', in the summer months of May, June, July, and August. From this it will be obvious that the projectors of the line had themselves at first no very large conceptions as to the scope of their project.

One day, in the spring of 1821, two strangers knocked at the door of Mr Pease's house in Darlington; and the message was brought to him that some persons from Killingworth wanted to speak with him. They were invited in, on which one of the visitors introduced himself as Nicholas Wood, viewer at Killingworth, and

* Mr Pease died at Darlington, on 31 July 1858, aged ninety-two.

then turning to his companion, he introduced him as George Stephenson, engine-wright, of the same place.

Mr Pease entered into conversation with his visitors, and was soon told their object. Stephenson had heard of the passing of the Stockton and Darlington Act, and desiring to increase his railway experience, and also to employ in some larger field the practical knowledge he had already gained, he determined to visit the known projector of the undertaking, with the view of being employed to carry it out. He had brought with him his friend Wood, for the purpose at the same time of relieving his diffidence, and supporting his application.

Mr Pease liked the appearance of his visitor: 'there was', as he afterwards remarked when speaking of Stephenson, 'such an honest, sensible look about him, and he seemed so modest and unpretending. He spoke in the strong Northumbrian dialect of his district, and described himself as "only the engine-wright at Killingworth; that's what he was".'

Mr Pease soon saw that our engineer was the very man for his purpose. The whole plans of the railway were still in an undetermined state, and Mr Pease was therefore glad to have the opportunity of profiting by Stephenson's experience. In the course of their conversation, the latter strongly recommended a *railway* in preference to a tramroad. They also discussed the kind of tractive power to be employed: Mr Pease stating that the company had based their whole calculations on the employment of *horse* power. 'I was so satisfied,' said he afterwards, 'that a horse upon an iron road would draw ten tons for one ton on a common road, that I felt sure that before long the railway would become the King's highway.' But Mr Pease was scarcely prepared for the bold assertion made by his visitor, that the locomotive engine with which he had been working the Killingworth Railway for many years past was worth fifty horses, and that engines made after a similar plan would yet entirely supersede all horse-power upon railroads. Stephenson was daily becoming more positive as to the superiority of his locomotive; and hence he strongly urged Mr Pease to adopt it. 'Come over to Killingworth,' said he, ' and see what my engines can do; seeing is believing, sir.' Mr Pease accordingly promised that on some early day he would go over to Killingworth, and take a look at the wonderful machine that was to supersede horses.

The result of the interview was, that Mr Pease promised to bring Stephenson's application for the appointment of engineer before the Directors, and to support it with his influence; whereon the two visitors prepared to take their leave, informing Mr Pease that they intended to return to Newcastle 'by nip'; that is, they expected to get a smuggled lift on the stage-coach, by tipping Jehu, for in those days the stage coachmen regarded all casual roadside passengers as their proper perquisites. They had, however, been so much engrossed by their conversation, that the lapse of time was forgotten, and when Stephenson and his friend made inquiries about the return coach, they found the last had left; and they had to walk the eighteen miles to Durham on their way back to Newcastle.

Mr Pease having made further inquiries respecting Stephenson's character and qualifications, and having received a very strong recommendation of him as the right man for the intended work, he brought the subject of his application before the directors of the Stockton and Darlington Company. They resolved to adopt his recommendation that a railway be formed instead of a tramroad; and they further requested Mr Pease to write to Stephenson, desiring him to undertake a re-survey of the line at the earliest practicable period.

A man was dispatched on a horse with the letter, and when he reached Killingworth he made diligent inquiry after the person named upon the address, 'George Stephenson, Esquire, Engineer'. No such person was known in the village. It is said that the man was on the point of giving up all further search, when the happy thought struck some of the colliers' wives who had gathered about him, that it must be 'Geordie the engine-wright' the man was in search of; and to Geordie's cottage he accordingly went, found him at home, and delivered the letter.

About the end of September, Stephenson went carefully over the line of the proposed railway, for the purpose of suggesting such improvements and deviations as he might consider desirable. He was accompanied by an assistant and a chainman, his son Robert entering the figures while his father took the sights. After being engaged in the work at intervals for about six weeks, Stephenson reported the result of his survey to the Board of Directors, and showed that by certain deviations, a line shorter by about three miles might be constructed at a considerable saving in expense, while at the same time more favourable gradients – an important consideration – would be secured.

It was, however, determined in the first place to proceed with the works at those parts of the line where no deviation was proposed; and the first rail of the Stockton and Darlington Railway was laid with considerable ceremony, near Stockton, on 23 May 1822.

It is worthy of note that Stephenson, in making his first estimate of the cost of forming the railway according to the instructions of the directors, set down, as part of the cost, £6,200 for stationary engines, not mentioning locomotives at all. The directors as yet confined their views to the employment only of horses for the haulage of the coals, and of fixed engines and ropes where horse-power was not applicable. The whole question of steam locomotive power was, in the estimation of the public, as well as of practical and scientific men, as yet in doubt. The confident anticipations of George Stephenson, as to the eventual success of locomotive engines, were regarded as mere speculations; and when he gave utterance to his views, as he frequently took the opportunity of doing, it even had the effect of shaking the confidence of some of his friends in the solidity of his judgement and his practical qualities as an engineer.

When Mr Pease discussed the question with Stephenson, his remark was, 'Come over and see my engines at Killingworth, and satisfy yourself as to the efficiency of the locomotive. I will show you the colliery books, that you may ascertain for yourself the actual cost of working. And I must tell you that the economy of the locomotive engine is no longer a matter of theory, but a matter of fact.' So confident was the tone in which Stephenson spoke of the success of his engines, and so important were the consequences involved in arriving at a correct conclusion on the subject, that Mr Pease at length resolved upon paying a visit to Killingworth in the summer of 1822, to see with his own eyes the wonderful new power so much vaunted by the engineer.

When Mr Pease arrived at Killingworth village, he inquired for George Stephenson, and was told that he must go over to the West Moor, and seek for a cottage by the roadside, with a dial over the door – 'that was where George Stephenson lived'. They soon found the house with the dial; and on knocking, the door was opened by Mrs Stephenson – his second wife (Elizabeth Hindmarsh), the daughter of a farmer at Black Callerton, whom he had married in 1820.* Her husband, she said, was not in the house at present, but

* The story has been told that George was a former suitor of Miss Hind-marsh, while occupying the position of a humble workman at Black Callerton, but that having been rejected by her, he made love to and married Fanny Henderson; and that long after the death of the latter,

she would send for him to the colliery. And in a short time Stephenson appeared before them in his working dress, just as he had come out of the pit.

He very soon had his locomotive brought up to the crossing close by the end of the cottage, made the gentlemen mount it, and showed them its paces. Harnessing it to a train of loaded waggons, he ran it along the railroad, and so thoroughly satisfied his visitors of its power and capabilities, that from that day Edward Pease was a declared supporter of the locomotive engine. In preparing the Amended Stockton and Darlington Act, at Stephenson's urgent request Mr Pease had a clause inserted, taking power to work the railway by means of locomotive engines, and to employ them for the haulage of passengers as well as of merchandise.* The Act was obtained in 1823, on which Stephenson was appointed the company's engineer at a salary of £300 per annum; and it was determined that the line should be constructed and open for traffic as soon as practicable.

He at once proceeded, accompanied by his assistants, with the working survey of the line, laying out every foot of the ground himself. Railway surveying was as yet in its infancy, and was slow and difficult work. It afterwards became a separate branch of railway business, and was entrusted to a special staff. Indeed on no subsequent line did George Stephenson take the sights through the spirit level with his own hands and eyes as he did on this railway. He started very early – dressed in a blue-tailed coat, breeches, and top-boots – and surveyed until dusk. He was not at any time particular as to his living; and during the survey, he took his chance of getting a little milk and bread at some cottager's house along the line, or occasionally joined in a homely dinner at some neighbouring farmhouse. The country people were accustomed to give him a hearty welcome when he appeared at their door; for he

* The first clause in any railway act, empowering the employment of locomotive engines for the working of passenger traffic.

when he had become a comparatively thriving man, he again made up to Miss Hindmarsh, and was on the second occasion accepted. This is the popular story, and different versions of it are current. Desirous of ascertaining the facts, the author called on Thomas Hindmarsh, Mrs Stephenson's brother, who assured him that George knew nothing of his sister until he (Hindmarsh) introduced him to her, at George's express request, about the year 1818 or 1819. The author was himself originally attracted by the much more romantic version of the story, and gave publicity to it many years since; but after Mr Hindmarsh's explicit statement, he thought fit to adopt the soberer, and, perhaps, the truer view.

was always full of cheery and homely talk, and, when there were children about the house, he had plenty of humorous chat for them as well as for their seniors.

After the day's work was over, George would drop in at Mr Pease's, to talk over the progress of the survey, and discuss various matters connected with the railway. Mr Pease's daughters were usually present; and on one occasion, finding the young ladies learning the art of embroidery, he volunteered to instruct them.* 'I know all about it,' said he; 'and you will wonder how I learnt it. I will tell you. When I was a brakesman at Killingworth, I learnt the art of embroidery while working the pitmen's buttonholes by the engine fire at nights.' He was never ashamed, but on the contrary rather proud, of reminding his friends of these humble pursuits of his early life. Mr Pease's family were greatly pleased with his conversation, which was always amusing and instructive; full of all sorts of experience, gathered in the oddest and most out-of-the-way places. Even at that early period, before he mixed in the society of educated persons, there was a dash of speculativeness in his remarks, which gave a high degree of originality to his conversation; and he would sometimes, in a casual remark, throw a flash of light upon a subject, which called up a train of pregnant suggestions.

One of the most important subjects of discussion at these meetings with Mr Pease, was the establishment of a manufactory at Newcastle for the building of locomotive engines. Up to this time all the locomotives constructed after Stephenson's designs, had been made by ordinary mechanics working among the collieries in the North of England. But he had long felt that the accuracy and style of their workmanship admitted of great improvement, and that upon this the more perfect action of the locomotive engine, and its general adoption, in a great measure depended. One great object that he had in view in establishing the proposed factory was, to concentrate a number of good workmen for the purpose of carrying out the improvements in detail which he was constantly making in his engine. He felt hampered by the want of efficient help from skilled mechanics, who could work out in a practical form the ideas of which his busy mind was always so prolific. Doubtless, too, he believed that the manufactory would prove a remunerative investment, and that, on the general adoption of the

* This incident, communicated to the author by the late Edward Pease, has since been made the subject of a fine picture by Mr A. Rankley, A.R.A., exhibited at the Royal Academy Exhibition of 1861.

railway system which he anticipated, he would derive solid advantages from the fact of his establishment being the only one of the kind for the special construction of locomotive engines.

Mr Pease approved of his design, and strongly recommended him to carry it into effect. But there was the question of means; and Stephenson did not think he had capital enough for the purpose. He told Mr Pease that he could advance £1,000 – the amount of the testimonial presented by the coal-owners for his safety-lamp invention, which he had still left untouched; but he did not think this sufficient for the purpose, and he thought that he should require at least another £1,000. Mr Pease had been very much struck with the successful performances of the Killingworth engine; and being an accurate judge of character, he believed that he could not go far wrong in linking a portion of his fortune with the energy and industry of George Stephenson. He consulted his friend Thomas Richardson in the matter; and the two consented to advance £500 each for the purpose of establishing the engine factory at Newcastle. A piece of land was accordingly purchased in Forth Street, in August 1823, on which a small building was erected – the nucleus of the gigantic establishment which was afterwards formed around it; and active operations were begun early in 1824.

While the Stockton and Darlington Railway works were in progress, our engineer had many interesting discussions with Mr Pease, on points connected with its construction and working, the determination of which in a great measure affected the formation and working of all future railways. The most important points were these: 1. The comparative merits of cast and wrought iron rails. 2. The gauge of the railway. 3. The employment of horse or engine power in working it, when ready for traffic.

The kind of rails to be laid down to form the permanent road was a matter of considerable importance. A wooden tramroad had been contemplated when the first Act was applied for; but Stephenson having advised that an iron road should be laid down, he was instructed to draw up a specification of the rails. He went before the directors to discuss with them the kind of material to be specified. He was himself interested in the patent for cast iron rails, which he had taken out in conjunction with Mr Losh in 1816; and, of course, it was to his interest that his articles should be used. But when requested to give his opinion on the subject, he frankly said to the directors, 'Well, gentlemen, to tell you the truth, although it would put £500 in my pocket to specify my own patent rails, I cannot do so after the experience I have had. If you take my advice, you will not lay down a single cast iron rail.' 'Why?' asked the directors. 'Because they will not stand the weight, and you will be at no end of expense for repairs and relays.' 'What kind of road, then,' he was asked, 'would you recommend?' 'Malleable rails, certainly,' said he; 'and I can recommend them with the more confidence from the fact that at Killingworth we have had some Swedish bars laid down – nailed to wooden sleepers – for a period of fourteen years, the waggons passing over them daily; and there they are, in use yet, whereas the cast rails are constantly giving way.'

The price of malleable rails was, however, so high – being then worth about £12 per ton as compared with cast iron rails at about £5 10s. – and the saving of expense was so important a consideration with the subscribers, that Stephenson was directed to provide, in the specification, that only one half of the rails required – or about 800 tons – should be of malleable iron, and the remainder of cast iron. The malleable rails were of the kind called 'fish-bellied', and weighed 28 lbs to the yard, being $2\frac{1}{4}$ inches broad at the top, with the upper flange $\frac{3}{4}$ inch thick. They were only 2 inches in depth at the points at which they rested on the chairs, and $3\frac{1}{4}$ inches in the middle or bellied part.

When forming the road, the proper gauge had also to be determined. What width was this to be? The gauge of the first tramroad laid down had virtually settled the point. The gauge of wheels of the common vehicles of the country – of the carts and waggons employed on common roads, which were first used on the tramroads – was about 4 feet $8\frac{1}{2}$ inches. And so the first tramroads were laid down of this gauge. The tools and machinery for constructing coal-waggons and locomotives were formed with this gauge in view. The Wylam waggon-way, afterwards the Wylam plate-way, the Killingworth railroad, and the Hetton railroad, were as nearly as possible on the same gauge. Some of the earth-waggons used to form the Stockton and Darlington road were brought from the Hetton railway; and others which were specially constructed were formed of the same dimensions, these being intended to be afterwards employed in the working of the traffic.

As the period drew near for the opening of the line, the question of the tractive power to be employed was anxiously discussed. At the Brusselton incline, fixed engines must necessarily be made use of; but with respect to the mode of working the railway generally, it was decided that horses were to be largely employed, and

arrangements were made for their purchase. The influence of Mr
Pease also secured that a fair trial should be given to the experiment of working the traffic by locomotive power; and three engines
were ordered from the firm of Stephenson and Co., Newcastle,
which were put in hand forthwith, in anticipation of the opening
of the railway. These were constructed after Mr Stephenson's most
matured designs, and embodied all the improvements which he had
contrived up to that time. No. 1 engine, the 'Locomotion', which
was first delivered, weighed about eight tons. It had one large flue
or tube through the boiler, by which the heated air passed direct
from the furnace at one end, lined with fire-bricks, to the chimney
at the other. The combustion in the furnace was quickened by the
adoption of the steam-blast in the chimney. The heat raised was
sometimes so great, and it was so imperfectly abstracted by the
surrounding water, that the chimney became almost red-hot. Such
engines, when put to their speed, were found capable of running at
the rate of from twelve to sixteen miles an hour; but they were
better adapted for the heavy work of hauling coal-trains at low
speeds – for which, indeed, they were specially constructed – than
for running at the higher speeds afterwards adopted. Nor was it
contemplated by the directors as possible, at the time when they
were ordered, that locomotives could be made available for the
purposes of passenger travelling. Besides, the Stockton and
Darlington Railway did not run through a district in which
passengers were supposed to be likely to constitute any considerable portion of the traffic.

We may easily imagine the anxiety felt by Mr Stephenson during
the progress of the works towards completion, and his mingled
hopes and doubts (though his doubts were but few) as to the issue
of this great experiment. When the formation of the line near
Stockton was well advanced, Mr Stephenson one day, accompanied
by his son Robert and John Dixon, made a journey of inspection
of the works. The party reached Stockton, and proceeded to dine
at one of the inns there. After dinner, Stephenson ventured on the
very unusual measure of ordering in a bottle of wine, to drink
success to the railway. John Dixon relates with pride the utterance
of the master on the occasion. 'Now, lads,' said he to the two young
men, 'I venture to tell you that I think you will live to see the day
when railways will supersede almost all other methods of conveyance in this country – when mail-coaches will go by railway, and
railroads will become the great highway for the king and all his
subjects. The time is coming when it will be cheaper for a working

man to travel upon a railway than to walk on foot. I know there are great and almost insurmountable difficulties to be encountered; but what I have said will come to pass as sure as you live. I only wish I may live to see the day, though I can scarcely hope for, as I know how slow all human progress is, and with what difficulty I have been able to get the locomotive thus far adopted, notwithstanding my more than ten years' successful experiment at Killingworth.' The result, however, outstripped even the most sanguine anticipations of Stephenson; and his son Robert, shortly after his return from America in 1827, saw his father's locomotive generally employed as the tractive power on railways.

The Stockton and Darlington line was opened for traffic on 27 September 1825. An immense concourse of people assembled from all parts to witness the ceremony of opening this first public railway. The powerful opposition which the project had encountered, the threats which were still uttered against the company by the road-trustees and others, who declared that they would yet prevent the line being worked, and perhaps the general unbelief as to its success which still prevailed, tended to excite the curiosity of the public as to the result. Some went to rejoice at the opening, some to see the 'bubble burst'; and there were many prophets of evil who would not miss the blowing up of the boasted travelling engine. The opening was, however, auspicious. The proceedings commenced at Brusselton Incline, about nine miles above Darlington, where the fixed engine drew a train of loaded waggons up the incline from the west, and lowered them on the east side. At the foot of the incline a locomotive was in readiness to receive them, Stephenson himself driving the engine. The train consisted of six waggons loaded with coals and flour; after these was the passenger-coach, filled with the directors and their friends, and then twenty-one waggons fitted up with temporary seats for passengers; and lastly came six waggon-loads of coals, making in all a train of thirty-eight vehicles. The local chronicler of the day almost went beside himself in describing the extraordinary event: 'The signal being given,' he says, 'the engine started off with this immense train of carriages; and such was its velocity, that in some parts the speed was frequently 12 miles an hour!' By the time it reached Stockton there were about 600 persons in the train or hanging on to the waggons, which must have gone at a safe and steady pace of from four to six miles an hour from Darlington. 'The arrival at Stockton,' it is added, 'excited a deep interest and admiration.'

The working of the line then commenced, and the results were such as to surprise even the most sanguine of its projectors. The traffic upon which they had formed their estimates of profit proved to be small in comparison with that which flowed in upon them which they had never dreamt of. Thus, what the company had principally relied upon for their receipts was the carriage of coals for land sale at the stations along the line, whereas the haulage of coals to the seaports for exportation to the London market was not contemplated as possible. When the Bill was before Parliament, Mr Lambton (afterwards Earl of Durham) succeeded in getting a clause inserted, limiting the charge for the haulage of all coal to Stockton-on-Tees for the purpose of shipment to $\frac{1}{2}d.$ per ton per mile; whereas a rate of $4d.$ per ton was allowed to be taken for all coals led upon the railway for land sale. Mr Lambton's object in enforcing the low rate of $\frac{1}{2}d.$ was to protect his own trade in coal exported from Sunderland and the northern ports. He believed, in common with everybody else, that the $\frac{1}{2}d.$ rate would effectually secure him against competition on the part of the Company; for it was not considered possible to lead coals at that price, and the proprietors of the railway themselves considered that such a rate would be utterly ruinous. The projectors never contemplated sending more than 10,000 tons a year to Stockton, and those only for shipment as ballast; they looked for their profits almost exclusively to the land sale. The result, however, was as surprising to them as it must have been to Mr Lambton. The $\frac{1}{2}d.$ rate which was forced upon them, instead of being ruinous, proved the vital element in the success of the railway. In the course of a few years, the annual shipment of coal, led by the Stockton and Darlington Railway to Stockton and Middlesbrough, was more than 500,000 tons; and it has since far exceeded this amount. Instead of being, as anticipated, a subordinate branch of traffic, it proved, in fact, the main traffic, while the land sale was merely subsidiary.

The anticipations of the company as to passenger traffic were in like manner more than realized. At first, passengers were not thought of; and it was only while the works were in progress that the starting of a passenger coach was seriously contemplated. The number of persons travelling between the two towns was very small; and it was not known whether these would risk their persons upon the iron road. It was determined, however, to make trial of a railway coach; and Mr Stephenson was authorized to have one built at Newcastle, at the cost of the company. This was done accordingly; and the first railway passenger carriage was built after our engineer's design. It was, however, a very modest, and indeed a somewhat uncouth machine, more resembling the caravans still to be seen at country fairs containing the 'Giant and the Dwarf' and other wonders of the world, than a passenger-coach of any extant form. A row of seats ran along each side of the interior, and a long deal table was fixed in the centre; the access being by means of a door at the back end, in the manner of an omnibus. This coach arrived from Newcastle the day before the opening, and formed part of the railway procession above described. Mr Stephenson was consulted as to the name of the coach, and he at once suggested 'The Experiment'; and by this name it was called. The Company's arms were afterwards painted on her side, with the motto 'Periculum privatum utilitas publica'. Such was the sole passenger-carrying stock of the Stockton and Darlington Company in the year 1825. But the 'Experiment' proved the forerunner of a mighty traffic: and long time did not elapse before it was displaced, not only by improved coaches (still drawn by horses), but afterwards by long trains of passenger-carriages drawn by locomotive engines.

'The Experiment' was fairly started as a passenger-coach on 10 October 1825, a fortnight after the opening of the line. It was drawn by one horse, and performed a journey daily each way between the two towns, accomplishing the distance of twelve miles in about two hours. The fare charged was a shilling without distinction of class; and each passenger was allowed fourteen pounds of luggage free. 'The Experiment' was not, however, worked by the company, but was let to contractors who worked it under an arrangement whereby toll was paid for the use of the line, rent of booking-cabins, etc.

The speculation answered so well, that several private coaching companies were shortly after got up by innkeepers at Darlington and Stockton, for the purpose of running other coaches upon the railroad; and an active competition for passenger traffic sprang up. 'The Experiment' being found too heavy for one horse to draw, besides being found an uncomfortable machine, was banished to the coal district. Its place was then supplied by other and better vehicles, though they were no other than old stage-coach bodies purchased by the company, and each mounted upon an under-frame with flange-wheels. These were let on hire to the coaching companies, who horsed and managed them under an arrangement as to tolls, in like manner as the 'Experiment' had been worked. Now began the distinction of inside and outside passengers, equivalent to first and second class, paying different fares. The competi-

tion with each other upon the railway, and with the ordinary
stage-coaches upon the road, soon brought up the speed, which
was increased to ten miles an hour – the mail-coach rate of travelling in those days, and considered very fast.

Mr Clephan, a native of the district, has described some of the
curious features of the competition between the rival coach companies: 'There were two separate coach companies in Stockton,
and amusing collisions sometimes occurred between the drivers –
who found on the rail a novel element for contention. Coaches cannot pass each other on the rail as on the road; and, as the line
was single, with four sidings in the mile, when two coaches met, or
two trains, or coach and train, the question arose which of the
drivers must go back? This was not always settled in silence. As to
trains, it came to be a sort of understanding that empty should
give way to loaded waggons; and as to trains and coaches, that the
passengers should have preference over coals; while coaches, when
they met, must quarrel it out. At length, midway between sidings,
a post was erected, and a rule was laid down that he who had
passed the pillar must go on, and the "coming man" go back. At
the Goose Pool and Early Nook, it was common for these coaches
to stop; and there, as Jonathan would say, passengers and coach-
men "liquored". One coach, introduced by an innkeeper, was a
compound of two mourning-coaches, an approximation to the real
railway-coach, which still adheres, with multiplying exceptions, to
the stage-coach type. One Dixon, who drove the "Experiment"
between Darlington and Shildon, is the inventor of carriage-
lighting on the rail. On a dark winter night, having compassion on
his passengers, he would buy a penny candle, and place it lighted
among them on the table of the "Experiment" – the first railway-
coach (which, by the way, ended its days at Shildon as a railway
cabin), being also the first coach on the rail (first, second, and third
class jammed all into one) that indulged its customers with light
in darkness.'

The traffic of all sorts increased so steadily and so rapidly that
considerable difficulty was experienced in working it satisfactorily.
It had been provided by the first Stockton and Darlington Act that
the line should be free to all parties who chose to use it at certain
prescribed rates, and that any person might put horses and
waggons on the railway, and carry for himself. But this arrangement led to increasing confusion and difficulty, and could not
continue in the face of a large and rapidly-increasing traffic. The
goods trains got so long that the carriers found it necessary to call

in the aid of the locomotive engine to help them on their way. Then mixed trains of passengers and merchandise began to run; and the result was that the railway company found it necessary to take the entire charge and working of the traffic. In course of time new coaches were specially built for the better accommodation of the public, until at length regular passenger trains were run, drawn by the locomotive engine, though this was not until after the Liverpool and Manchester Company had established this as a distinct branch of their traffic.

The three Stephenson locomotives were from the first regularly employed to work the coal trains; and their proved efficiency for this purpose led to the gradual increase of the locomotive power. The speed of the engines – slow though it seems now – was in those days regarded as something marvellous. A race actually came off between No. 1 engine, the 'Locomotion', and one of the stage-coaches travelling from Darlington to Stockton by the ordinary road; and it was regarded as a great triumph of mechanical skill that the locomotive reached Stockton first, beating the stage-coach by about a hundred yards! The same engine continued in good working order in the year 1846, when it headed the railway procession on the opening of the Middlesbrough and Redcar Railway, travelling at the rate of about fourteen miles an hour. This engine, the first that travelled upon the first public railway, has recently been placed upon a pedestal in front of the railway station at Darlington.

For some years, however, the principal haulage of the line was performed by horses. The inclination of the gradients being to-wards the sea, this was perhaps the cheapest mode of traction, so long as the traffic was not very large. The horse drew the train along the level road, until, on reaching a descending gradient, down which the train ran by its own gravity, the animal was un-harnessed, and, when loose, he wheeled round to the other end of the waggons, to which a 'dandy-cart' was attached, its bottom being only a few inches from the rail. Bringing his step into unison with the speed of the train, the horse learnt to leap nimbly into his place in this waggon, which was usually fitted with a well-filled hay-rack.

The details of the working were gradually perfected by experi-ence, the projectors of the line being scarcely conscious at first of the importance and significance of the work which they had taken in hand, and little thinking that they were laying the foundations of a system which was yet to revolutionize the internal communi-

cations of the world, and confer the greatest blessings on mankind.
It is important to note that the commercial results of the enterprise were considered satisfactory from the opening of the railway.
Besides conferring a great public benefit upon the inhabitants of
the district and throwing open entirely new markets for coal, the
profits derived from the traffic created by the railway yielded
increasing dividends to those who had risked their capital in the
undertaking, and thus held forth an encouragement to the projectors of railways generally, which was not without an important
effect in stimulating the projection of similar enterprises in other
districts. These results, as displayed in the annual dividends, must
have been eminently encouraging to the astute commercial men
of Liverpool and Manchester, who were then engaged in the prosecution of their railway. Indeed, the commercial success of the
Stockton and Darlington Company may be justly characterized as
the turning-point of the railway system.

Before leaving this subject, we cannot avoid alluding to one of
its most remarkable and direct results – the creation of the town
of Middlesbrough-on-Tees. When the railway was opened in 1825,
the site of this future metropolis of Cleveland was occupied by one
solitary farmhouse and its outbuildings. All round was pastureland
or mud-banks; scarcely another house was within sight. In 1829
some of the principal proprietors of the railway joined in the purchase of about 500 or 600 acres of land five miles below Stockton –
the site of the modern Middlesbrough – for the purpose of there
forming a new seaport for the shipment of coals brought to the
Tees by the railway. The line was accordingly extended thither;
docks were excavated; a town sprang up; churches, chapels, and
schools were built, with a custom-house, mechanics' institute,
banks, shipbuilding yards, and iron-factories. In ten years a busy
population of some 6,000 persons (since increased to about 23,000)
occupied the site of the original farmhouse.* More recently, the

---

* Middlesbrough does not furnish the only instance of the extraordinary
increase of population in certain localities, occasioned by railways. Hartle-
pool, in the same neighbourhood, has in thirty years increased from 1,330
to above 15,000; and Stockton-on-Tees from 7,763 to above 16,000. In 1831
Crewe was a little village with 295 inhabitants: it now numbers upwards of
10,000. Rugby and Swindon have quadrupled their population in the same
time. The railway has been the making of Southampton, and added 30,000
to its formerly small number of inhabitants. In like manner the railway has
taken London to the sea-side, and increased the population of Brighton
from 40,000 to nearly 100,000. That of Folkestone has been trebled. New
and populous suburbs have sprung up all round London. The population of

discovery of vast stores of ironstone in the Cleveland Hills, closely adjoining Middlesbrough, has tended still more rapidly to augment the population and increase the commercial importance of the place.

It is pleasing to relate, in connection with this great work – the Stockton and Darlington Railway, projected by Edward Pease and executed by George Stephenson – that when Mr Stephenson became a prosperous and a celebrated man, he did not forget the friend who had taken him by the hand, and helped him on in his early days. He continued to remember Mr Pease with gratitude and affection, and that gentleman, to the close of his life, was proud to exhibit a handsome gold watch, received as a gift from his celebrated protégé, bearing these words: 'Esteem and gratitude: from George Stephenson to Edward Pease.'

Stratford-le-Bow and West Ham was 11,580 in 1831; it is now nearly 40,000. Reigate has been trebled in size, and Redhill has been created by the railway. Blackheath, Forest Hill, Sydenham, New Cross, Wimbledon, and a number of populous places round London, may almost be said to have sprung into existence since the extension of railways to them within the last thirty years.

CHAPTER IX — THE LIVERPOOL AND MANCHESTER RAILWAY PROJECTED

THE rapid growth of the trade and manufactures of South Lancashire gave rise, about the year 1821, to the project of a tramroad for the conveyance of goods between Liverpool and Manchester. Since the construction of the Bridgewater Canal by Brindley, some fifty years before, the increase in the business transacted between the two towns had become quite marvellous. The steam-engine, the spinning-jenny, and the canal, working together, had accumulated in one focus a vast aggregate of population, manufactures, and trade.

Such was the expansion of business caused by the inventions to which we have referred, that the navigation was found altogether inadequate to accommodate the traffic, which completely outgrew all the Canal Companies' appliances of wharves, boats, and horses. Cotton lay at Liverpool for weeks together, waiting to be removed; and it occupied a longer time to transport the cargoes from Liverpool to Manchester than it had done to bring them across the Atlantic from the United States to England. Carts and waggons were tried, but proved altogether insufficient. Sometimes manufacturing operations had to be suspended altogether, and during a frost, when the canals were frozen up, the communication was entirely stopped. The consequences were often disastrous, alike to operatives, merchants, and manufacturers.

Expostulation with the Canal Companies was of no use. They were overcrowded with business at their own prices, and disposed to be very dictatorial. When the Duke first constructed his canal, he had to encounter the fierce opposition of the Irwell and Mersey Navigation, whose monopoly his new line of water conveyance threatened to interfere with.* But the innovation of one generation often becomes the obstruction of the next. The Duke's agents would scarcely listen to the remonstrances of the Liverpool merchants and Manchester manufacturers, and the Bridgewater Canal was accordingly, in its turn, denounced as a monopoly.

Under these circumstances, any new mode of transit between the two towns which offered a reasonable prospect of relief was certain to receive a cordial welcome. The scheme of a tramroad was, however, so new and comparatively untried, that it is not surprising that the parties interested should have hesitated before committing themselves to it. Mr Sandars, a Liverpool merchant, was among the first to broach the subject. He had suffered in his business, in common with many others, from the insufficiency of the existing modes of communication, and was ready to give consideration to any plan presenting elements of practical efficiency which proposed a remedy for the generally admitted grievance. Having caused inquiry to be made as to the success which had attended the haulage of heavy coal trains by locomotive power on the northern railways, he was led to the opinion that the same means might be equally efficient in conducting the increasing traffic in merchandise between Liverpool and Manchester. He ventilated the subject among his friends, and about the beginning of 1821 a committee was formed for the purpose of bringing the scheme of a railroad before the public.

The novel project having become noised abroad, attracted the attention of the friends of railways in other quarters. Tramroads were by no means new expedients for the transit of heavy articles. The Croydon and Wandsworth Railway, laid down by William Jessop as early as the year 1801, had been regularly used for the conveyance of lime and stone in waggons hauled by mules or donkeys from Merstham to London. The sight of this humble railroad in 1813 led Sir Richard Phillips in his 'Morning Walk to Kew' to anticipate the great advantages which would be derived by the nation from the general adoption of Blenkinsop's engine for the conveyance of mails and passengers at ten or even fifteen miles an hour. In the same year we find Mr Lovell Edgworth, who had for fifty years been advocating the superiority of tram or rail roads over common roads, writing to James Watt (7 August 1813): 'I have always thought that steam would become the universal lord, and that we should in time scorn post-horses; an iron railroad would be a cheaper thing than a road upon the common construction.'

* *Lives of the Engineers*, vol. i, p. 371.

Thomas Gray, of Nottingham, was another speculator on the same subject. Though he was no mechanic nor inventor, he had an enthusiastic belief in the powers of the railroad system. Being a native of Leeds, he had, when a boy, seen Blenkinsop's locomotive at work on the Middleton cogged railroad, and from an early period he seems to have entertained almost as sanguine views on the subject as Sir Richard Phillips. It would appear that Gray was residing in Brussels in 1816, when the project of a canal from Charleroi, for the purpose of connecting Holland with the mining districts of Belgium, was the subject of discussion; and, in conversation with Mr John Cockerill and others, he took the opportunity of advocating the superior advantages of a railway. He was absorbed for some time with the preparation of a pamphlet on the subject. He shut himself up, secluded from his wife and relations, declining to give them any information as to his mysterious studies, beyond the assurance that his scheme 'would revolutionize the whole face of the material world and of society'. In 1820 Mr Gray published the result of his studies in his *Observations on a General Iron Railway*, in which, with great cogency, he urged the superiority of a locomotive railway over common roads and canals, pointing out, at the same time, the advantages to all classes of the community of this mode of conveyance for merchandise and persons. In this book Mr Gray suggested a railway between Manchester and Liverpool, 'which', he observed, 'would employ many thousands of the distressed population of Lancashire'. The treatise must have met with a ready sale, as we find that two years later it had passed into a fourth edition. In 1822 Mr Gray added diagrams to the book, showing, in one, suggested lines of railway connecting the principal towns of England, and in another, the principal towns of Ireland.

These speculations show that the subject of railways was gradually becoming familiar to the public mind, and that thoughtful men were anticipating with confidence the adoption of steam-power for the purposes of railway traction. At the same time, a still more profitable class of labourers was at work – first, men like Stephenson, who were engaged in improving the locomotive and making it a practicable and economical working power; and next, those like Edward Pease of Darlington, and Joseph Sandars of Liverpool, who were organizing the means of laying down the railways. Mr William James, of West Bromwich, belonged to the active class of projectors. He was a man of considerable social influence, of an active temperament, and had from an early period

taken a warm interest in the formation of tramroads. Acting as
land-agent for gentlemen of property in the mining districts, he
had laid down several tramroads in the neighbourhood of Birmingham, Gloucester, and Bristol; and he published many pamphlets
urging their formation in other places. At one period of his life he
was a large iron-manufacturer. The times, however, went against
him. It was thought he was too bold, some considered him even
reckless, in his speculations; and he lost almost his entire fortune.
He continued to follow the business of a land-agent, and it was
while engaged in making a survey for one of his clients in the
neighbourhood of Liverpool early in 1821, that he first heard of the
project of a railway between that town and Manchester. He at once
called upon Mr Sandars, and offered his services as surveyor of the
proposed line, and his offer was accepted.

A trial survey was then begun, but it was conducted with great
difficulty, the inhabitants of the district entertaining the most
violent prejudices against the scheme. In some places Mr James
and his surveying party even encountered personal violence. The
farmers stationed men at the field-gates with pitchforks, and sometimes with guns, to drive them back. At St Helens, one of the
chainmen was laid hold of by a mob of colliers, and threatened to
be hurled down a coal-pit. A number of men, women, and children,
collected and ran after the surveyors wherever they made their
appearance, bawling nicknames and throwing stones at them. As
one of the chainmen was climbing over a gate one day, a labourer
made at him with a pitchfork, and ran it through his clothes into
his back; other watchers running up, the chainman, who was more
stunned than hurt, took to his heels and fled. But that mysterious-
looking instrument – the theodolite – most excited the fury of the
natives, who concentrated on the man who carried it their fiercest
execrations and most offensive nicknames.

A powerful fellow, a noted bruiser, was hired by the surveyors to
carry the instrument, with a view to its protection against all
assailants; but one day an equally powerful fellow, a St Helens
collier, cock of the walk in his neighbourhood, made up to the
theodolite bearer to wrest it from him by sheer force. A battle took
place, the collier was soundly pummelled, but the natives poured
in volleys of stones upon the surveyors and their instruments, and
the theodolite was smashed to pieces.

An outline-survey having at length been made, notices were
published of an intended application to Parliament. In the mean
time Mr James proceeded to Killingworth to see Stephenson's loco-

motives at work. Stephenson was not at home at the time, but James saw his engines, and was very much struck by their power and efficiency. He saw at a glance the magnificent uses to which the locomotive might be applied. 'Here,' said he, 'is an engine that will, before long, effect a complete revolution in society.' Returning to Moreton-in-the-Marsh, he wrote to Mr Losh (Stephenson's partner in the patent) expressing his admiration of the Killingworth engine. 'It is,' said he, 'the greatest wonder of the age, and the forerunner, as I firmly believe, of the most important changes in the internal communications of the kingdom.' Shortly after, Mr James, accompanied by his two sons, made a second journey to Killingworth, where he met both Losh and Stephenson. The visitors were at once taken to where the locomotive was working, and invited to mount it. The uncouth and extraordinary appearance of the machine, as it came snorting along, was somewhat alarming to the youths, who expressed their fears lest it should burst; and they were with some difficulty induced to mount.

The engine went through its usual performances, dragging a heavy load of coal-waggons at about six miles an hour, with apparent ease, at which Mr James expressed his extreme satisfaction, and declared to Mr Losh his opinion that Stephenson 'was the greatest practical genius of the age', and that, 'if he developed the full powers of that engine (the locomotive), his fame in the world would rank equal with that of Watt.' Mr James informed Stephenson and Losh of his survey of the proposed tramroad between Liverpool and Manchester, and did not hesitate to state that he would thenceforward advocate the construction of a locomotive railroad instead of the tramroad which had originally been proposed.

Stephenson and Losh were naturally desirous of enlisting James's good services on behalf of their patent locomotive, for as yet it had proved comparatively unproductive. They believed that he might be able so to advocate it in influential quarters as to ensure its more extensive adoption, and with this object they proposed to give him an interest in the patent. Accordingly they assigned him one-fourth of any profits which might be derived from the use of the patent locomotive on any railways constructed south of a line drawn across England from Liverpool to Hull. The arrangement, however, led to no beneficial results. Mr James endeavoured to introduce the engine on the Moreton-in-Marsh Railway; but it was opposed by the engineer of the line, and the attempt failed. He next urged that a locomotive should be sent for trial upon the Merstham tramroad; but, anxious though Stephenson was respecting its extended employment, he was too cautious to risk an experiment which might only bring discredit upon the engine; and the Merstham road being only laid with cast iron plates, which would not bear its weight, the invitation was declined.

It turned out that the first survey of the Liverpool and Manchester line was very imperfect, and it was determined to have a second and more complete one made in the following year. Robert Stephenson was sent over by his father to Liverpool to assist in this survey. He was present with Mr James on the occasion on which he tried to lay out the line across Chat Moss, a proceeding which was not only difficult but dangerous. The Moss was very wet at the time, and only its edges could be ventured on. Mr James was a heavy, thick-set man; and one day, when endeavouring to obtain a stand for his theodolite, he felt himself suddenly sinking. He immediately threw himself down, and rolled over and over until he reached firm ground again, in a sad mess. Other attempts which he subsequently made to enter upon the Moss for the same purpose, were abandoned for the same reason – the want of a solid stand for the theodolite.

On 4 October 1822, we find Mr James writing to Mr Sandars, 'I came last night to send my aid, Robert Stephenson, to his father, and to-morrow I shall pay off Evans and Hamilton, two other assistants. I have now only Messrs. Padley and Clarke to finish the copy of plans for Parliament, which will be done in about a week or nine days' time.' It would appear, however, that, notwithstanding all his exertions, Mr James was unable to complete his plans and estimates in time for the ensuing Session; and another year was thus lost. The Railroad Committee became impatient at the delay. Mr James's financial embarrassments reached their climax; and, what with illness and debt, he was no longer in a position to fulfil his promises to the Committee. They were, therefore, under the necessity of calling to their aid some other engineer.

Mr Sandars had by this time visited George Stephenson at Killingworth, and, like all who came within reach of his personal influence, was charmed with him at first sight. The energy which he had displayed in carrying on the works of the Stockton and Darlington Railway, now approaching completion; his readiness to face difficulties, and his practical ability in overcoming them; the enthusiasm which he displayed on the subject of railways and railway locomotion, concurred in satisfying Mr Sandars that he was, of all men, the best calculated to help forward the Liverpool undertaking at this juncture. On his return he stated this opinion to the Committee, who approved his recommendation, and George Stephenson was unanimously appointed engineer of the projected railway.

It will be observed that Mr Sandars had held to his original purpose with great determination and perseverance, and he gradually succeeded in enlisting on his side an increasing number of influential merchants and manufacturers both at Liverpool and Manchester. Early in 1824 he published a pamphlet, in which he strongly urged the great losses and interruptions to the trade of the district by the delays in the forwarding of merchandise; and in the same year he had a Public Declaration drawn up, and signed by upwards of 150 of the principal merchants of Liverpool, setting forth that they considered 'the present establishments for the transport of goods quite inadequate, and that a new line of conveyance has become absolutely necessary to conduct the increasing trade of the country with speed, certainty, and economy'.

A public meeting was then held to consider the best plan to be adopted, and resolutions were passed in favour of a railroad. A committee was appointed to take the necessary measures; but, as if reluctant to enter upon their arduous struggle with the 'vested interests', they first waited on Mr Bradshaw, the Duke of Bridgewater's canal agent, in the hope of persuading him to increase the means of conveyance, as well as to reduce the charges; but they were met by an unqualified refusal. They suggested the expediency of a railway, and invited Mr Bradshaw to become a proprietor of shares in it. But his reply was – 'All or none!' The canal proprietors, confident in their imagined security, ridiculed the proposed railway as a chimera. It had been spoken about years before, and nothing had come of it then: it would be the same now.

In order to form a better opinion as to the practicability of the railroad, a deputation of gentlemen interested in the project proceeded to Killingworth, to inspect the engines which had been so long in use there. They first went to Darlington, where they found the works of the Stockton line in progress, though still unfinished. Proceeding next to Killingworth with Mr Stephenson, they there witnessed the performances of his locomotive engines. The result of their visit was, on the whole, so satisfactory, that on their report being delivered to the committee at Liverpool, it was finally determined to form a company of proprietors for the construction of a double line of railway between Liverpool and Manchester.

The first prospectus of the scheme was dated 29 October 1824, and had attached to it the names of the leading merchants of Liverpool and Manchester. It was a modest document, very unlike the inflated balloons which were sent up by railway speculators in succeeding years. It set forth as its main object the establishment of a safe and cheap mode of transit for merchandise, by which the conveyance of goods between the two towns would be effected in five or six hours (instead of thirty-six hours by the canal), while the charges would be reduced one-third. On looking at the prospectus now, it is curious to note that, while the advantages anticipated from the carriage of merchandise were strongly insisted upon, the conveyance of passengers – which proved to be the chief source of profit – was only very cautiously referred to. 'As a cheap and expeditious means of conveyance for travellers,' says the prospectus in conclusion, 'the railway holds out the fair prospect of a public accommodation, the magnitude and importance of which cannot be immediately ascertained.' The estimated expense of forming the line was set down at £400,000, a sum which was eventually found quite inadequate. The subscription list when opened was filled up without difficulty.

While the project was still under discussion, its promoters, desirous of removing the doubts which existed as to the employment of steam power on the proposed railway, sent a second deputation to Killingworth for the purpose of again observing the action of Stephenson's engines. The cautious projectors of the railway were not yet quite satisfied; and third journey was made to Killingworth, in January 1825, by several gentlemen of the committee, accompanied by practical engineers, for the purpose of being personal eye-witnesses of what steam-carriages were able to perform upon a railway. There they saw a train, consisting of a locomotive and loaded waggons, weighing in all 54 tons, travelling at the average rate of about 7 miles an hour, the greatest speed being about $9\frac{1}{2}$ miles an hour. But when the engine was run with only one waggon attached containing twenty gentlemen, five of whom were engineers, the speed attained was from 10 to 12 miles an hour.

In the mean time the survey was proceeded with, in the face of great opposition from the proprietors of the lands through which the railway was intended to pass. The prejudices of the farming and labouring classes were strongly excited against the persons employed upon the ground, and it was with the greatest difficulty that the levels could be taken. At one place, Stephenson was driven off the ground by the keepers, and threatened to be ducked in the pond if found there again. The farmers also turned out their men to watch the surveying party, and prevent them entering upon any lands where they had the power of driving them off.

One of the proprietors declared that he would order his game-keepers to shoot or apprehend any persons attempting a survey over his property. But one moonlight night a survey was obtained by the following ruse. Some men, under the orders of the surveying party, were set to fire off guns in a particular quarter; on which all the gamekeepers on the watch made off in that direction, and they were drawn away to such a distance in pursuit of the supposed poachers, as to enable a rapid survey to be made during their absence.

When the canal companies found that the Liverpool merchants were determined to proceed with their scheme – that they had completed their survey, and were ready to apply to Parliament for an Act to enable them to form the railway – they at last reluctantly, and with a bad grace, made overtures of conciliation. They promised to employ steam-vessels both on the Mersey and on the Canal. One of the companies offered to reduce its length by three miles, at a considerable outlay. At the same time they made a show of lowering their rates. But it was too late; for the project of the railway had now gone so far that the promoters (who might have been conciliated by such overtures at an earlier period) felt they were fully committed to it, and that now they could not well draw back. Besides, the remedies offered by the canal companies could only have had the effect of staving off the difficulty for a brief season, the absolute necessity of forming a new line of communication between Liverpool and Manchester becoming more urgent from year to year. Arrangements were therefore made for proceeding with the bill in the parliamentary session of 1825.

On this becoming known, the canal companies prepared to resist the measure tooth and nail. The public were appealed to on the subject; pamphlets were written and newspapers were hired to revile the railway. It was declared that its formation would prevent cows grazing and hens laying. The poisoned air from the loco-motives would kill birds as they flew over them, and render the preservation of pheasants and foxes no longer possible. House-holders adjoining the projected line were told that their houses would be burnt up by the fire thrown from the engine-chimneys; while the air around would be polluted by clouds of smoke. There would no longer be any use for horses; and if railways extended,

the species would become extinguished, and oats and hay be
rendered unsaleable commodities. Travelling by rail would be
highly dangerous, and country inns would be ruined. Boilers would
burst and blow passengers to atoms. But there was always this
consolation to wind up with – that the weight of the locomotive
would completely prevent its moving, and that railways, even if
made, could *never* be worked by steam-power.

Indeed, when Mr Stephenson, at the interviews with counsel,
held previous to the Liverpool and Manchester bill going into
Committee of the House of Commons, confidently stated his expectation of being able to impel his locomotive at the rate of 20
miles an hour, Mr William Brougham, who was retained by the
promoters to conduct their case, frankly told him that if he did
not moderate his views, and bring his engine within a *reasonable*
speed, he would 'inevitably damn the whole thing, and be himself
regarded as a maniac fit only for Bedlam'.

The idea thrown out by Stephenson, of travelling at a rate of
speed double that of the fastest mail-coach, appeared at the time
so preposterous that he was unable to find any engineer who would
risk his reputation in supporting such 'absurd views'. Speaking of
his isolation at the time, he subsequently observed, at a public
meeting of railwaymen in Manchester: 'He remembered the time
when he had very few supporters in bringing out the railway
system – when he sought England over for an engineer to support
him in his evidence before Parliament, and could find only one
man, James Walker, but was afraid to call that gentleman, because he knew nothing about railways. He had then no one to tell
his tale to but Mr Sandars, of Liverpool, who did listen to him, and
kept his spirits up; and his schemes had at length been carried out
only by dint of sheer perseverance.'

George Stephenson's idea was at that time regarded as but the
dream of a chimerical projector. It stood before the public friend-
less, struggling hard to gain a footing, scarcely daring to lift itself
into notice for fear of ridicule. The civil engineers generally rejected the notion of a Locomotive Railway; and when no leading
man of the day could be found to stand forward in support of the
Killingworth mechanic, its chances of success must indeed have
been pronounced but small.

When such was the hostility of the civil engineers, no wonder
the reviewers were puzzled. The *Quarterly*, in an able article in
support of the projected Liverpool and Manchester Railway, while
admitting its *absolute necessity*, and insisting that there was no

choice left but a railroad, on which the journey between Liverpool and Manchester, whether performed by horses or engines, would always be accomplished 'within the day', nevertheless scouted the idea of travelling at a greater speed than eight or nine miles an hour. Adverting to a project for forming a railway to Woolwich, by which passengers were to be drawn by locomotive engines, moving with twice the velocity of ordinary coaches, the reviewer observed: 'What can be more palpably absurd and ridiculous than the prospect held out of locomotives travelling *twice as fast* as stage-coaches! We would as soon expect the people of Woolwich to suffer themselves to be fired off upon one of Congreve's ricochet rockets, as trust themselves to the mercy of such a machine going at such a rate. We will back old Father Thames against the Woolwich Railway for any sum. We trust that Parliament will, in all railways it may sanction, limit the speed to *eight or nine miles an hour*, which we entirely agree with Mr Sylvester is as great as can be ventured on with safety.'

At length the survey was completed, the plans were deposited, the requisite preliminary arrangements were made, and the promoters of the scheme applied to Parliament for the necessary powers to construct the railway. The Bill went into Committee of the Commons on 21 March 1825. There was an extraordinary array of legal talent on the occasion, but especially on the side of the opponents to the measure; their counsel including Mr (afterwards Baron) Alderson, Mr (afterwards Baron) Parke, Mr Harrison, and Mr Erle. The counsel for the Bill were Mr Adam, Mr Serjeant Spankie, Mr William Brougham, and Mr Joy.

Evidence was taken at great length as to the difficulties and delays in forwarding raw material of all kinds from Liverpool to Manchester, as also in the conveyance of manufactured goods from Manchester to Liverpool. The evidence adduced in support of the Bill on these grounds was overwhelming. The utter inadequacy of the existing modes of conveyance to carry on satisfactorily the large and rapidly-growing trade between the two towns was fully proved. But then came the gist of the promoter's case – the evidence to prove the practicability of a railroad to be worked by locomotive power. Mr Adam, in his opening speech, referred to the cases of the Hetton and the Killingworth railroads, where heavy goods were safely and economically transported by means of locomotive engines. 'None of the tremendous consequences,' he observed, 'have ensued from the use of steam in land carriage that have been stated. The horses have not started, nor the cows ceased

to give their milk, nor have ladies miscarried at the sight of these
things going forward at the rate of four miles and a half an hour.'
Notwithstanding the petition of two ladies alleging the great
danger to be apprehended from the bursting of the locomotive
boilers, he urged the safety of the high-pressure engine when the
boilers were constructed of wrought iron; and as to the rate at
which they could travel, he expressed his full conviction that such
engines 'could supply force to drive a carriage at the rate of five
or six miles an hour'.

The taking of the evidence as to the impediments thrown in the
way of trade and commerce by the existing system extended over
a month, and it was 21 April before the Committee went into the
engineering evidence, which was the vital part of the question.

On the 25th George Stephenson was called into the witness-box.
It was his first appearance before a Committee of the House of
Commons, and he well knew what he had to expect. He was aware
that the whole force of the opposition was to be directed
against him; and if they could break down his evidence, the canal
monopoly might yet be upheld for a time. Many years afterwards,
when looking back at his position on this trying occasion, he said:
'When I went to Liverpool to plan a line from thence to Manchester, I pledged myself to the directors to attain a speed of
10 miles an hour. I said I had no doubt the locomotive might be
made to go much faster, but that we had better be moderate at the
beginning. The directors said I was quite right; for that if, when
they went to Parliament, I talked of going at a greater rate than
10 miles an hour, I should put a cross upon the concern. It was not
an easy task for me to keep the engine down to 10 miles an hour,
but it must be done, and I did my best. I had to place myself in
that most unpleasant of all positions – the witness-box of a Parliamentary Committee. I was not long in it, before I began to wish
for a hole to creep out at! I could not find words to satisfy either
the Committee or myself. I was subjected to the cross-examination
of eight or ten barristers, purposely, as far as possible, to bewilder
me. Some member of the Committee asked if I was a foreigner, and
another hinted that I was mad. But I put up with every rebuff, and
went on with my plans, determined not to be put down.'

Mr Stephenson stood before the Committee to prove what the
public opinion of that day held to be impossible. The self-taught
mechanic had to demonstrate the practicability of accomplishing
that which the most distinguished engineers of the time regarded
as impracticable. Clear though the subject was to himself, and

familiar as he was with the powers of the locomotive, it was no easy task for him to bring home his convictions, or even to convey his meaning, to the less informed minds of his hearers. In his strong Northumbrian dialect, he struggled for utterance, in the face of the sneers, interruptions, and ridicule of the opponents of the measure, and even of the Committee, some of whom shook their heads and whispered doubts as to his sanity, when he energetically avowed that he could make the locomotive go at the rate of 12 miles an hour! It was so grossly in the teeth of all the experience of honourable members, that the man 'must certainly be labouring under a delusion!'

And yet his large experience of railways and locomotives, as described by himself to the Committee, entitled this 'untaught, inarticulate genius', as he has so well been styled, to speak with confidence on such a subject. Beginning with his experience as a brakesman at Killingworth in 1803, he went on to state that he was appointed to take the entire charge of the steam-engines in 1813, and had superintended the railroads connected with the numerous collieries of the Grand Allies from that time downwards. He had laid down or superintended the railways at Burradon, Mount Moor, Springwell, Bedlington, Hetton, and Darlington, besides improving those at Killingworth, South Moor, and Derwent Crook. He had constructed fifty-five steam-engines, of which sixteen were locomotives. Some of these had been sent to France. The engines constructed by him for the working of the Killingworth Railroad, eleven years before, had continued steadily at work ever since, and fulfilled his most sanguine expectations. He was prepared to prove the safety of working high-pressure locomotives on a railroad, and the superiority of this mode of transporting goods over all others. As to speed, he said he had recommended 8 miles an hour with 20 tons, and 4 miles an hour with 40 tons; but he was quite confident that much more might be done. Indeed, he had no doubt they might go at the rate of 12 miles. As to the charge that locomotives on a railroad would so terrify the horses in the neighbourhood, that to travel on horseback or to plough the adjoining fields would be rendered highly dangerous, the witness said that horses learnt to take no notice of them, though there *were* horses that would shy at a wheelbarrow. A mailcoach was likely to be more shied at by horses than a locomotive. In the neighbourhood of Killingworth, the cattle in the fields went on grazing while the engines passed them, and the farmers made no complaints.

Mr Alderson, who had carefully studied the subject, and was well skilled in practical science, subjected the witness to a protracted and severe cross-examination as to the speed and power of the locomotive, the stroke of the piston, the slipping of the wheels upon the rails, and various other points of detail. Mr Stephenson insisted that no slipping took place, as attempted to be extorted from him by the counsel. He said, 'It is impossible for slipping to take place so long as the adhesive weight of the wheel upon the rail is greater than the weight to be dragged after it.' As to accidents, Stephenson said he knew of none that had occurred with his engines. There had been one, he was told, at the Middleton Colliery, near Leeds, with a Blenkinsop engine. The driver had been in liquor, and put a considerable load on the safety-valve, so that upon going forward the engine blew up and the man was killed. But he added, if proper precautions had been used with that boiler, the accident could not have happened. The following cross-examination occurred in reference to the question of speed:

'Of course,' he was asked, 'when a body is moving upon a road, the greater the velocity the greater the momentum that is generated?' 'Certainly.' – 'What would be the momentum of 40 tons moving at the rate of 12 miles an hour?' 'It would be very great.' – 'Have you seen a railroad that would stand that?' 'Yes.' – 'Where?' 'Any railroad that would bear going 4 miles an hour: I mean to say, that if it would bear the weight at 4 miles an hour, it would bear it at 12.' – 'Taking it at 4 miles an hour, do you mean to say that it would not require a stronger railway to carry the same weight 12 miles an hour?' 'I will give an answer to that. I dare say every person has been over ice when skating, or seen persons go over, and they know that it would bear them better at a greater velocity than it would if they went slower; when they go quick, the weight in a measure ceases.' – 'Is not that upon the hypothesis that the railroad is perfect?' 'It is; and I mean to make it perfect.'

It is not necessary to state that to have passed the ordeal of so severe a cross-examination scatheless, needed no small amount of courage, intelligence, and ready shrewdness on the part of the witness. Nicholas Wood, who was present on the occasion, has since stated that the point on which Stephenson was hardest pressed was that of speed. 'I believe,' he says, 'that it would have lost the Company their Bill if he had gone beyond 8 or 9 miles an hour. If he had stated his intention of going 12 or 15 miles an hour, not a single person would have believed it to be practicable.'

The Committee also seem to have entertained considerable alarm as to the high rate of speed which had been spoken of, and proceeded to examine the witness further on the subject. They supposed the case of the engine being upset when going at 9 miles an hour, and asked what, in such a case, would become of the cargo astern. To which the witness replied that it would not be upset. One of the members of the Committee pressed the witness a little further. He put the following case: 'Suppose, now, one of these engines to be going along a railroad at the rate of 9 or 10 miles an hour, and that a cow were to stray upon the line and get in the way of the engine; would not that, think you, be a very awkward circumstance?' 'Yes,' replied the witness, with a twinkle in his eye, 'very awkward – *for the coo!*' The honourable member did not proceed further with his cross-examination; to use a railway phrase, he was 'shunted'. Another asked if animals would not be very much frightened by the engine passing them, especially by the glare of the red-hot chimney? 'But how would they know that it wasn't painted?' said the witness.

On the following day, the engineer was subjected to a very severe examination. On that part of the scheme with which he was most practically conversant, his evidence was clear and conclusive. Now, he had to give evidence on the plans made by his surveyors, and the estimates which had been founded on such plans. So long as he was confined to locomotive engines and iron railroads, with the minutest details of which he was more familiar than any man living, he felt at home, and in his element. But when the designs of bridges and the cost of constructing them had to be gone into, the subject being in a great measure new to him, his evidence was much less satisfactory.

Mr Alderson cross-examined him at great length on the plans of the bridges, the tunnels, the crossings of the roads and streets, and the details of the survey, which, it soon clearly appeared, were in some respects seriously at fault. It seems that, after the plans had been deposited, Stephenson found that a much more favourable line might be made; and he made his estimates accordingly, supposing that Parliament would not confine the Company to the precise plan which had been deposited. This was felt to be a serious blot in the parliamentary case, and one very difficult to be got over.

For three entire days was our engineer subjected to this cross-examination. He held his ground bravely, and defended the plans

and estimates with remarkable ability and skill; but it was clear
they were imperfect, and the result was on the whole damaging
to the measure.

The case of the opponents was next gone into, in the course of
which the counsel indulged in strong vituperation against the witnesses for the Bill. One of them spoke of the utter impossibility of
making a railway upon so treacherous a material as Chat Moss,
which was declared to be an immense mass of pulp, and nothing
else. 'It actually,' said Mr Harrison, 'rises in height, from the rain
swelling it like a sponge, and sinks again in dry weather; and if a
boring instrument is put into it, it sinks immediately by its own
weight. The making of an embankment out of this pulpy, wet moss,
is no very easy task. Who but Mr Stephenson would have thought
of entering into Chat Moss, carrying it out almost like wet dung?
It is ignorance almost inconceivable. It is perfect madness, in a
person called upon to speak on a scientific subject, to propose such
a plan. . . . Every part of this scheme shows that this man has
applied himself to a subject of which he has no knowledge, and to
which he has no science to apply.' Then adverting to the proposal
to work the intended line by means of locomotives, the learned
gentleman proceeded: 'When we set out with the original prospectus, we were to gallop, I know not at what rate; I believe it was
at the rate of 12 miles an hour. My learned friend, Mr Adam,
contemplated – possibly alluding to Ireland – that some of the
Irish members would arrive in the waggons to a division. My
learned friend says that they would go at the rate of 12 miles an
hour with the aid of the devil in the form of a locomotive, sitting
as postilion on the fore horse, and an honourable member sitting
behind him to stir up the fire, and keep it at full speed. But the
speed at which these locomotive engines are to go has slackened:
Mr Adam does not go faster now than 5 miles an hour. The learned
serjeant (Spankie) says he should like to have 7, but he would be
content to go 6. I will show he cannot go 6; and probably, for any
practical purposes, I may be able to show that I can keep up with
him *by the canal* . . . Locomotive engines are liable to be operated
upon by the weather. You are told they are affected by rain, and
an attempt has been made to cover them; but the wind will affect
them; and any gale of wind which would affect the traffic on the
Mersey would render it *impossible* to set off a locomotive engine,
either by poking of the fire, or keeping up the pressure of the steam
till the boiler was ready to burst.' How amusing it now is to read
these extraordinary views as to the formation of a railway over

Near Liverpool looking towards Manchester

Chat Moss, and the impossibility of starting a locomotive engine in the face of a gale of wind!

Evidence was called to show that the house property passed by the proposed railway would be greatly deteriorated – in some places almost destroyed; that the locomotive engines would be terrible nuisances, in consequence of the fire and smoke vomited forth by them; and that the value of land in the neighbourhood of Manchester alone would be deteriorated by no less than £20,000! Evidence was also given at great length showing the utter impossibility of forming a road of any kind upon Chat Moss. A Manchester builder, who was examined, could not imagine the feat possible, unless by arching it across in the manner of a viaduct from one side to the other. It was the old story of 'nothing like leather'. But the opposition mainly relied upon the evidence of the leading engineers – not, like Stephenson, self-taught men, but regular professionals. One of these, Mr Francis Giles, C.E., had been twenty-two years an engineer, and could speak with some authority. His testimony was mainly directed to the utter impossibility of forming a railway over Chat Moss. *'No engineer in his senses,'* said he, 'would go through Chat Moss if he wanted to make a railroad from Liverpool to Manchester. . . . In my judgement *a railroad certainly cannot be safely made over Chat Moss without going to the bottom of the Moss.* The soil ought all to be taken out, undoubtedly; in doing which, it will not be practicable to approach each end of the cutting, as you make it, with the carriages. No carriages would stand upon the Moss short of the bottom. My estimate for the whole cutting and embankment over Chat Moss is £270,000, nearly, at those quantities and those prices which are decidedly correct. . . . It will be necessary to take this Moss completely out at the bottom, in order to make a solid road.'

When the engineers had given their evidence, Mr Alderson summed up in a speech which extended over two days. He declared Mr Stephenson's plan to be 'the most absurd scheme that ever entered into the head of man to conceive. My learned friends,' said he, 'almost endeavoured to stop my examination; they wished me to put in the plan, but I had rather have the exhibition of Mr Stephenson in that box. I say he never had a plan – I believe he never had one – I do not believe he is capable of making one. His is a mind perpetually fluctuating between opposite difficulties: he neither knows whether he is to make bridges over roads or rivers, of one size or of another; or to make embankments, or cuttings, or inclined planes, or in what way the thing is to be carried into effect.

Whenever a difficulty is pressed, as in the case of a tunnel, he gets out of it at one end, and when you try to catch him at that, he gets out at the other.' Mr Alderson proceeded to declaim against the gross ignorance of this so-called engineer, who proposed to make 'impossible ditches by the side of an impossible railway' upon Chat Moss; 'I care not,' he said, 'whether Mr Giles is right or wrong in his estimate, for whether it be effected by means of piers raised up all the way for four miles through Chat Moss, whether they are to support it on beams of wood or by erecting masonry, or whether Mr Giles shall put a solid bank of earth through it, in all these schemes there is not one found like that of Mr Stephenson's, namely, to cut impossible drains on the side of this road; and it is sufficient for me to suggest and to show, that this scheme of Mr Stephenson's is impossible or impracticable, and that no other scheme, if they proceed upon this line, can be suggested which will not produce enormous expense. I think that has been irrefragably made out. Every one knows Chat Moss – every one knows that the iron sinks immediately on its being put upon the surface. I have heard of culverts, which have been put upon the Moss, which, after having been surveyed the day before, have the next morning disappeared; and that a house (a poet's house, who may be supposed in the habit of building castles even in the air), storey after storey, as fast as one is added, the lower one sinks! There is nothing, it appears, except long sedgy grass, and a little soil to prevent its sinking into the shades of eternal night. I have now done, sir, with Chat Moss, and there I leave this railroad.'

The case of the principal petitioners against the bill occupied many more days, and on its conclusion the committee proceeded to divide on the preamble, which was carried by a majority of only *one* – 37 voting for it, and 36 against it. The clauses were next considered, and on a division the first clause, empowering the Company to make the railway, was lost by a majority of 19 to 13. In like manner, the next clause, empowering the Company to take land, was lost; on which the Bill was withdrawn.

Thus ended this memorable contest, which had extended over two months – carried on throughout with great pertinacity and skill, especially on the part of the opposition, who left no stone unturned to defeat the measure. The want of a third line of communication between Liverpool and Manchester had been clearly proved; but the engineering evidence in support of the proposed railway having been thrown almost entirely upon Stephenson, who fought this, the most important part of the battle, single-handed, was not brought out so clearly as it would have been, had he secured more efficient engineering assistance – which he was not able to do, as the principal engineers of that day were against the locomotive railway. The obstacles thrown in the way of the survey by the landowners and canal companies, by which the plans were rendered exceedingly imperfect, also tended in a great measure to defeat the Bill.

The rejection of the Bill was probably the most severe trial George Stephenson underwent in the whole course of his life. The circumstances connected with the defeat of the measure, the errors in the levels, his rigid cross-examination, followed by the fact of his being superseded by another engineer, all told fearfully upon him, and for some time he was as much weighed down as if a personal calamity of the most serious kind had befallen him.

Stephenson had been so terribly abused by the leading counsel for the opposition in the course of the proceedings before the Committee – stigmatized by them as an ignoramus, a fool, and a maniac – that even his friends seem for a time to have lost faith in him and in the locomotive system, whose efficiency he nevertheless continued to uphold. Things never looked blacker for the success of the railway system than at the close of this great parliamentary struggle. And yet it was on the very eve of its triumph.

The Committee of Directors appointed to watch the measure in Parliament were so determined to press on the project of a railway, even though it should have to be worked merely by horse-power, that the bill had scarcely been thrown out ere they met in London to consider their next step. They called their parliamentary friends together to consult as to future proceedings; and the result was that they went back to Liverpool determined to renew their application to Parliament in the ensuing session.

It was not considered desirable to employ Mr Stephenson in making the new survey. He had not as yet established his reputation as an engineer beyond the boundaries of his own district; and the promoters of the Bill had doubtless felt the disadvantages of this in the course of their parliamentary struggle. They therefore resolved now to employ engineers of the highest established reputation, as well as the best surveyors that could be obtained. In accordance with these views they engaged Messrs. George and John Rennie to be the engineers of the railway; and Mr Charles Vignolles was appointed to prepare the plans and sections. The line which was eventually adopted differed somewhat from that surveyed by Mr Stephenson. The principal parks and game-preserves of the district were carefully avoided. The promoters thus hoped to get rid of the opposition of the most influential of the resident land-owners. The crossing of certain of the streets of Liverpool was also avoided, and the entrance contrived by means of a tunnel and an inclined plane. The new line stopped short of the river Irwell at the Manchester end, by which the objections grounded on an illegal interruption to the canal or river traffic were in some measure removed. The opposition of the Duke of Bridgewater's trustees was also got rid of, and the Marquis of Stafford became a subscriber for a thousand shares. With reference to the use of the locomotive engine, the promoters, remembering with what effect the objections to it had been urged by the opponents of the Bill, intimated, in their second prospectus, that 'as a guarantee of their good faith towards the public they will not require any clause empowering them to use it; or they will submit to such restrictions in the employment of it as Parliament may impose.'

The survey of the new line having been completed, the plans were deposited, the standing orders duly complied with, and the Bill went before Parliament. The same counsel appeared for the promoters, but the examination of witnesses was not nearly so protracted as on the previous occasion. The preamble was declared proved by a majority of 43 to 18. On the third reading in the House of Commons, an animated, and what now appears a very amusing discussion took place. The Hon. Edward Stanley moved that the Bill be read that day six months; and in his speech he undertook to prove that the railway trains would take *ten hours* on the journey, and that they could only be worked by horses. Sir Isaac Coffin seconded the motion, and in doing so denounced the project as a most flagrant imposition. He would not consent to see widows' premises invaded; and 'What, he would like to know, was to be done with all those who had advanced money in making and repairing turnpike-roads? What was to become of coach-makers and harness-makers, coach-masters and coach-men, inn-keepers, horse-breeders, and horse-dealers? Was the house aware of the smoke and the noise, the hiss and the whirl, which locomotive engines, passing at the rate of 10 or 12 miles an hour, would occasion? Neither the cattle ploughing in the fields or grazing in the meadows could behold them without dismay. Iron would be raised in price 100 per cent, or more probably exhausted altogether! It would be the greatest nuisance, the most complete disturbance of quiet and comfort in all parts of the kingdom, that the ingenuity of man could invent!'

Mr Huskisson and other speakers, though unable to reply to such arguments as these, strongly supported the Bill; and it was carried on the third reading by a majority of 88 to 41. The Bill passed the House of Lords almost unanimously, its only opponents being the Earl of Derby and his relative the Earl of Wilton.

CHAPTER X — CHAT MOSS — CONSTRUCTION OF THE LIVERPOOL AND MANCHESTER RAILWAY

THE appointment of principal engineer to the railway was taken into consideration at the first meeting of the directors held at Liverpool subsequent to the passing of the Act. The magnitude of the proposed works, and the vast consequences involved in their experiment, were deeply impressed upon their minds; and they resolved to secure the services of a resident engineer of proved experience and ability. Their attention was naturally directed to Mr Stephenson; at the same time they desired to have the benefit of the Messrs. Rennie's professional assistance in superintending the works. Mr George Rennie had an interview with the Board on the subject, at which he proposed to undertake the chief super-intendence, making six visits in each year, and stipulating that he should have the appointment of the resident engineer. But the responsibility attaching to the direction in the matter of the efficient carrying on of the works, would not admit of their being influenced by ordinary punctilios on the occasion; and they accord-

ingly declined this proposal, and proceeded to appoint Mr Stephenson their principal engineer at a salary of £1,000 per annum.

He at once removed his residence to Liverpool, and made
arrangements to commence the works. He began with the 'impossible thing' – to do that which the most distinguished engineers of
the day had declared that 'no man in his senses would undertake
to do' – namely, to make the road over Chat Moss! It was indeed
a most formidable undertaking; and the project of carrying a railway along, under, or over such a material as that of which it
consisted, would certainly never have occurred to an ordinary
mind. Michael Drayton supposed the Moss to have had its origin
at the Deluge. Nothing more impassable could have been imagined
than that dreary waste; and Mr Giles only spoke the popular feeling of the day when he declared that no carriage could stand on it
'short of the bottom'. In this bog, singular to say, Mr Roscoe, the
accomplished historian of the Medicis, buried his fortune in the
hopeless attempt to cultivate a portion of it which he had bought.

Chat Moss is an immense peat bog of about twelve square miles
in extent. Unlike the bogs or swamps of Cambridge and Lincoln-
shire, which consist principally of soft mud or silt, this bog is a vast
mass of spongy vegetable pulp, the result of the growth and decay
of ages. The spagni, or bog-mosses, cover the entire area; one year's
growth rising over another, the old growths not entirely decaying,
but remaining partially preserved by the antiseptic properties
peculiar to peat. Hence the remarkable fact that, although a semi-
fluid mass, the surface of Chat Moss rises above the level of the
surrounding country. Like a turtle's back, it declines from the
summit in every direction, having from thirty to forty feet gradual
slope to the solid land on all sides. From the remains of trees,
chiefly alder and birch, which have been dug out of it, and which
must have previously flourished upon the surface of soil now
deeply submerged, it is probable that the sand and clay base on
which the bog rests is saucer-shaped, and so retains the entire mass
in position. In rainy weather, such is its capacity for water that it
sensibly swells, and rises in those parts where the moss is the
deepest. This occurs through the capillary attraction of the fibres
of the submerged moss, which is from 20 to 30 feet in depth, while
the growing plants effectually check evaporation from the surface.
This peculiar character of the Moss has presented an insuperable
difficulty in the way of reclaiming it by any system of extensive
drainage – such as by sinking shafts, and pumping up the water by
steam power, as has been proposed. Supposing a shaft of 30 feet

deep to be sunk, it has been calculated that this would only be effectual for draining a circle of about 100 yards, the water running down an incline of about 5 to 1; for it was found in the course of draining the bog, that a ditch 3 feet deep only served to drain a space of less than 5 yards on each side, and two ditches of this depth, 10 yards apart, left a portion of the Moss between them scarcely affected by the drains.

The three resident engineers selected by Mr Stephenson to super-intend the construction of the line, were Joseph Locke, William Allcard, and John Dixon. The last was appointed to that portion which lay across the Moss, neither of the other two envying his lot. On Mr Dixon's arrival, about July 1826, Mr Locke proceeded to show him over the length he was to take charge of, and to install him in office. When they reached Chat Moss, Mr Dixon found that the line had already been staked out and the levels taken in detail by the aid of planks laid upon the bog. The cutting of the drains along each side of the proposed road had also been commenced; but the soft pulpy stuff had up to this time flowed into the drains and filled them up as fast as they were cut. Proceeding across the Moss, on the first day's inspection, the new resident, when about half-way over, slipped off the plank on which he walked, and sank to his knees in the bog. Struggling only sent him the deeper, and he might have disappeared altogether, but for the workmen, who hastened to his assistance upon planks, and rescued him from his perilous position. Much disheartened, he desired to return, and even thought of giving up the job; but Mr Locke assured him that the worst part was now past; so the new resident plucked up heart again, and both floundered on until they reached the further edge of the Moss, wet and plastered over with bog-sludge. Mr Dixon's companions endeavoured to comfort him by the assurance that he might avoid similar perils, by walking upon 'pattens', or boards fastened to the soles of his feet, as they had done when taking the levels, and as the workmen did when engaged in making drains in the softest parts of the Moss. The resident engineer was sorely puzzled in the outset by the problem of constructing a road for heavy locomotives, with trains of passengers and goods, upon a bog which he had found incapable of supporting his own weight!

Mr Stephenson's idea was, that such a road might be made to *float* upon the bog, simply by means of a sufficient extension of the bearing surface. As a ship, or a raft, capable of sustaining heavy loads floated in water, so in his opinion, might a light road be floated upon a bog, which was of considerably greater consistency than water. Long before the railway was thought of, Mr Roscoe had adopted the remarkable expedient of fitting his plough-horses with flat wooden soles or pattens, to enable them to walk upon the Moss land which he had brought into cultivation. These pattens were fitted on by means of a screw apparatus, which met in front of the foot and was easily fastened. The mode by which these pattens served to sustain the horse is capable of easy explanation, and it will be observed that the *rationale* likewise explains the floating of a railway train. The foot of an ordinary farm-horse presents a base of about five inches diameter, but if this base be enlarged to seven inches – the circles being to each other as the squares of the diameters – it will be found that, by this slight enlargement of the base, a circle of nearly double the area has been secured; and consequently the pressure of the foot upon every unit of ground upon which the horse stands has been reduced one half. In fact, this contrivance has an effect tantamount to setting the horse upon eight feet instead of four.

Apply the same reasoning to the ponderous locomotive, and it will be found, that even such a machine may be made to stand upon a bog, by means of a similar extension of the bearing surface. Suppose the engine to be 20 feet long and 5 feet wide, thus covering a surface of 100 square feet, and, provided the bearing has been extended by means of cross sleepers supported on a matting of heath and branches of trees covered with a few inches of gravel, the pressure of an engine of 20 tons will be only equal to about 3 pounds per inch over the whole surface on which it stands. Such was George Stephenson's idea in contriving his floating road – something like an elongated raft across the Moss; and we shall see that he steadily kept it in view in carrying the work into execution.

The first thing done was to form a footpath of ling or heather along the proposed road, on which a man might walk without risk of sinking. A single line of temporary railway was then laid down, formed of ordinary cross-bars about 3 feet long and an inch square, with holes punched through them at the ends and nailed down to temporary sleepers. Along this way ran the waggons in which were conveyed the materials requisite to form the permanent road. These waggons carried about a ton each, and they were propelled by boys running behind them along the narrow iron rails. The boys became so expert that they would run the 4 miles across at the rate of 7 or 8 miles an hour without missing a step; if they had done so, they would have sunk in many places up to their middle. A comparatively slight extension of the bearing surface being found sufficient to enable the bog to bear this temporary line, the circumstance was a source of increased confidence and hope to our engineer in proceeding with the formation of the permanent roadway alongside.

The digging of drains had been proceeding for some time along each side of the intended line; but they filled up almost as soon as dug, the sides flowing in, and the bottom rising up. It was only in some of the drier parts of the bog that a depth of three or four feet could be reached. The surface-ground between the drains, containing the intertwined roots of heather and long grass, was left untouched, and upon this was spread branches of trees and hedge-cuttings. In the softest places, rude gates or hurdles, some 8 or 9 feet long by 4 feet wide, interwoven with heather, were laid in double thicknesses, their ends overlapping each other; and upon this floating bed was spread a thin layer of gravel, on which the sleepers, chairs, and rails were laid in the usual manner. Such was the mode in which the road was formed upon the Moss.

It was found, however, after the permanent way had been thus laid, that there was a tendency to sinking at those parts where the bog was softest. In ordinary cases, where a bank subsides, the sleepers are packed up with ballast or gravel; but in this case the ballast was dug away and removed in order to lighten the road, and the sleepers were packed instead with cakes of dry turf or bundles of heath. By these expedients the subsided parts were again floated up to the level, and an approach was made towards a satisfactory road. But the most formidable difficulties were encountered at the centre and towards the edges of the Moss; and it required no small degree of ingenuity and perseverance on the part of the engineer successfully to overcome them.

The Moss, as already observed, was highest in the centre, and it there presented a sort of hunchback with a rising and falling gradient. At that point it was found necessary to cut deeper drains in order to consolidate the ground between them on which the road was to be formed. But, as at other places, the deeper the cutting the more rapid was the flow of fluid bog into the drain, the bottom rising up almost as fast as it was removed. To meet this emergency, numbers of empty tar-barrels were brought from Liverpool; and as soon as a few yards of drain were dug, the barrels were laid down end to end, firmly fixed to each other by strong slabs laid over the joints, and nailed. They were then covered over with clay, and thus formed an underground sewer of wood instead of bricks. This expedient was found to answer the purpose intended, and the road across the centre of the Moss having been so prepared, it was then laid with the permanent materials.

The greatest difficulty was, however, experienced in forming an embankment upon the edge of the bog at the Manchester end. Moss as dry as it could be cut, was brought up in small waggons, by men and boys, and emptied so as to form an embankment; but the bank had scarcely been raised three or four feet in height, when the stuff broke through the heathery surface of the bog and sank out of sight. More moss was brought up and emptied with no better result; and for weeks the filling was continued without any visible embankment having been made. It was the duty of the resident engineer to proceed to Liverpool every fortnight to obtain the wages for the workmen employed under him; and on these occasions he was required to colour up, on a section drawn to a working scale suspended against the wall of the directors' room, the amount of excavation and embankment from time to time executed. But on many of these occasions, Mr Dixon had no progress whatever to show for the money expended on the Chat Moss embankment. Sometimes, indeed, the visible work done was *less* than it had appeared a fortnight or a month before!

The directors now became seriously alarmed, and feared that the evil prognostications of the eminent engineers were about to be fulfilled. The resident engineer was even called upon to supply an estimate of the cost of forming an embankment of solid stuff throughout, as also of the cost of piling the roadway, and in effect constructing a four-mile viaduct of timber across the Moss, from twenty to thirty feet high from the foundation. The expense appalled the directors, and the question arose, whether the work was to be proceeded with or *abandoned*!

Mr Stephenson afterwards described the alarming position of affairs at a public dinner at Birmingham (23 December 1837), on the occasion of a piece of plate being presented to his son, upon the completion of the London and Birmingham Railway. He related the anecdote, he said, for the purpose of impressing upon the minds of those who heard him the necessity of perseverance.

'After working for weeks and weeks,' said he, 'in filling in materials to form the road, there did not yet appear to be the least sign of our being able to raise the solid embankment one single inch; in short we went on filling in without the slightest apparent effect. Even my assistants began to feel uneasy, and to doubt of the success of the scheme. The directors, too, spoke of it as a hopeless task: and at length they became seriously alarmed, so much so,

indeed, that a board meeting was held on Chat Moss to decide
whether I should proceed any further. They had previously taken
the opinion of other engineers, who reported unfavourably. An
immense outlay had been incurred; and great loss would have been
occasioned had the scheme been then abandoned, and the line
taken by another route. So the directors were *compelled* to allow me
to go on with my plans, of the ultimate success of which I myself
never for one moment doubted.'

During the progress of this part of the works, the Worsley and
Trafford men, who lived near the Moss, and plumed themselves
upon their practical knowledge of bog-work, declared the completion of the road to be utterly impracticable. 'If you knew as much
about Chat Moss as we do,' they said, 'you would never have
entered on so rash an undertaking; and depend upon it, all you
have done and are doing will prove abortive. You must give up
the idea of a floating railway, and either fill the Moss hard from
the bottom, or deviate so as to avoid it altogether.' Such were the
conclusions of science and experience.

In the midst of all these alarms and prophecies of failure,
Stephenson never lost heart, but held to his purpose. His motto
was 'Persevere!' 'You must go on filling in,' he said; 'there is no
other help for it. The stuff emptied in is doing its work out of sight,
and if you will but have patience, it will soon begin to show.' And
so the filling in went on; several hundreds of men and boys were
employed to skin the Moss all round for many thousand yards, by
means of sharp spades, called by the turf cutters 'tommy-spades';
and the dried cakes of turf were afterwards used to form the embankment, until at length as the stuff sank and rested upon the
bottom, the bank gradually rose above the surface, and slowly
advanced onwards, declining in height and consequently in weight,
until it became joined to the floating road already laid upon the
Moss. In the course of forming the embankment, the pressure of
the bog turf tipped out of the waggons caused a copious stream of
bog-water to flow from the end of it, in colour resembling Barclay's
double stout; and when completed, the bank looked like a long
ridge of tightly pressed tobacco-leaf. The compression of the turf
may be imagined from the fact that 670,000 cubic yards of raw
moss formed only 277,000 cubic yards of embankment at the completion of the work.

At the western, or Liverpool end of the Chat Moss, there was a
like embankment; but, as the ground there was solid, little difficulty was experienced in forming it, beyond the loss of substance

caused by the oozing out of the water held by the moss-earth.

At another part of the Liverpool and Manchester line, Parr Moss was crossed by an embankment about 1½ mile in extent. In the immediate neighbourhood was found a large excess of cutting, which it would have been necessary to 'put out in spoil-banks' (according to the technical phrase); but the surplus clay, stone, and shale, were tipped, waggon after waggon, into Parr Moss, until a solid but concealed embankment, from fifteen to twenty-five feet high, was formed, although to the eye it appears to be laid upon the level of the adjoining surface, as at Chat Moss.

The road across Chat Moss was finished by 1 January 1830, when the first experimental train of passengers passed over it, drawn by the 'Rocket'; and it turned out that, instead of being the most expensive part of the line, it was about the cheapest. The total cost of forming the line over the Moss was £28,000, whereas Mr Giles's estimate was £270,000! It also proved to be one of the best portions of the railway. Being a floating road, it was smooth and easy to run upon, just as Dr Arnott's water-bed is soft and easy to lie upon – the pressure being equal at all points. There was, and still is, a sort of springiness in the road over the Moss, such as is felt in passing along a suspended bridge; and those who looked along the line as a train passed over it, said they could observe a waviness, such as precedes and follows a skater upon ice.

During the progress of these works the most ridiculous rumours were set afloat. The drivers of the stage-coaches who feared for their calling, brought the alarming intelligence into Manchester from time to time, that 'Chat Moss was blown up!' 'Hundreds of men and horses had sunk, and the works were completely abandoned!' The engineer himself was declared to have been swallowed up in the Serbonian bog; and 'railways were at an end for ever!'

In the construction of the railway, Mr Stephenson's capacity for organizing and directing the labours of a large number of workmen of all kinds eminently displayed itself. A vast quantity of ballast-waggons had to be constructed, and implements and materials collected, before the army of necessary labourers could be efficiently employed at the various points of the line. There were not at that time, as there are now, large contractors possessed of railway plant, capable of executing earthworks on a large scale. The first railway engineer had not only to contrive the plant, but to organize and direct the labour. The labourers themselves had to be trained to their work; and it was on the Liverpool and Manchester line that Mr Stephenson organized the staff of that mighty band of railway navvies, whose handiworks will be the wonder and admiration of succeeding generations. Looking at their gigantic traces, the men of some future age may be found to declare of the engineer and of his workmen, that 'there were giants in those days'.

Although the works of the Liverpool and Manchester Railway are of a much less formidable character than those of many lines that have since been constructed, they were then regarded as of the most stupendous description. Indeed, the like of them had not before been executed in England. It had been our engineer's original intention to carry the railway from the north end of Liverpool, round the red-sandstone ridge on which the upper part of the town is built, and also round the higher rise of the coal formation at Rainhill, by following the natural levels. But the opposition of the landowners having forced the line more to the south, it was rendered necessary to cut through the hills, and go over the high grounds instead of round them. The first consequence of this alteration in the plans was the necessity for constructing a tunnel under the town of Liverpool $1\frac{1}{2}$ mile in length; the second, a long and deep cutting through the red-sandstone rock at Olive Mount; and the third and most serious of all, was the necessity for surmounting the Whiston and Sutton hills by inclined planes of 1 in 96. The line was also, by the same forced deviation, prevented passing through the Lancashire coalfield, and the engineer was compelled to carry it across the Sankey valley, at a point where the waters of the brook had dug out an excessively deep channel through the marl-beds of the district.

The principal difficulty was experienced in pushing on the works connected with the formation of the tunnel under Liverpool, 2,200 yards in length. The blasting and hewing of the rock were vigorously carried on night and day; and the engineer's practical experience in the collieries here proved of great use to him. Many obstacles had to be encountered and overcome in the formation of the tunnel, the rock varying in hardness and texture at different parts. In some places the miners were deluged by water, which surged from the soft blue shale found at the lowest level of the tunnel. In other places, beds of wet sand were cut through; and there careful propping and pinning were necessary to prevent the roof from tumbling in, until the masonry to support it could be erected. On one occasion, while the engineer was absent from Liverpool, a mass of loose moss-earth and sand fell from the roof, which had been insufficiently propped. The miners withdrew from the work; and on Stephenson's return, he found them in a refractory state, refusing to re-enter the tunnel. He induced them, however, by his example, to return to their labours; and when the roof had been secured, the work went on again as before. When there was danger, he was always ready to share it with the men; and gathering confidence from his fearlessness, they proceeded vigorously with the undertaking, boring and mining their way towards the light.

The Olive Mount cutting was the first extensive stone cutting executed on any railway, and to this day it is one of the most formidable. It is about two miles long, and in some parts 80 feet deep. It is a narrow ravine or defile cut out of the solid rock; and not less than 480,000 cubic yards of stone were removed from it. Mr Vignolles, afterwards describing it, said it looked as if it had been dug out by giants.

The crossing of so many roads and streams involved the necessity for constructing an unusual number of bridges. There were not fewer than sixty-three, under or over the railway, on the thirty miles between Liverpool and Manchester. Up to this time, bridges had been applied generally to high roads where inclined approaches were of comparatively small importance, and in determining the rise of his arch the engineer selected any headway he thought proper. Every consideration was indeed made subsidiary to constructing the bridge itself, and the completion of one large structure of this sort was regarded as an epoch in engineering history. Yet here, in the course of a few years, no fewer than sixty-three bridges were constructed on one line of railway! Mr Stephenson early found that the ordinary arch was inapplicable in certain cases, where the headway was limited, and yet the level of the railway must be preserved. In such cases he employed simple cast iron beams, by which he safely bridged gaps of moderate width, economizing headway, and introducing the use of a new material of the greatest possible value to the railway engineer. The bridges of masonry upon the line were of many kinds; several of them askew bridges, and others, such as those at Newton and over the Irwell at Manchester, straight and of considerable dimensions; but the principal piece of masonry was the Sankey viaduct.

This fine work is principally of brick, with stone facings. It consists of nine arches of fifty feet span each. The massive piers are supported on two hundred piles driven deep into the soil; and they rise to a great height, the coping of the parapet being seventy feet above the level of the valley, in which flow the Sankey brook and canal. Its total cost was about £45,000.

By the end of 1828 the directors found they had expended

£460,000 on the works, and that they were still far from completion. They looked at the loss of interest on this large investment,
and began to grumble at the delay. They desired to see their capital
becoming productive; and in the spring of 1829 they urged the
engineer to push on the works with increased vigour. Mr Cropper,
one of the directors, who took an active interest in their progress,
said to Stephenson one day, 'Now, George, thou must get on with
the railway, and have it finished without further delay; thou must
really have it ready for opening by the first day of January next.'
'Consider the heavy character of the works, sir, and how much we
have been delayed by the want of money, not to speak of the wet-
ness of the weather: it is impossible.' 'Impossible!' rejoined Cropper; 'I wish I could get Napoleon to thee – he would tell thee there
is no such word as "impossible" in the vocabulary.' 'Tush!' exclaimed Stephenson, with warmth; 'don't speak to me about
Napoleon! Give me men, money, and materials, and I will do what
Napoleon couldn't do – drive a railway from Liverpool to Manchester over Chat Moss!'

The works made rapid progress in the course of the year 1829.
Double sets of labourers were employed on Chat Moss and at other
points, by night and day, the night-shifts working by torch and
fire-light; and at length, the work advancing at all points, the
directors saw their way to the satisfactory completion of the
undertaking.

It may well be supposed that Mr Stephenson's time was fully
occupied in superintending the extensive, and for the most part
novel works, connected with the railway, and that even his extraordinary powers of labour and endurance were taxed to the utmost
during the four years that they were in progress. Almost every
detail in the plans was directed and arranged by himself. Every
bridge, from the simplest to the most complicated, including the
then novel structure of the 'skew bridge', iron girders, siphons,
fixed engines, and the machinery for working the tunnel at the
Liverpool end, had to be thought out by his own head, and reduced to definite plans under his own eyes. Besides all this, he had
to design the working plant in anticipation of the opening of the
railway. He must be prepared with waggons, trucks, and carriages,
himself superintending their manufacture. The permanent road,
turntables, switches, and crossings, in short, the entire structure
and machinery of the line, from the turning of the first sod to the
running of the first train of carriages upon the railway, were
executed under his immediate supervision. And it was in the midst

of this vast accumulation of work and responsibility that the battle of the locomotive engine had to be fought, a battle, not merely against material difficulties, but against the still more trying obstructions of deeply-rooted mistrust and prejudice on the part of a considerable minority of the directors.

He had no staff of experienced assistants, not even a staff of draughtsmen in his office, but only a few pupils learning their business; and he was frequently without even their help. The time of his engineering inspectors was fully occupied in the actual super-intendence of the works at different parts of the line; and he took care to direct all their more important operations in person. The principal draughtsman was Mr Thomas Gooch, a pupil he had brought with him from Newcastle. 'I may say,' writes Mr Gooch, 'that nearly the whole of the working and other drawings, as well as the various land-plans for the railway, were drawn by my own hand. They were done at the Company's office in Clayton Square during the day, from instructions supplied in the evenings by Mr Stephenson, either by word of mouth, or by little rough hand-sketches on letter-paper. The evenings were also generally devoted to my duties as secretary, in writing (mostly from his own dicta-tion) his letters and reports, or in making calculations and estimates. The mornings before breakfast were not infrequently spent by me in visiting and lending a helping hand in the tunnel and other works near Liverpool, the untiring zeal and perseverance of George Stephenson never for an instant flagging and inspiring with a like enthusiasm all who were engaged under him in carrying forward the works.'*

The usual routine of his life at this time – if routine it might be called – was, to rise early, by sunrise in summer and before it in winter, and thus 'break the back of the day's work' by midday. While the tunnel under Liverpool was in progress, one of his first duties in a morning before breakfast was to go over the various shafts, clothed in a suitable dress, and inspect their progress at

---

* Mr Gooch's letter to the author, 13 December 1861. Referring to the preparations of the plans and drawings, Mr Gooch adds, 'When we consider the extensive sets of drawings which most engineers have since found it right to adopt in carrying out similar works, it is not the least surprising feature in George Stephenson's early professional career, that he should have been able to confine himself to so limited a number as that which could be supplied by the hands of one person in carrying out the construc-tion of the Liverpool and Manchester Railway; and this may still be said, after full allowance is made for the alteration of system involved by the adoption of the large contract system.'

different points; on other days he would visit the extensive work-shops at Edgehill, where most of the 'plant' for the line was in course of manufacture. Then, returning to his house, in Upper Parliament Street, Windsor, after a hurried breakfast, he would ride along the works to inspect their progress, and push them on with greater energy where needful. On other days he would prepare for the much less congenial engagement of meeting the Board, which was often a cause of great anxiety and pain to him; for it was difficult to satisfy men of all tempers, and some of these not of the most generous sort. On such occasions he might be seen with his right-hand thumb thrust through the topmost button-hole of his coat-breast, vehemently hitching his right shoulder, as was his habit when labouring under any considerable excitement. Oc-casionally he would take an early ride before breakfast, to inspect the progress of the Sankey viaduct. He had a favourite horse, brought by him from Newcastle, called 'Bobby' – so tractable that, with his rider on his back, he would walk up to a locomotive with the steam blowing off, and put his nose against it without shying. 'Bobby', saddled and bridled, was brought to Mr Stephenson's door betimes in the morning; and mounting him, he would ride the fifteen miles to Sankey, putting up at a little public-house which then stood upon the banks of the canal. There he had his breakfast of 'crowdie', which he made with his own hands. It consisted of oatmeal stirred into a basin of hot water, a sort of porridge, which was supped with cold sweet milk. After this frugal breakfast, he would go upon the works, and remain there, riding from point to point for the greater part of the day. When he returned before midday, he examined the pay-sheets in the different departments, sent in by the assistant engineers, or by the foremen of the work-shops. To all these he gave his most careful personal attention, requiring when necessary a full explanation of the items.

After a late dinner, which occupied very short time and was always of a plain and frugal description, he disposed of his corre-spondence, or prepared sketches of drawings, and gave instruc-tions as to their completion. He would occasionally refresh himself for this evening work by a short doze, which, however, he would never admit had exceeded the limits of 'winking', to use his own term. Mr Frederick Swanwick, who officiated as his secretary, after the appointment of Mr Gooch as Resident Engineer to the Bolton and Leigh Railway, has informed us that he then remarked – what in after years he could better appreciate – the clear, terse, and vigorous style of Mr Stephenson's dictation. There was nothing superfluous in it; but it was close, direct, and to the point, in short, thoroughly business-like. And if, in passing through the pen of the amanuensis, his meaning happened in any way to be distorted or modified, it did not fail to escape his detection, though he was always tolerant of any liberties taken with his own form of expression, so long as the words written down conveyed his real meaning.

His letters and reports written, and his sketches of drawings made and explained, the remainder of the evening was usually devoted to conversation with his wife and those of his pupils who lived under his roof, and constituted, as it were, part of the family. He then delighted to test the knowledge of his young companions, and to question them upon the principles of mechanics. If they were not quite 'up to the mark' on any point, there was no escaping detection by evasive or specious explanations. These always brought out the verdict, 'Ah! you know nought about it now; but think it over again, and tell me when you understand it.' If there were even partial success in the reply, it was at once acknowledged, and a full explanation given, to which the master would add illustrative examples for the purpose of impressing the principle more deeply upon the pupil's mind.

It was not so much his object and purpose to 'cram' the minds of the young men committed to his charge with the *results* of knowledge, as to stimulate them to educate themselves – to induce them to develop their mental and moral powers by the exercise of their own free energies, and thus acquire that habit of self-thinking and self-reliance which is the spring of all true manly action. In a word, he sought to bring out and invigorate the *character* of his pupils. He felt that he himself had been made stronger and better through his encounters with difficulty; and he would not have the road of knowledge made too smooth and easy for them. 'Learn for yourselves, think for yourselves,' he would say: 'make yourselves masters of principles, persevere, be industrious, and there is then no fear of you.' And not the least emphatic proof of the soundness of this system of education, as conducted by Mr Stephenson, was afforded by the after history of these pupils themselves. There was not one of those trained under his eye who did not rise to eminent usefulness and distinction as an engineer. He sent them forth into the world braced with the spirit of manly self-help – inspired by his own noble example; and they repeated in their after career the lessons of earnest effort and persistent industry which his daily life had taught them.

Stephenson's evenings at home were not, however, exclusively devoted either to business or to the graver exercises above referred to. He would often indulge in cheerful conversation and anecdote, falling back from time to time upon the struggles and difficulties of his early life. The not unfrequent winding up of his story addressed to the young men about him, was, 'Ah! ye young fellows don't know what *wark* is in these days!' Mr Swanwick takes pleasure in recalling to mind how seldom, if ever, a cross or captious word, or an angry look, marred the enjoyment of those evenings. The presence of Mrs Stephenson gave them an additional charm: amiable, kind-hearted, and intelligent, she shared quietly in the pleasure of the party; and the atmosphere of comfort which always pervaded her home contributed in no small degree to render it a centre of cheerful, hopeful intercourse, and of earnest, honest industry. She was a wife who well deserved, what she through life retained, the strong and unremitting affection of her husband.

When Mr Stephenson retired for the night, it was not always that he permitted himself to sink into slumber. Like Brindley, he worked out many a difficult problem in bed; and for hours he would turn over in his mind and study how to overcome some obstacle, or to mature some project, on which his thoughts were bent. Some remark inadvertently dropped by him at the breakfast-table in the morning, served to show that he had been stealing some hours from the past night in reflection and study. Yet he would rise at his accustomed early hour, and there was no abatement of his usual energy in carrying on the business of the day.

CHAPTER XI — ROBERT STEPHENSON'S RESIDENCE IN COLOMBIA, AND RETURN — THE BATTLE OF THE LOCOMOTIVE — THE 'ROCKET'

WE return to the career of Robert Stephenson, who had been absent from England during the construction of the Liverpool railway, but was shortly about to join his father and take part in 'the battle of the locomotive', which was now impending.

On his return from Edinburgh College in the summer of 1823, he had assisted in the survey of the Stockton and Darlington line; and when the Locomotive Engine Works were started in Forth Street, Newcastle, he took an active part in that concern. 'The factory,' he says, 'was in active operation early in 1824; I left England for Colombia in June of that year, having finished drawing the designs of the Brusselton stationary engines for the Stockton and Darlington Railway before I left.'*

Speculation was very rife at the time; and among the most promising adventures were the companies organized for the purpose of working the gold and silver mines of South America. Great difficulty was experienced in finding mining engineers capable of carrying out those projects, and young men of even the most

* Letter to the author.

moderate experience were eagerly sought after. The Colombian Mining Association of London offered an engagement to young Stephenson, to go out to Mariquita and take charge of the engineering operations of that company. Robert was himself desirous of accepting it, but his father said it would first be necessary to ascertain whether the proposed change would be for his good. His health had been very delicate for some time, partly occasioned by his rapid growth, but principally because of his close application to work and study. Father and son together called upon Dr Headlam, the eminent physician of Newcastle, to consult him on the subject. During the examination which ensued, Robert afterwards used to say that he felt as if he were upon trial for life or death. To his great relief, the doctor pronounced that a temporary residence in a warm climate was the very thing likely to be most beneficial to him. The appointment was accordingly accepted, and, before many weeks had passed, Robert Stephenson set sail for South America.

After a tolerably prosperous voyage he landed at La Guayra, on the north coast of Venezuela, on 23 July, from thence proceeding to Caracas, the capital of the district, about fifteen miles inland. There he remained for two months, unable to proceed in consequence of the wretched state of the roads in the interior. He contrived, however, to make occasional excursions in the neighbourhood, with an eye to the mining business on which he had come. About the beginning of October he set out for Bogota, the capital of Colombia or New Granada. The distance was about 1,200 miles, through a very difficult region, and it was performed entirely upon mule-back after the fashion of the country.

In the course of the journey Robert visited many of the districts reported to be rich in minerals, but he met with few traces except of copper, iron, and coal, with occasional indications of gold and silver. He found the people ready to furnish information, which, however, when tested, usually proved worthless. A guide, whom he employed for weeks, kept him buoyed up with the hope of richer mining quarters than he had yet seen; but when he professed to be able to show him mines of 'brass, steel, alcohol, and pinchbeck', Stephenson discovered him to be an incorrigible rogue, and immediately dismissed him. At length our traveller reached Bogota, and after an interview with Mr Illingworth, the commercial manager of the mining Company, he proceeded to Honda, crossed the Magdalena, and shortly after reached the site of his intended operations on the eastern slopes of the Andes.

Mr Stephenson used afterwards to speak in glowing terms of this

his first mule-journey in South America. Everything was entirely new to him. The variety and beauty of the indigenous plants, the luxurious tropical vegetation, the appearance, manners, and dress of the people, and the mode of travelling, were altogether different from everything he had before seen. His own travelling garb also must have been strange even to himself. 'My hat,' he says, 'was of plaited grass, with a crown nine inches in height, surrounded by a brim of six inches; a white cotton suit; and a *ruana* of blue and crimson plaid, with a hole in the centre for the head to pass through. This cloak is admirably adapted for the purpose, amply covering the rider and mule, and at night answering the purpose of a blanket in the net-hammock, which is made from fibres of the aloe, and which every traveller carries before him on his mule, and suspends to the trees or in houses, as occasion may require.' The part of the journey which seems to have made the most lasting impression on his mind was that between Bogota and the mining district in the neighbourhood of Mariquita. As he ascended the slopes of the mountain-range, and reached the first step of the table-land, he was struck beyond expression with the noble view of the valley of the Magdalena behind him, so vast that he failed in attempting to define the point at which the course of the river blended with the horizon. Like all travellers in the district, he noted the remarkable changes of climate and vegetation, as he rose from the burning plains towards the fresh breath of the mountains. From an atmosphere as hot as that of an oven he passed into delicious cool air; until, in his onward and upward journey, a still more temperate region was reached, the very perfection of climate. Before him rose the majestic Cordilleras, forming a rampart against the western skies, at certain times of the day looking black, sharp, and, at their summit, almost as even as a wall.

Our engineer took up his abode for a time at Mariquita, a fine old city, though then greatly decayed. During the period of the Spanish dominion, it was an important place, most of the gold and silver convoys passing through it on their way to Cartagena, there to be shipped in galleons for Europe. The mountainous country to the west was rich in silver, gold, and other metals, and it was Mr Stephenson's object to select the best site for commencing operations for the Company. With this object he 'prospected' about in all directions, visiting long-abandoned mines, and analysing specimens obtained from many quarters. The mines eventually fixed upon as the scene of his operations were those of La Manta and Santa Anna, long before worked by the Spaniards, though, in consequence of the luxuriance and rapidity of the vegetation, all traces of the old workings had become completely overgrown and lost. Everything had to be begun anew. Roads had to be cut to the mines, machinery to be erected, and the ground opened up, in course of which some of the old adits were hit upon. The native peons or labourers were not accustomed to work, and at first they usually contrived to desert when they were not watched, so that very little progress could be made until the arrival of the expected band of miners from England. The authorities were by no means helpful, and the engineer was driven to an old expedient with the object of overcoming this difficulty. 'We endeavour all we can,' he says, in one of his letters, 'to make ourselves popular, and this we find most effectually accomplished by "regaling the venal beasts".'* He also gave a ball at Mariquita, which passed off with éclat, the governor from Honda, with a host of friends, honouring it with their presence. It was, indeed, necessary to 'make a party' in this way, as other schemers were already trying to undermine the Colombian company in influential directions. The engineer did not exaggerate when he said, 'The uncertainty of transacting business in this country is perplexing beyond description.'

At last, his party of miners arrived from England, but they gave him even more trouble than the peons had done. They were rough, drunken, and sometimes altogether ungovernable. He set them to work at the Santa Anna mine without delay, and at the same time took up his abode among them, 'to keep them,' he said, 'if possible, from indulging in the detestable vice of drunkenness, which, if not put a stop to, will eventually destroy themselves, and involve the mining association in ruin.' To add to his troubles, the captain of the miners displayed a very hostile and insubordinate spirit, quarrelled and fought with the men, and was insolent to the engineer himself. The captain and his gang, being Cornishmen, told Robert to his face, that because he was a North-country man, and not born in Cornwall it was impossible he should know anything of mining. Disease also fell upon him, first fever, and then visceral derangement, followed by a return of his 'old complaint, a feeling of oppression in the breast'. No wonder that in the midst of these troubles he should longingly speak of returning to his native land. But he stuck to his post and his duty, kept up his courage, and by a mixture of mildness and firmness, and the display of great coolness of judgement, he contrived to keep the men to their work, and gradually to carry forward the enterprise which he had under-

* Letter to Mr Illingworth, 25 September 1825.

taken. By the beginning of July 1826, we find that quietness and order had been restored, and the works were proceeding more satisfactorily, though the yield of silver was not as yet very promising. Mr Stephenson calculated that at least three years' diligent and costly operations would be needed to render the mines productive.

In the mean time he removed to the dwelling which had been erected for his accommodation at Santa Anna. It was a structure speedily raised after the fashion of the country. The walls were of split and flattened bamboo, tied together with the long fibres of a dried climbing plant; the roof was of palm-leaves, and the ceiling of reeds. When an earthquake shook the district – for earthquakes were frequent – the inmates of such a fabric merely felt as if shaken in a basket, without sustaining any harm. In front of the cottage lay a woody ravine, extending almost to the base of the Andes, gorgeously clothed in primeval vegetation – magnolias, palms, bamboos, tree-ferns, acacias, cedars; and, towering over all, the great almendrons, with their smooth, silvery stems, bearing aloft noble clusters of pure white blossom. The forest was haunted by myriads of gay insects, butterflies with wings of dazzling lustre, birds of brilliant plumage, humming-birds, golden orioles, toucans, and a host of solitary warblers. But the glorious sunsets seen from his cottage-porch more than all astonished and delighted the young engineer; and he was accustomed to say that, after having witnessed them, he was reluctant to accuse the ancient Peruvians of idolatry.

But all these natural beauties failed to reconcile him to the harassing difficulties of his situation, which continued to increase rather than diminish. He was hampered by the action of the Board at home, who gave ear to hostile criticisms on his reports; and, although they afterwards made handsome acknowledgement of his services, he felt his position to be altogether unsatisfactory. He therefore determined to leave at the expiry of his three years' engagement, and communicated his decision to the directors accordingly. On receiving his letter, the Board, through Mr Richardson, of Lombard Street, one of the directors, communicated with his father at Newcastle, representing that if he would allow his son to remain in Colombia the Company would make it 'worth his while'. To this the father gave a decided negative, and intimated that he himself needed his son's assistance, and that he must return at the expiry of this three years' term, a decision, writes Robert, 'at which I feel much gratified, as it is clear that he is as anxious to

have me back in England as I am to get there'.* At the same time,
Edward Pease, a principal partner in the Newcastle firm, privately
wrote Robert to the following effect, urging his return home: 'I can
assure thee that thy business at Newcastle, as well as thy father's
engineering, have suffered very much from thy absence, and, unless thou soon return, the former will be given up, as Mr Longridge
is not able to give it that attention it requires; and what *is* done
is not done with credit to the house.' The idea of the manufactory
being given up, which Robert had laboured so hard to establish
before leaving England, was painful to him in the extreme, and he
wrote to the manager of the Company, strongly urging that
arrangements should be made for him to leave without delay. In
the mean time he was again laid prostrate by another violent attack
of aguish fever; and when able to write in June 1827, he expressed
himself as 'completely wearied and worn down with vexation'.

At length, when he was sufficiently recovered from his attack
and able to travel, he set out on his voyage homeward in the
beginning of August. At Mompox, on his way down the river
Magdalena, he met Mr Bodmer, his successor, with a fresh party of
miners from England, on their way up the country to the quarters
which he had just quitted. Next day, six hours after leaving
Mompox, a steamboat was met ascending the river, with Bolivar
the Liberator on board, on his way to St Bogota; and it was a
mortification to our engineer that he had only a passing sight of
that distinguished person. It was his intention, on leaving Mariquita, to visit the Isthmus of Panama on his way home, for the
purpose of inquiring into the practicability of cutting a canal to
unite the Atlantic and Pacific – a project which then formed the
subject of considerable public discussion; but his presence being so
anxiously desired at home, he determined to proceed to New York
without delay.

Arrived at the port of Cartagena, he had to wait some time for a
ship. The delay was very irksome to him, the more so as the city
was then desolated by the ravages of the yellow fever. While sitting
one day in the large, bare, comfortless public room of the miserable
hotel at which he put up, he observed two strangers, whom he at
once perceived to be English. One of the strangers was a tall, gaunt
man, shrunken and hollow-looking, shabbily dressed, and apparently poverty-stricken. On making inquiry, he found it was
Trevithick, the builder of the first railroad locomotive! He was
returning home from the gold-mines of Peru penniless. He had

* Letter to Mr Illingworth, 9 April 1827.

left England in 1816, with powerful steam-engines, intended for the drainage and working of the Peruvian mines. He met with almost a royal reception on his landing at Lima. A guard of honour was appointed to attend him, and it was even proposed to erect a statue of Don Ricardo Trevithick in solid silver. It was given forth in Cornwall that his emoluments amounted to £100,000, a year,* and that he was making a gigantic fortune. Great, therefore, was Robert Stephenson's surprise to find this potent Don Ricardo in the inn at Cartagena, reduced almost to his last shilling, and unable to proceed further. He had indeed realized the truth of the Spanish proverb, that 'a silver-mine brings misery, a gold-mine ruin'. He and his friend had lost everything in their journey across the country from Peru. They had forded rivers and wandered through forests, leaving all their baggage behind them, and had reached thus far with little more than the clothes upon their backs. Almost the only remnant of precious metal saved by Trevithick was a pair of silver spurs, which he took back with him to Cornwall. Robert Stephenson lent him £50 to enable him to reach England; and though he was afterwards heard of as an inventor there, he had no further part in the ultimate triumph of the locomotive.

But Trevithick's misadventures on this occasion had not yet ended, for before he reached New York he was wrecked, and Robert Stephenson with him. The following is the account of the voyage, 'big with adventures', as given by the latter in a letter to his friend Illingworth: 'At first we had very little foul weather, and indeed were for several days becalmed among the islands, which was so far fortunate, for a few degrees further north the most tremendous gales were blowing, and they appear (from our future information) to have wrecked every vessel exposed to their violence. We had two examples of the effects of the hurricane; for, as we sailed north we took on board the remains of two crews found floating about on dismantled hulls. The one had been nine days without food of any kind, except the carcasses of two of their companions who had died a day or two previously from fatigue and hunger. The other crew had been driven about for six days, and were not so dejected, but reduced to such a weak state that they were obliged to be drawn on board our vessel by ropes. A brig bound for Havannah took part of the men, and we took the remainder. To attempt any description of my feelings on witnessing such scenes would be in vain. You will not be surprised to learn that I felt somewhat uneasy at the thought that we were so far

* *Geological Transactions of Cornwall*, i.222.

from England, and that I also might possibly suffer similar shipwreck; but I consoled myself with the hope that fate would be
more kind to us. It was not so much so, however, as I had flattered
myself; for on voyaging towards New York, after we had made the
land; we ran aground about midnight. The vessel soon filled with
water, and, being surrounded by the breaking surf, the ship was
soon split up, and before morning our situation became perilous.
Masts and all were cut away to prevent the hull rocking; but all
we could do was of no avail. About 8 o'clock on the following
morning, after a most miserable night, we were taken off the
wreck, and were so fortunate as to reach the shore. I saved my
minerals, but Empson lost part of his botanical collection. Upon
the whole, we got off well; and, had I not been on the American
side of the Atlantic, I "guess" I would not have gone to sea again.'

After a short tour in the United States and Canada, Robert
Stephenson and his friend took ship for Liverpool, where they
arrived at the end of November, and at once proceeded to Newcastle. The factory was by no means in a prosperous state. During
the time Robert had been in America it had been carried on at a
loss; and Edward Pease, much disheartened, wished to retire, but
George Stephenson was unable to buy him out, and the establishment had to be carried on in the hope that the locomotive might
yet be established in public estimation as a practical and economical working power. Robert Stephenson immediately instituted a
rigid inquiry into the working of the concern, unravelled the
accounts, which had fallen into confusion during his father's
absence at Liverpool: and he soon succeeded in placing the affairs
of the factory in a more healthy condition. In all this he had the
hearty support of his father, as well as of the other partners.

The works of the Liverpool and Manchester Railway were now
approaching completion. But, singular to say, the directors had
not yet decided as to the tractive power to be employed in working
the line when opened for traffic. The differences of opinion among
them were so great as apparently to be irreconcilable. It was necessary, however, that they should come to some decision without
further loss of time; and many Board meetings were accordingly
held to discuss the subject. The old-fashioned and well-tried
system of horse haulage was not without its advocates; but, looking at the large amount of traffic which there was to be conveyed, and
at the probable delay in the transit from station to station if this
method were adopted, the directors, after a visit made by them to
the Northumberland and Durham railways in 1828, came to the

conclusion that the employment of horse-power was inadmissible.

Fixed engines had many advocates; the locomotive very few: it stood as yet almost in a minority of one – George Stephenson. The prejudice against the employment of the latter power had even increased since the Liverpool and Manchester Bill underwent its first ordeal in the House of Commons. In proof of this, we may mention that the Newcastle and Carlisle Railway Act was conceded in 1829, on the express condition that it should *not* be worked by locomotives, but by horses only.

Grave doubts existed as to the practicability of working a large traffic by means of travelling engines. The most celebrated engineers offered no opinion on the subject. They did not believe in the locomotive, and would scarcely take the trouble to examine it. The ridicule with which George Stephenson had been assailed by the barristers before the Parliamentary Committee had not been altogether distasteful to them. Perhaps they did not relish the idea of a man who had picked up his experience in Newcastle coal-pits appearing in the capacity of a leading engineer before Parliament, and attempting to establish a new system of internal communication in the country. The directors could not disregard the adverse and conflicting views of the professional men whom they consulted. But Mr Stephenson had so repeatedly and earnestly urged upon them the propriety of making a trial of the locomotive before coming to any decision against it, that they at length authorized him to proceed with the construction of one of his engines by way of experiment. In their report to the proprietors at their annual meeting on 27 March 1828, they state that they had, after due consideration, authorized the engineer 'to prepare a locomotive engine, which, from the nature of its construction and from the experiments already made, he is of opinion will be effective for the purposes of the Company, without proving an annoyance to the public'. The locomotive thus ordered was placed upon the line in 1829, and was found of great service in drawing the waggons full of marl from the two great cuttings.

In the mean time the discussion proceeded as to the kind of power to be permanently employed for the working of the railway. The directors were inundated with schemes of all sorts for facilitating locomotion. The projectors of England, France, and America, seemed to be let loose upon them. There were plans for working the waggons along the line by water-power. Some proposed hydrogen, and others carbonic acid gas. Atmospheric pressure had its eager advocates. And various kinds of fixed and locomotive steam-power were suggested. Thomas Gray urged his plan of a greased road with cog rails; and Messrs. Vignolles and Ericsson recommended the adoption of a central friction rail, against which two horizontal rollers under the locomotive, pressing upon the sides of this rail, were to afford the means of ascending the inclined planes. The directors felt themselves quite unable to choose from amidst this multitude of projects. The engineer expressed himself as decidedly as heretofore in favour of smooth rails and locomotive engines, which, he was confident, would be found the most economical and by far the most convenient moving power that could be employed. The Stockton and Darlington Railway being now at work, another deputation went down personally to inspect the fixed and locomotive engines on that line, as well as at Hetton and Killingworth. They returned to Liverpool with much information; but their testimony as to the relative merits of the two kinds of engines was so contradictory, that the directors were as far from a decision as ever.

They then resolved to call to their aid two professional engineers of high standing, who should visit the Darlington and Newcastle railways, carefully examine both modes of working – the fixed and the locomotive – and report to them fully on the subject. The gentlemen selected were Mr Walker of Limehouse and Mr Rastrick of Stourbridge. After carefully examining the modes of working the northern railways, they made their report to the directors in the spring of 1829. They concurred in the opinion that the cost of an establishment of fixed engines would be somewhat greater than that of locomotives to do the same work; but thought the annual charge would be less if the former were adopted. They calculated that the cost of moving a ton of goods thirty miles by fixed engines would be 6·40d., and by locomotives, 8·36d. – assuming a profitable traffic to be obtained both ways. At the same time it was admitted that there appeared more ground for expecting improvements in the construction and working of locomotives than of stationary engines. On the whole, however, and looking especially at the computed annual charge of working the road on the two systems on a large scale, the two reporting engineers were of opinion that fixed engines were preferable, and accordingly recommended their adoption. And, in order to carry the system recommended by them into effect, they proposed to divide the railroad between Liverpool and Manchester into nineteen stages of about a mile and a half each, with twenty-one engines fixed at the different points to work the trains forward.

Such was the result, so far, of George Stephenson's labours. Two of the best practical engineers of the day concurred in reporting substantially in favour of the employment of fixed engines. Not a single professional man of eminence supported the engineer in his preference for locomotive over fixed engine power. He had scarcely an adherent, and the locomotive system seemed on the eve of being abandoned. Still he did not despair. With the profession as well as public opinion against him – for the most frightful stories were abroad respecting the dangers, the unsightliness, and the nuisance which the locomotive would create – Stephenson held to his purpose. Even in this, apparently the darkest hour of the locomotive, he did not hesitate to declare that locomotive railroads would, before many years had passed, be 'the great highways of the world'.

He urged his views upon the directors in all ways, and, as some of them thought, at all seasons. He pointed out the greater convenience of locomotive power for the purposes of a public highway, likening it to a series of short unconnected chains, any one of which could be removed and another substituted without interruption to the traffic; whereas the fixed engine system might be regarded in the light of a continuous chain extending between the two termini, the failure of any link of which would derange the whole.* He represented to the Board that the locomotive was yet capable of great improvements, if proper inducements were held out to inventors and machinists to make them; and he pledged himself that, if time were given him, he would construct an engine that should satisfy their requirements, and prove itself capable of working heavy loads along the railway with speed, regularity, and safety. At length, influenced by his persistent earnestness not less than by his arguments, the directors, at the suggestion of Mr Harrison, determined to offer a prize of £500 for the best locomotive engine, which, on a certain day, should be produced on the railway,

---

* The arguments used by Mr Stephenson with the directors, in favour of the locomotive engine, were afterwards collected and published in 1830 by Robert Stephenson and Joseph Locke, as 'compiled from the Reports of Mr George Stephenson'. The pamphlet was entitled, *Observations on the Comparative Merits of Locomotive and Fixed Engines*. Robert Stephenson, speaking of the authorship many years after, said, 'I believe I furnished the facts and the arguments, and Locke put them into shape. Locke was a very flowery writer, whereas my style was rather bald and unattractive; so he was the editor of the pamphlet, which excited a good deal of attention among engineers at the time.'

and perform certain specified conditions in the most satisfactory manner.*

It was now felt that the fate of railways in a great measure depended upon the issue of this appeal to the mechanical genius of England. When the advertisement of the prize for the best locomotive was published, scientific men began more particularly to direct their attention to the new power which was thus struggling into existence. In the mean time public opinion on the subject of railway working remained suspended, and the progress of the undertaking was watched with intense interest.

During the progress of the discussion with reference to the kind of power to be employed, Mr Stephenson was in constant communication with his son Robert, who made frequent visits to Liverpool for the purpose of assisting his father in the preparation of his reports to the Board on the subject. They had also many conversations as to the best mode of increasing the powers and perfecting the mechanism of the locomotive. These became more frequent and interesting, when the prize was offered for the best locomotive, and the working plans of the engine which they proposed to construct came to be settled.

One of the most important considerations in the new engine was the arrangement of the boiler and the extension of its heating surface to enable steam enough to be raised rapidly and con-

* The conditions were these:
1. The engine must effectually consume its own smoke.
2. The engine, if of six tons weight, must be able to draw after it, day by day, twenty tons weight (including the tender and water-tank) at *ten miles* an hour, with a pressure of steam on the boiler not exceeding fifty pounds to the square inch.
3. The boiler must have two safety-valves, neither of which must be fastened down, and one of them be completely out of the control of the engineman.
4. The engine and boiler must be supported on springs, and rest on six wheels, the height of the whole not exceeding fifteen feet to the top of the chimney.
5. The engine, with water, must not weigh more than six tons; but an engine of less weight would be preferred on its drawing a proportionate load behind it; if only four and a half tons, then it might be put on only four wheels. The Company to be at liberty to test the boiler, etc., by a pressure of one hundred and fifty pounds to the square inch.
6. A mercurial gauge must be affixed to the machine, showing the steam pressure above forty-five pounds per square inch.
7. The engine must be delivered, complete and ready for trial, at the Liverpool end of the railway, not later than 1 October 1829.
8. The price of the engine must not exceed £550.

tinuously, for the purpose of maintaining high rates of speed, the effect of high-pressure engines being ascertained to depend mainly upon the quantity of steam which the boiler can generate, and upon its degree of elasticity when produced. The quality of steam so generated, it will be obvious, must depend chiefly upon the quantity of fuel consumed in the furnace, and by necessary consequence, upon the high rate of temperature maintained there.

It will be remembered that in Stephenson's first Killingworth engines he invented and applied the ingenious method of stimulating combustion in the furnace, by throwing the waste steam into the chimney after performing its office in the cylinders, thus accelerating the ascent of the current of air, greatly increasing the draught, and consequently the temperature of the fire. This plan was adopted by him, as we have already seen, as early as 1815; and it was so successful that he himself attributed to it the greater economy of the locomotive as compared with horse-power. Hence the continuance of its use upon the Killingworth railway.

Though the adoption of the steam-blast greatly quickened combustion and contributed to the rapid production of high-pressure steam, the limited amount of heating surface presented to the fire was still felt to be an obstacle to the complete success of the locomotive engine. Mr Stephenson endeavoured to overcome this by lengthening the boilers and increasing the surface presented by the flue-tubes. The 'Lancashire Witch', which he built for the Bolton and Leigh Railway, and used in forming the Liverpool and Manchester Railway embankments, was constructed with a double tube, each of which contained a fire and passed longitudinally through the boiler. But this arrangement necessarily led to a considerable increase in the weight of the engine, which amounted to about twelve tons; and as six tons was the limit allowed for engines admitted to the Liverpool competition, it was clear that the time was come when the Killingworth locomotive must undergo a further important modification.

For many years previous to this period, ingenious mechanics had been engaged in attempting to solve the problem of the best and most economical boiler for the production of high-pressure steam. As early as 1803, Mr Woolf patented a tubular boiler, which was extensively employed at the Cornish mines, and was found greatly to facilitate the production of steam, by the extension of the heating surface. The ingenious Trevithick, in his patent of 1815, seems also to have entertained the idea of employing a boiler constructed of 'small perpendicular tubes', with the same object of increasing the heating surface. These tubes were to be closed at the bottom, and open into a common reservoir, from which they were to receive their water, and where the steam of all the tubes was to be united.

About the same time George Stephenson was trying the effect of introducing small tubes in the boilers of his locomotives, with the object of increasing their evaporative power. Thus, in 1829, he sent to France two engines constructed at the Newcastle works for the Lyons and St Etienne Railway, in the boilers of which tubes were placed containing water. The heating surface was thus found to be materially increased; but the expedient was not successful, for the tubes, becoming furred with deposit, shortly burned out and were removed. It was then that M. Seguin, the engineer of the railway, pursuing the same idea, adopted his plan of employing horizontal tubes through which the heated air passed in streamlets. Mr Henry Booth, the secretary of the Liverpool and Manchester Railway, without any knowledge of M. Seguin's proceedings, next devised his plan of a tubular boiler, which he brought under the notice of Mr Stephenson, who at once adopted it, and settled the mode in which the fire-box and tubes were to be mutually arranged and connected. This plan was adopted in the construction of the celebrated 'Rocket' engine, the building of which was immediately proceeded with at the Newcastle works.

The principal circumstances connected with the construction of the 'Rocket', as described by Robert Stephenson to the author, may be briefly stated. The tubular principle was adopted in a more complete manner than had yet been attempted. Twenty-five copper tubes, each three inches in diameter, extended from one end of the boiler to the other, the heated air passing through them on its way to the chimney; and the tubes being surrounded by the water of the boiler, it will be obvious that a large extension of the *heating surface* was thus effectually secured. The principal difficulty was in fitting the copper tubes within the boiler so as to prevent leakage. They were made by a Newcastle coppersmith, and soldered to brass screws which were screwed into the boiler ends, standing out in great knobs. When the tubes were thus fitted, and the boiler was filled with water, hydraulic pressure was applied; but the water squirted out at every joint, and the factory floor was soon flooded. Robert went home in despair; and in the first moment of grief, he wrote to his father that the whole thing was a failure. By return of post came a letter from his father, telling him that despair was not to be thought of – that he must 'try again'; and he suggested a mode of overcoming the difficulty, which his son had already anticipated and proceeded to adopt. It was, to bore clean holes in the boiler ends, fit in the smooth copper tubes as tightly as possible, solder up, and then raise the steam. This plan succeeded perfectly, the expansion of the copper tubes completely filling up all interstices, and producing a perfectly watertight boiler, capable of withstanding extreme internal pressure.

The mode of employing the steam-blast for the purpose of increasing the draught in the chimney, was also the subject of numerous experiments. When the engine was first tried, it was thought that the blast in the chimney was not strong enough to keep up the intensity of the fire in the furnace, so as to produce high-pressure steam in sufficient quantity. The expedient was therefore adopted of hammering the copper tubes at the point at which they entered the chimney, whereby the blast was considerably sharpened; and on a further trial it was found that the draught was increased to such an extent as to enable abundance of steam to be raised. The rationale of the blast may be simply explained by referring to the effect of contracting the pipe of a water-hose, by which the force of the jet of water is proportionately increased. Widen the nozzle of the pipe, and the force is in like manner diminished. So is it with the steam-blast in the chimney of the locomotive.

Doubts were, however, expressed whether the greater draught secured by the contraction of the blast-pipe was not counterbalanced in some degree by the negative pressure upon the piston. A series of experiments was made with pipes of different diameters; the amount of vacuum produced being determined by a glass tube open at both ends, which was fixed to the bottom of the smokebox, and descended into a bucket of water. As the rarefaction took place, the water would of course rise in the tube; and the height to which it rose above the surface of the water in the bucket was made the measure of the amount of rarefaction. These experiments proved that a considerable increase of draught was obtained by the contraction of the orifice; accordingly, the two blast-pipes opening from the cylinders into either side of the 'Rocket' chimney, and turned up within it, were contracted slightly below the area of the steam-ports; and before the engine left the factory, the water rose in the glass tube three inches above the water in the bucket.

The other arrangements of the 'Rocket' were briefly these: the boiler was cylindrical with flat ends, 6 feet in length, and 3 feet 4 inches in diameter. The upper half of the boiler was used as a reservoir for the steam, the lower half being filled with water.

Through the lower part, 25 copper tubes of 3 inches diameter extended, which were open to the fire-box at one end, and to the chimney at the other. The fire-box, or furnace, 2 feet wide and 3 feet high, was attached immediately behind the boiler, and was also surrounded with water. The cylinders of the engine were placed on each side of the boiler, in an oblique position, one end being nearly level with the top of the boiler at its after end, and the other pointing towards the centre of the foremost or driving pair of wheels, with which the connection was directly made from the piston-rod, to a pin on the outside of the wheel. The engine, together with its load of water, weighed only $4\frac{1}{4}$ tons, and was supported on four wheels, not coupled. The tender was four-wheeled, and similar in shape to a waggon, the foremost part holding the fuel, and the hind part a water-cask.

When the 'Rocket' was finished, it was placed upon the Killingworth railway for the purpose of experiment. The new boiler arrangement was found perfectly successful. The steam was raised rapidly and continuously, and in a quantity which then appeared marvellous. The same evening Robert despatched a letter to his father at Liverpool, informing him, to his great joy, that the 'Rocket' was 'all right', and would be in complete working trim by the day of trial. The engine was shortly after sent by waggon to Carlisle, and thence shipped for Liverpool.

The time so much longed for by George Stephenson had now arrived, when the merit of the passenger locomotive was to be put to a public test. He had fought the battle for it until now almost single-handed. Engrossed by his daily labours and anxieties, and harassed by difficulties and discouragements which would have crushed the spirit of a less resolute man, he had held firmly to his purpose through good and through evil report. The hostility which he experienced from some of the directors opposed to the adoption of the locomotive, was the circumstance that caused him the greatest grief of all; for where he had looked for encouragement, he found only carping and opposition. But his pluck never failed him; and now the 'Rocket' was upon the ground, to prove, to use his own words, 'whether he was a man of his word or not'.

Great interest was felt at Liverpool, as well as throughout the country, in the approaching competition. Engineers, scientific men, and mechanics, arrived from all quarters to witness the novel display of mechanical ingenuity on which such great results depended. The public generally were no indifferent spectators either. The inhabitants of Liverpool, Manchester, and the adjacent towns felt that the successful issue of the experiment would confer upon them individual benefits and local advantages almost incalculable, while populations at a distance waited for the results with almost equal interest.

On the day appointed for the great competition of locomotives at Rainhill, the following engines were entered for the prize:

1. Messrs. Braithwaite and Ericsson's* 'Novelty'.
2. Mr Timothy Hackworth's 'Sanspareil'.
3. Messrs. R. Stephenson and Co.'s 'Rocket'.
4. Mr Burstall's 'Perseverance'.

Another engine was entered by Mr Brandreth of Liverpool – the 'Cycloped', weighing 3 tons, worked by a horse in a frame, but it could not be admitted to the competition. The above were the only four exhibited, out of a considerable number of engines constructed in different parts of the country in anticipation of this contest, many of which could not be satisfactorily completed by the day of trial.

The ground on which the engines were to be tried was a level piece of railroad, about two miles in length. Each was required to make twenty trips, or equal to a journey of 70 miles, in the course of the day; and the average rate of travelling was to be not under 10 miles an hour. It was determined that, to avoid confusion, each engine should be tried separately, and on different days.

The day fixed for the competition was 1 October, but to allow sufficient time to get the locomotives into good working order, the directors extended it to the 6th. On the morning of the 6th, the ground at Rainhill presented a lively appearance, and there was as much excitement as if the St Leger were about to be run. Many thousand spectators looked on, among whom were some of the first engineers and mechanicians of the day. A stand was provided for the ladies; the 'beauty and fashion' of the neighbourhood were present, and the side of the railroad was lined with carriages of all descriptions.

It was quite characteristic of the Stephensons, that, although their engine did not stand first on the list for trial, it was the first that was ready; and it was accordingly ordered out by the judges for an experimental trip. Yet the 'Rocket' was by no means 'the

---

* The inventor of this engine was a Swede, who afterwards proceeded to the United States, and there achieved considerable distinction as an engineer. His Caloric Engine has so far proved a failure, but his iron cupola vessel, the 'Monitor', must be admitted to have been a remarkable success in its way.

favourite' with either the judges or the spectators. A majority of
the judges was strongly predisposed in favour of the 'Novelty', and
nine-tenths of those present were against the 'Rocket' because of
its appearance. Nearly every person favoured some other engine,
so that there was nothing for the 'Rocket' but the practical test.
The first trip which it made was quite successful. It ran about
12 miles, without interruption, in about 53 minutes.

The 'Novelty' was next called out. It was a light engine, very
compact in appearance, carrying the water and fuel upon the same
wheels as the engine. The weight of the whole was only 3 tons and
1 hundredweight. A peculiarity of this engine was that the air was
driven or *forced* through the fire by means of bellows. The day
being now far advanced, and some dispute having arisen as to the
method of assigning the proper load for the 'Novelty', no particular experiment was made, further than that the engine traversed
the line by way of exhibition, occasionally moving at the rate of
24 miles an hour. The 'Sanspareil', constructed by Mr Timothy
Hackworth, was next exhibited; but no particular experiment was
made with it on this day.

The contest was postponed until the following day, but before
the judges arrived on the ground, the bellows for creating the blast
in the 'Novelty' gave way, and it was found incapable of going
through its performance. A defect was also detected in the boiler of
the 'Sanspareil'; and some further time was allowed to get it
repaired. The large number of spectators who had assembled to
witness the contest were greatly disappointed at this postpone-
ment; but, to lessen it, Stephenson again brought out the 'Rocket',
and, attaching to it a coach containing thirty persons, he ran them
along the line at the rate of from 24 to 30 miles an hour, much to
their gratification and amazement. Before separating, the judges
ordered the engine to be in readiness by eight o'clock on the following morning, to go through its definitive trial according to the
prescribed conditions.

On the morning of 8 October, the 'Rocket' was again ready for
the contest. The engine was taken to the extremity of the stage,
the fire-box was filled with coke, the fire lighted, and the steam
raised until it lifted the safety-valve loaded to a pressure of 50
pounds to the square inch. This proceeding occupied fifty-seven
minutes. The engine then started on its journey, dragging after it
about 13 tons weight in waggons, and made the first ten trips
backwards and forwards along the two miles of road, running the
35 miles, including stoppages, in one hour and 48 minutes. The

second ten trips were in like manner performed in 2 hours and 3 minutes. The maximum velocity attained during the trial trip was 29 miles an hour, or about three times the speed that one of the judges of the competition had declared to be the limit of possibility. The average speed at which the whole of the journeys were performed was 15 miles an hour, or 5 miles beyond the rate specified in the conditions published by the Company. The entire performance excited the greatest astonishment among the assembled spectators; the directors felt confident that their enterprise was now on the eve of success; and George Stephenson rejoiced to think that in spite of all false prophets and fickle counsellors, the locomotive system was now safe. When the 'Rocket', having performed all the conditions of the contest, arrived at the 'grandstand' at the close of its day's successful run, Mr Cropper – one of the directors favourable to the fixed-engine system – lifted up his hands, and exclaimed, 'Now has George Stephenson at last delivered himself!'

Neither the 'Novelty' nor the 'Sanspareil' was ready for trial until the 10th, on the morning of which day an advertisement appeared, stating that the former engine was to be tried on that day, when it would perform more work than any engine upon the ground. The weight of the carriages attached to it was only about 7 tons. The engine passed the first post in good style; but in returning, the pipe from the forcing-pump burst and put an end to the trial. The pipe was afterwards repaired, and the engine made several trips by itself, in which it was said to have gone at the rate of from 24 to 28 miles an hour.

The 'Sanspareil' was not ready until the 13th; and when its boiler and tender were filled with water, it was found to weigh 4 cwt. beyond the weight specified in the published conditions as the limit of four-wheeled engines; nevertheless the judges allowed it to run on the same footing as the other engines, to enable them to ascertain whether its merits entitled it to favourable consideration. It travelled at the average speed of about 14 miles an hour, with its load attached; but at the eighth trip the cold-water pump got wrong, and the engine could proceed no further.

It was determined to award the premium to the successful engine on the following day, the 14th, on which occasion there was an unusual assemblage of spectators. The owners of the 'Novelty' pleaded for another trial; and it was conceded. But again it broke down. The owner of the 'Sanspareil' also requested the opportunity for making another trial of his engine. But the judges had now had enough of failures; and they declined, on the ground that not only was the engine above the stipulated weight, but that it was constructed on a plan which they could not recommend for adoption by the directors of the Company. One of the principal practical objections to this locomotive was the enormous quantity of coke consumed or wasted by it – about 692 lbs per hour when travelling – caused by the sharpness of the steam-blast in the chimney, which blew a large proportion of the burning coke into the air.

The 'Perseverance' was found unable to move at more than five or six miles an hour; and it was withdrawn from the contest at an early period. The 'Rocket' was thus the only engine that had performed, and more than performed, all the stipulated conditions; and its owners were declared to be fully entitled to the prize of £500, which was awarded to the Messrs. Stephenson and Booth accordingly. And further, to show that the engine had been working quite within its powers, Mr Stephenson ordered it to be brought upon the ground and detached from all incumbrances, when, in making two trips, it was found to travel at the astonishing rate of 35 miles an hour.

The 'Rocket' had thus eclipsed the performances of all locomotive engines that had yet been constructed, and outstripped even the sanguine expectations of its constructors. It satisfactorily answered the report of Messrs. Walker and Rastrick; and established the efficiency of the locomotive for working the Liverpool and Manchester Railway, and indeed all future railways. The 'Rocket' showed that a new power had been born into the world, full of activity and strength, with boundless capability of work. It was the simple but admirable contrivance of the steam-blast, and its combination with the multitubular boiler, that at once gave the locomotive a vigorous life, and secured the triumph of the railway system.* It has been well observed, that this wonderful ability to increase and multiply its powers of performance with the emergency that demands them, has made this giant engine the noblest creation of human wit, the very lion among machines. The success of the Rainhill experiment, as judged by the public, may be inferred from the fact that the shares of the Company immediately rose 10 per cent, and nothing more was heard of the proposed twenty-one fixed engines, engine-houses, ropes, etc. All this cumbersome apparatus was thenceforward effectually disposed of.

Very different now was the tone of those directors who had

* 'The Rocket' is now to be seen at the Museum of Patents at Kensington, where it is carefully preserved.

distinguished themselves by the persistency of their opposition to Mr Stephenson's plans. Coolness gave way to eulogy, and hostility to unbounded offers of friendship – after the manner of many men who run to the help of the strong. Deeply though the engineer had felt aggrieved by the conduct pursued towards him during this eventful struggle, by some from whom forbearance was to have been expected, he never entertained towards them in after life any angry feelings; on the contrary, he forgave all. But though the directors afterwards passed unanimous resolutions eulogizing 'the great skill and unwearied energy' of their engineer, he himself, when speaking confidentially to those with whom he was most intimate, could not help pointing out the difference between his 'foul-weather and fair-weather friends'. Mr Gooch says of him that though naturally most cheerful and kind-hearted in his disposition, the anxiety and pressure which weighed upon his mind during the construction of the railway, had the effect of making him occasionally impatient and irritable, like a spirited horse touched by the spur; though his original good-nature from time to time shone through it all. When the line had been brought to a successful completion, a very marked change in him became visible. The irritability passed away, and when difficulties and vexations arose they were treated by him as matters of course, and with perfect composure and cheerfulness.

CHAPTER XII — OPENING OF THE LIVERPOOL AND MANCHESTER RAILWAY, AND EXTENSION OF THE RAILWAY SYSTEM

THE directors of the Railway now began to see daylight; and they derived encouragement from the skilful manner in which their engineer had overcome the principal difficulties of the undertaking. He had formed a solid road over Chat Moss, and thus achieved one 'impossibility'; and he had constructed a locomotive that could run at a speed of 30 miles an hour, thus vanquishing a still more formidable difficulty.

A single line of way was completed over Chat Moss by 1 January 1830; and on that day, the 'Rocket' with a carriage full of directors, engineers, and their friends, passed along the greater part of the road between Liverpool and Manchester. Mr Stephenson continued to direct his close attention to the improvement of the details of the locomotive, every successive trial of which proved more satisfactory. In this department he had the benefit of the able and unremitting assistance of his son, who, in the workshops at Newcastle, directly superintended the construction of the new engines required for the public working of the railway. He did not by any means rest satisfied with the success, decided though it was, which had been achieved by the 'Rocket'. He regarded it but in the light of a successful experiment; and every succeeding engine placed upon the railway exhibited some improvement on its predecessors. The arrangement of the parts, and the weight and proportions of the engines, were altered, as the experience of each successive day, or week, or month, suggested; and it was soon found that the performances of the 'Rocket' on the day of trial had been greatly within the powers of the locomotive.

The first entire trip between Liverpool and Manchester was performed on 14 June 1830, on the occasion of a Board meeting being held at the latter town. The train was on this occasion drawn by the 'Arrow', one of the new locomotives, in which the most recent improvements had been adopted. Mr Stephenson himself drove the engine, and Captain Scoresby, the circumpolar navigator, stood beside him on the foot-plate, and minuted the speed of the train. A great concourse of people assembled at both termini, as well as along the line, to witness the novel spectacle of a train of carriages dragged by an engine at a speed of 17 miles an hour. On the return journey to Liverpool in the evening, the 'Arrow' crossed Chat Moss at a speed of nearly 27 miles an hour, reaching its destination in about an hour and a half.

In the mean time Mr Stephenson and his assistants were diligently occupied in making the necessary preliminary arrangements for the conduct of the traffic against the time when the line should be ready for opening. The experiments made with the object of carrying on the passenger traffic at quick velocities were of an especially harassing and anxious character. Every week, for nearly three months before the opening, trial trips were made to Newton and back, generally with two or three trains following each other, and carrying altogether from 200 to 300 persons. These trips were usually made on Saturday afternoons, when the works could be more conveniently stopped and the line cleared. In these experiments Mr Stephenson had the able assistance of Mr Henry Booth, the secretary of the Company, who contrived many of the arrangements in the rolling-stock, not the least valuable of which was his invention of the coupling screw, still in use on all passenger railways.

At length the line was finished, and ready for the public ceremony of the opening, which took place on 15 September 1830, and attracted a vast number of spectators. The completion of the railway was justly regarded as an important national event, and the opening was celebrated accordingly. The Duke of Wellington, then Prime Minister, Sir Robert Peel, and Mr Huskisson, one of the members for Liverpool, were among the number of distinguished public personages present.

Eight locomotive engines, constructed at the Stephenson works, had been delivered and placed upon the line, the whole of which had been tried and tested weeks before, with perfect success. The several trains of carriages accommodated in all about 600 persons. The procession was cheered in its progress by thousands of spectators – through the deep ravine of Olive Mount; up the Sutton incline; over the great Sankey viaduct, beneath which a great multitude of persons had assembled – carriages filling the narrow lanes, and barges crowding the river; the people below gazing with wonder and admiration at the trains which sped along the line, far above their heads, at the rate of some 24 miles an hour.

At Parkside, about 17 miles from Liverpool, the engines stopped to take in water. Here a deplorable accident occurred to one of the illustrious visitors, which threw a deep shadow over the subsequent proceedings of the day. The 'Northumbrian' engine, with the carriage containing the Duke of Wellington, was drawn up on one line, in order that the whole of the trains on the other line might pass in review before him and his party. Mr Huskisson had alighted from the carriage, and was standing on the opposite road, along which the 'Rocket' was observed rapidly coming up. At this moment the Duke of Wellington, between whom and Mr Huskisson some coolness had existed, made a sign of recognition, and held out his hand. A hurried but friendly grasp was given; and before it was loosened there was a general cry from the bystanders of 'Get in, get in!' Flurried and confused, Mr Huskisson endeavoured to get round the open door of the carriage, which projected over the opposite rail; but in so doing he was struck down by the 'Rocket', and falling with his leg doubled across the rail, the limb was instantly crushed. His first words, on being raised, were, 'I have met my death', which unhappily proved true, for he expired that same evening in the parsonage of Eccles. It was cited at the time as a remarkable fact, that the 'Northumbrian' engine, driven by George Stephenson himself, conveyed the wounded body of the unfortunate gentleman a distance of about 15 miles in 25 minutes, or at the rate of 36 miles an hour. This incredible speed burst upon the world with the effect of a new and unlooked-for phenomenon.

The accident threw a gloom over the rest of the day's proceedings. The Duke of Wellington and Sir Robert Peel expressed a wish that the procession should return to Liverpool. It was, however, represented to them that a vast concourse of people had assembled at Manchester to witness the arrival of the trains; that report would exaggerate the mischief, if they did not complete the journey; and that a false panic on that day might seriously affect future railway travelling and the value of the Company's property.

The party consented accordingly to proceed to Manchester, but on the understanding that they should return as soon as possible, and refrain from further festivity.

As the trains approached Manchester, crowds of people were found covering the banks, the slopes of the cuttings, and even the railway itself. The multitude, become impatient and excited by the rumours which reached them, had outflanked the military, and all order was at an end. The people clambered about the carriages, holding on by the door-handles, and many were tumbled over; but, happily, no fatal accident occurred. At the Manchester station, the political element began to display itself; placards about 'Peterloo', etc., were exhibited, and brickbats were thrown at the carriage containing the Duke. On the carriages coming to a stand in the Manchester station the Duke did not descend, but remained seated, shaking hands with the women and children who were pushed forward by the crowd. Shortly after, the trains returned to Liverpool, which they reached, after considerable interruptions, in the dark, at a late hour.

On the following morning the railway was opened for public traffic. The first train of 140 passengers was booked and sent on to Manchester, reaching it in the allotted period of two hours; and from that time the traffic has regularly proceeded from day to day until now.

It is scarcely necessary that we should speak at any length of the commercial results of the Liverpool and Manchester Railway. Suffice it to say that its success was complete and decisive. The anticipations of its projectors were, however, in many respects at fault. They had based their calculations almost entirely on the heavy merchandise traffic – such as coal, cotton, and timber – relying little upon passengers; whereas the receipts derived from the conveyance of passengers far exceeded those derived from merchandise of all kinds, which, for a time continued a subordinate branch of the traffic.

For some time after the public opening of the line, Mr Stephenson's ingenuity continued to be employed in devising improved methods for securing the safety and comfort of the travelling public. Few are aware of the thousand minute details which have to be arranged – the forethought and contrivance that have to be exercised – to enable the traveller by railway to accomplish his journey in safety. After the difficulties of constructing a level road over bogs, across valleys, and through deep cuttings, have been overcome, the maintenance of the way has to be provided for with continuous care. Every rail with its fastenings must be complete, to prevent risk of accident; and the road must be kept regularly ballasted up to the level, to diminish the jolting of vehicles passing over it at high speeds. Then the stations must be protected by signals observable from such a distance as to enable the train to be stopped in event of an obstacle, such as a stopping or shunting train being in the way. For some years the signals employed on the Liverpool railway were entirely given by men with flags of different colours stationed along the line; there were no fixed signals, nor electric telegraphs; but the traffic was nevertheless worked quite as safely as under the more elaborate and complicated system of telegraphing which has since been established.

From an early period it became obvious that the iron road as originally laid down was far too weak for the heavy traffic which it had to carry. The line was at first laid with fish-bellied rails weighing thirty-five pounds to the yard, calculated only for horse-traffic, or, at most, for engines like the 'Rocket', of very light weight. But as the power and the weight of the locomotives were increased, it was found that such rails were quite insufficient for the safe conduct of the traffic, and it therefore became necessary to re-lay the road with heavier and stronger rails at considerably increased expense.

The details of the carrying stock had in like manner to be settled by experience. Everything had, as it were, to be begun from the beginning. The coal-waggon, it is true, served in some degree as a model for the railway-truck; but the railway passenger-carriage was an entirely novel structure. It had to be mounted upon strong framing, of a peculiar kind, supported on springs to prevent jolting. Then there was the necessity for contriving some method of preventing hard bumping of the carriage-ends when the train was pulled up; and hence the contrivance of buffer-springs and spring frames. For the purpose of stopping the train, brakes on an improved plan were also contrived, with new modes of lubricating the carriage axles, on which the wheels revolved at an unusually high velocity. In all these arrangements, Mr Stephenson's inventiveness was kept constantly on the stretch; and though many improvements in detail have been effected since his time, the foundations were then laid by him of the present system of conducting railway traffic. As an illustration of the inventive ingenuity which he displayed in providing for the working of the Liverpool line, we may mention his contrivance of the Self-acting Brake. He early entertained the idea that the momentum of the running train might

itself be made available for the purpose of checking its speed. He
proposed to fit each carriage with a brake which should be called
into action immediately on the locomotive at the head of the train
being pulled up. The impetus of the carriages carrying them forward, the buffer-springs would be driven home, and, at the same
time, by a simple arrangement of the mechanism, the brakes would
be called into simultaneous action; thus the wheels would be
brought into a state of sledge, and the train speedily stopped. This
plan was adopted by Mr Stephenson before he left the Liverpool
and Manchester Railway, though it was afterwards discontinued;
but it is a remarkable fact, that this identical plan, with the addition of a centrifugal apparatus, has quite recently been revived by
M. Guérin, a French engineer, and extensively employed on foreign
railways, as the best method of stopping railway trains in the
most efficient manner and in the shortest time.

Finally, Mr Stephenson had to attend to the improvement of
the power and speed of the locomotive – always the grand object
of his study – with a view to economy as well as regularity of
working. In the 'Planet' engine, delivered upon the line immediately subsequent to the public opening, all the improvements
which had up to that time been contrived by him and his son were
introduced in combination – the blast-pipe, the tubular boiler,
horizontal cylinders inside the smoke-box, the cranked axle, and
the fire-box firmly fixed to the boiler. The first load of goods conveyed from Liverpool to Manchester by the 'Planet' was 80 tons
in weight, and the engine performed the journey against a strong
head-wind in $2\frac{1}{2}$ hours. On another occasion, the same engine
brought up a cargo of voters from Manchester to Liverpool, during
a contested election, within a space of sixty minutes! The 'Samson',
delivered in the following year, exhibited still further improvements, the most important of which was that of *coupling* the fore
and hind wheels of the engine. By this means, the adhesion of the
wheels on the rails was more effectually secured, and thus the full
hauling power of the locomotive was made available. The 'Samson',
shortly after it was placed upon the line, dragged after it a train
of waggons weighing 150 tons at a speed of about 20 miles an hour;
the consumption of coke being reduced to only about a third of a
pound per ton per mile.

The success of the Liverpool and Manchester experiment
naturally excited great interest. People flocked to Lancashire from
all quarters to see the steam-coach running upon a railway at three
times the speed of a mail-coach, and to enjoy the excitement of

actually travelling in the wake of an engine at that incredible velocity. The travellers returned to their respective districts full of the wonders of the locomotive, considering it to be the greatest marvel of the age. Railways are familiar enough objects now, and our children who grow up in their midst may think little of them; but thirty years since it was an event in one's life to see a locomotive, and to travel for the first time upon a public railroad.

The practicability of railway locomotion being now proved, and its great social and commercial advantages ascertained, the general extension of the system was merely a question of time, money, and labour. Although the legislature took no initiative step in the direction of railway extension, the public spirit and enterprise of the country did not fail it at this juncture. The English people, though they may be defective in their capacity for organization, are strong in individualism; and not improbably their admirable qualities in the latter respect detract from their efficiency in the former. Thus, in all times, their greatest enterprises have not been planned by officialism and carried out upon any regular system, but have sprung, like their constitution, their laws, and their entire industrial arrangements, from the force of circumstances and the individual energies of the people.

The mode of action in the case of railway extension was characteristic and national. The execution of the new lines was undertaken entirely by joint-stock associations of proprietors, after the manner of the Stockton and Darlington, and Liverpool and Manchester companies. These associations are conformable to our national habits, and fit well into our system of laws. They combine the power of vast resources with individual watchfulness and motives of self-interest; and by their means gigantic undertakings, which otherwise would be impossible to any but kings and emperors with great national resources at command, were carried out by the co-operation of private persons. And the results of this combination of means and of enterprise have been truly marvellous. Within the life of the present generation, the private citizens of England engaged in railway extension have, in the face of Government obstructions, and without taking a penny from the public purse, executed a system of communications involving works of the most gigantic kind, which, in their total mass, their cost, and their public utility, far exceed the most famous national undertakings of any age or country.

Mr Stephenson, was of course, actively engaged in the construction of the numerous railways now projected by the joint-

Working Shaft of the West Kilsby Tunnel

stock companies. The desire for railway extension principally pervaded the manufacturing districts, especially after the successful
opening of the Liverpool and Manchester line. The commercial
classes of the larger towns soon became eager for a participation in
the good which they had so recently derided. Railway projects
were set on foot in great numbers, and Manchester became a centre
from which main lines and branches were started in all directions.
The interest, however, which attaches to these later schemes is of
a much less absorbing kind than that which belongs to the earlier
history of the railway and the steps by which it was mainly
established. We naturally sympathize more keenly with the early
struggles of a great principle, its trials and its difficulties, than with
its after stages of success; and, however gratified and astonished
we may be at its consequences, the interest is in a great measure
gone when its triumph has become a matter of certainty.

The commercial results of the Liverpool and Manchester line
were so satisfactory, and indeed so greatly exceeded the expectations of its projectors, that many of the abandoned projects of the
speculative year 1825 were forthwith revived. An abundant crop of
engineers sprang up, ready to execute railways of any extent. Now
that the Liverpool and Manchester line had been made, and the
practicability of working it by locomotive power had been proved,
it was as easy for engineers to make railways and to work them, as
it was for navigators to find America after Columbus had made the
first voyage. Mr Francis Giles attached himself to the Newcastle
and Carlisle and London and Southampton projects. Mr Brunel
appeared as engineer of the line projected between London and
Bristol; and Mr Braithwaite, the builder of the 'Novelty' engine,
acted in the same capacity for a railway from London to Col-
chester.

The first lines constructed subsequent to the opening of the
Liverpool and Manchester Railway, were mostly in connection
with it, and principally in the county of Lancaster. Thus a branch
was formed from Bolton to Leigh, and another from Leigh to
Kenyon, where it formed a junction with the main line between
Liverpool and Manchester. Branches to Wigan on the north, and
to Runcorn Gap and Warrington on the south of the same line,
were also formed. A continuation of the latter, as far south as
Birmingham, was shortly after projected under the name of the
Grand Junction Railway.

The last mentioned line was projected as early as the year 1824,
when the Liverpool and Manchester scheme was under discussion,

and Mr Stephenson then published a report on the subject. The plans were deposited, but the Bill was thrown out through the opposition of the landowners and canal proprietors. When engaged in making the survey, Stephenson called upon some of the land-owners in the neighbourhood of Nantwich to obtain their assent, and was greatly disgusted to learn that the agents of the canal companies had been before him, and described the locomotive to the farmers as a most frightful machine, emitting a breath as poisonous as the fabled dragon of old; and telling them that if a bird flew over the district where one of these engines passed, it would inevitably drop down dead! The application for the Bill was renewed in 1826, and again failed; and at length it was determined to wait the issue of the Liverpool and Manchester experiment. The act was eventually obtained in 1833.

When it was proposed to extend the advantages of railways to the population of the midland and southern counties of England, an immense amount of alarm was created in the minds of the country gentlemen. They did not relish the idea of private indivi-duals, principally resident in the manufacturing districts, invading their domains; and they everywhere rose up in arms against the 'new-fangled roads'. Colonel Sibthorpe openly declared his hatred of the 'infernal railroads', and said that he 'would rather meet a highwayman, or see a burglar on his premises, than an engineer!' The impression which prevailed in the rural districts was, that fox-covers and game-preserves would be seriously prejudiced by the formation of railroads; that agricultural communications would be destroyed, land thrown out of cultivation, landowners and farmers reduced to beggary, the poor-rates increased through the number of persons thrown out of employment by the railways, and all this in order that Liverpool, Manchester, and Birmingham shopkeepers and manufacturers might establish a monstrous monopoly in railway traffic.

The inhabitants of even some of the large towns were thrown into a state of consternation by the proposal to provide them with the accommodation of a railway. The line from London to Bir-mingham would naturally have passed close to the handsome town of Northampton, and was so projected; but the inhabitants of the shire, urged on by the local press, and excited by men of influence and education, opposed the project, and succeeded in forcing the promoters, in their survey of the line, to pass the town at a distance. When the first railway through Kent was projected, the line was laid out so as to pass by Maidstone, the county town. But it had not a single supporter among the townspeople, while the landowners for many miles round combined to oppose it. In like manner, the line projected from London to Bristol was strongly denounced by the inhabitants of the intermediate districts; and when the first Bill was thrown out, Eton assembled under the presidency of the Marquis of Chandos to congratulate the country upon its defeat.

During the time that the works of the Liverpool and Manchester line were in progress, our engineer was consulted respecting a short railway proposed to be formed between Leicester and Swannington, for the purpose of opening up a communication between the town of Leicester and the coal-fields in the western part of the county. The projector of this undertaking had some difficulty in getting the requisite capital subscribed for, the Leicester townspeople who had money being for the most part interested in canals. George Stephenson was invited to come upon the ground and survey the line. He did so, and then the projector told him of the difficulty he had in finding subscribers to the concern. 'Give me a sheet,' said Stephenson, 'and I will raise the money for you in Liverpool.' The engineer was as good as his word, and in a short time the sheet was returned with the subscription complete. Mr Stephenson was then asked to undertake the office of engineer for the line, but his answer was that he had thirty miles of railway in hand, which were enough for any engineer to attend to properly. Was there any person he could recommend? 'Well,' said he, 'I think my son Robert is competent to undertake the thing.' Would Mr Stephenson be answerable for him? 'Oh, yes, certainly.' And Robert Stephenson, at twenty-seven years of age, was installed engineer of the line accordingly.

The requisite Parliamentary powers having been obtained, Robert Stephenson proceeded with the construction of the railway, about 16 miles in length, towards the end of 1830. The works were comparatively easy, excepting at the Leicester end, where the young engineer encountered his first stiff bit of tunnelling. The line passed underground for $1\frac{3}{4}$ mile, and 500 yards of its course lay in loose dry running sand. The presence of this material rendered it necessary for the engineer first to construct a wooden tunnel to support the soil while the brickwork was being executed. This proved sufficient, and the whole was brought to a successful termination within a reasonable time. While the works were in progress, Robert kept up a regular correspondence with his father at Liverpool, consulting him on all points in which his greater experience

was likely to be of service. Like this father, Robert was very observant, and always ready to seize opportunity by the forelock. It
happened that the estate of Snibston, near Ashby-de-la-Zouch,
was advertised for sale; and the young engineer's experience as a
coal-viewer and practical geologist suggested to his mind that coal
was most probably to be found underneath. He communicated his
views to his father on the subject. The estate lay in the immediate
neighbourhood of the railway; and if the conjecture proved correct,
the finding of coal would necessarily greatly enhance its value. He
accordingly requested his father to come over to Snibston and look
at the property, which he did; and after a careful inspection of the
ground, he arrived at the same conclusion as his son.

The large manufacturing town of Leicester, about fourteen miles
distant, had up to that time been exclusively supplied with coal
brought by canal from Derbyshire; and Mr Stephenson saw that
the railway under construction from Swannington to Leicester,
would furnish him with a ready market for any coals which he
might find at Snibston. Having induced two of his Liverpool friends
to join him in the venture, the Snibston estate was purchased in
1831: and shortly after, Stephenson removed his home from Liverpool to Alton Grange, for the purpose of superintending the sinking
of the pit. He travelled thither by gig with his wife, his favourite
horse 'Bobby' performing the journey by easy stages.

Sinking operations were immediately begun, and proceeded
satisfactorily until the old enemy, water, burst in upon the workmen, and threatened to drown them out. But by means of efficient
pumping-engines, and the skilful casing of the shaft with segments
of cast iron – a process called 'tubbing',* which Mr Stephenson was
the first to adopt in the Midland counties – it was eventually made
water-tight, and the sinking proceeded. When a depth of 166 feet
had been reached, a still more formidable difficulty presented
itself – one which had baffled former sinkers in the neighbourhood,
and deterred them from further operations. This was a remarkable
bed of whinstone or greenstone, which had originally been poured
out as a sheet of burning lava over the denuded surface of the coal
measures; indeed it was afterwards found that it had turned to
cinders one part of the seam of coal with which it had come in

---

* Tubbing is now adopted in many cases as a substitute for brick-walling.
The tubbing consists of short portions of cast-iron cylinder fixed in segments. Each weighs about 4½ cwt., is about 3 or 4 feet long, and about ⅜ of
an inch thick. These pieces are fitted closely together, length under length,
and form an impermeable wall along the side of the pit.

contact. The appearance of this bed of solid rock was so unusual a
circumstance in coal-mining, that some experienced sinkers urged
Stephenson to proceed no further, believing the occurrence of the
dyke at that point to be altogether fatal to his enterprise. But, with
his faith still firm in the existence of coal underneath, he fell back
on his old motto of 'Persevere'. He determined to go on boring;
and down through the solid rock he went until, twenty-two feet
lower, he came upon the coal measures. In the mean time, however, lest the boring at that point should prove unsuccessful, he
had commenced sinking another pair of shafts about a quarter of a
mile west of the 'fault'; and after about nine months' labour he
reached the principal seam, called the 'main coal'.

The works were then opened out on a large scale, and Mr
Stephenson had the pleasure and good fortune to send the first
train of main coal to Leicester by railway. The price was immediately reduced to about 8s. a ton, effecting a pecuniary saving
to the inhabitants of the town of about £40,000 per annum, or
equivalent to the whole amount then collected in Government
taxes and local rates, besides giving an impetus to the manufacturing prosperity of the place, which has continued down to the
present day. The correct principles upon which the mining operations at Snibston were conducted offered a salutary example to the
neighbouring colliery owners. The numerous improvements there
introduced were freely exhibited to all, and they were afterwards
reproduced in many forms all over the Midland counties, greatly to
the advantage of the mining interest.

Nor was Mr Stephenson less attentive to the comfort and well-
being of those immediately dependent upon him – the workpeople
of the Snibston colliery and their families. Unlike many of those
large employers who have 'sprung from the ranks', he was one of
the kindest and most indulgent of masters. He would have a fair
day's work for a fair day's wages; but he never forgot that the
employer had his duties as well as his rights. First of all, he
attended to the proper home accommodation of his workpeople.
He erected a village of comfortable cottages, each provided with a
snug little garden. He was also instrumental in erecting a church
adjacent to the works, as well as Church schools for the education
of the colliers' children; and with that broad catholicity of senti-
ment which distinguished him, he further provided a chapel and a
school-house for the use of the Dissenting portion of the colliers
and their families – an example of benevolent liberality which was
not without a salutary influence upon the neighbouring employers.

CHAPTER XIII – ROBERT STEPHENSON CONSTRUCTS THE LONDON AND BIRMINGHAM RAILWAY

OF the numerous extensive projects which followed close upon the completion of the Liverpool and Manchester line, and the Locomotive triumph at Rainhill, that of a railway between London and Birmingham was the most important. The scheme originated at the latter place in 1830. Two committees were formed, and two plans were proposed. One was of a line to London by way of Oxford, and the other by way of Coventry. The simple object of the promoters of both schemes being to secure the advantages of railway communication with the metropolis, they wisely determined to combine their strength to secure it. They then resolved to call George Stephenson to their aid, and requested him to advise them as to the two schemes which were before them. After a careful examination of the country, Mr Stephenson reported in favour of the Coventry route, when the Lancashire gentlemen, who were the principal subscribers to the project, having every confidence in his judgement, supported his decision, and the line recommended by him was adopted accordingly.

At the meeting of the promoters held at Birmingham to determine on the appointment of the engineer for the railway, there was a strong party in favour of associating with Mr Stephenson a gentleman with whom he had been brought into serious collision in the course of the Liverpool and Manchester undertaking. When the offer was made to him that he should be joint engineer with the other, he requested leave to retire and consider the proposal with his son. The father was in favour of accepting it. His struggle heretofore had been so hard that he could not bear the idea of missing so promising an opportunity of professional advancement. But the son, foreseeing the jealousies and heartburnings which the joint engineership would most probably create, recommended his father to decline the connection. George adopted the suggestion, and returning to the Committee, he announced to them his decision; on which the promoters decided to appoint him the engineer of the undertaking in conjunction with his son.

This line, like the Liverpool and Manchester, was very strongly opposed, especially by the landowners. Numerous pamphlets were published, calling on the public to 'beware of the bubbles', and holding up the promoters of railways to ridicule. They were compared to St John Long and similar quacks, and pronounced fitter for Bedlam than to be left at large. The canal proprietors, land-owners, and road trustees, made common cause against them. The failure of railways was confidently predicted – indeed, it was elaborately attempted to be proved that they had failed; and it was industriously spread abroad that the locomotive engines, having been found useless and highly dangerous on the Liverpool and Manchester line, were immediately to be abandoned in favour of horses – a rumour which the directors of the Company thought it necessary publicly to contradict.

Public meetings were held in all the counties through which the line would pass between London and Birmingham, at which the project was denounced, and strong resolutions against it were passed. The attempt was made to conciliate the landlords by explanations, but all such efforts proved futile, the owners of nearly seven-eighths of the land being returned as dissentients. 'I remember,' said Robert Stephenson, describing the opposition, 'that we called one day on Sir Astley Cooper, the eminent surgeon, in the hope of overcoming his aversion to the railway. He was one of our most inveterate and influential opponents. His country house at Berkhampsted was situated near the intended line, which passed through part of his property. We found a courtly, fine-looking old gentleman, of very stately manners, who received us kindly and heard all we had to say in favour of the project. But he was quite inflexible in his opposition to it. No deviation or improvement that we could suggest had any effect in conciliating him. He was opposed to railways generally, and to this in particular. "Your scheme," said he, "is preposterous in the extreme. It is of so extravagant a character, as to be positively absurd. Then look at the recklessness of your proceedings! You are proposing to cut up our estates in all directions for the purpose of making an unnecessary road. Do you think for one moment of the destruction of property involved by it? Why, gentlemen, if this sort of thing be permitted to go on, you will in a very few years *destroy the noblesse*!" We left the honourable baronet without having produced the slightest effect upon him, excepting perhaps, it might be, increased exasperation against our scheme. I could not help observing to my companions as we left the house, "Well, it is really provoking to find one who has been made a 'Sir' for cutting that wen out of George the Fourth's neck, charging us with contemplating the destruction of the *noblesse*, because we propose to confer upon him the benefits of a railroad".'

Such being the opposition of the owners of land, it was with the greatest difficulty that an accurate survey of the line could be made. At one point the vigilance of the landowners and their servants was such that the surveyors were effectually prevented taking the levels by the light of day; and it was only at length accomplished at night by means of dark lanterns. There was one clergyman, who made such alarming demonstrations of his opposition, that the extraordinary expedient was resorted to of surveying his property during the time he was engaged in the pulpit. This was managed by having a strong force of surveyors in readiness to commence their operations, who entered the clergyman's grounds on one side the moment they saw him fairly off them on the other. By a well-organized and systematic arrangement each man concluded his allotted task just as the reverend gentleman concluded his sermon; so that, before he left the church, the deed was done, and the sinners had all decamped. Similar opposition was offered at many other points, but ineffectually. The laborious application of Robert Stephenson was such, that in examining the country to ascertain the best line, he walked the whole distance between London and Birmingham upwards of twenty times.

When the Bill went before the Committee of the Commons in 1832, a formidable array of evidence was produced. All the railway experience of the day was brought to bear in support of the measure, and all that interested opposition could do was set in

motion against it. The necessity for an improved mode of communication between London and Birmingham was clearly demonstrated; and the engineering evidence was regarded as quite
satisfactory. Not a single fact was proved against the utility of the
measure, and the Bill passed the Committee, and afterwards the
third reading in the Commons, by large majorities.

It was then sent to the Lords, and went into Committee, when a
similar mass of testimony was again gone through. But it had been
evident, from the opening of the proceedings, that the fate of the
Bill had been determined before even a word of the evidence had
been heard. At that time the committees were open to all peers;
and the promoters of the Bill found, to their dismay, many of the
lords who were avowed opponents of the measure as landowners,
sitting as judges to decide its fate. Their principal object seemed
to be, to bring the proceedings to a termination as quickly as
possible. An attempt at negotiation was indeed made in the course
of the proceedings in committee, but failed, and the Bill was
thrown out.

As the result had been foreseen, measures were taken to neutralize the effect of this decision as regarded future operations. Not
less than £32,000 had been expended in preliminary and parliamentary expenses up to this stage; but the promoters determined
not to look back, and forthwith made arrangements for prosecuting
the Bill in the next session. Strange to say, the Bill then passed
both Houses silently and almost without opposition. The mystery
was afterwards solved by the appearance of a circular issued by
the directors of the company, in which it was stated, that they had
opened 'negotiations' with the most influential of their opponents;
that 'these measures had been successful to a greater extent than
they had ventured to anticipate; and the most active and formidable had been conciliated'. An instructive commentary on the
mode by which these noble lords and influential landed proprietors
had been 'conciliated', was the simple fact that the estimate for
land was nearly trebled, and that the owners were paid about
£750,000 for what had been originally estimated at £250,000.

The landowners having thus been 'conciliated', the promoters of
the measure were permitted to proceed with the formation of their
great highway. Robert Stephenson was, with the sanction of his
father, appointed sole engineer; and steps were at once taken by
him to make the working survey, to prepare the working drawings,
and arrange for the construction of the railway. Eighty miles of
the road were shortly under contract; having been let within the

estimates; and the works were in satisfactory progress by the
beginning of 1834.

The difficulties encountered in their construction were very
great; the most formidable of them originating in the character of
the works themselves. Extensive tunnels had to be driven through
unknown strata, and miles of underground excavation had to be
carried out in order to form a level road from valley to valley,
under the intervening ridges. This kind of work was the newest of
all to the contractors of that day. Robert Stephenson's experience
in the collieries of the North rendered him well fitted to grapple
with such difficulties; yet even he, with all his practical knowledge,
could scarcely have foreseen the serious obstacles which he was
called upon to encounter in executing the formidable cuttings,
embankments, and tunnels of the London and Birmingham Railway. It would be an uninteresting, as it would be a fruitless task,
to attempt to describe the works in detail; but a general outline of
their extraordinary character and extent may not be out of place.

The length of railway to be constructed between London and
Birmingham was $112\frac{1}{2}$ miles. The line crossed a series of low-lying
districts separated from each other by considerable ridges of hills;
and it was the object of the engineer to cross the valleys at as high,
and the hills at as low, elevations as possible. The high ground was
therefore cut down and the 'stuff' led into embankments, in some
places of great height and extent, so as to form a road upon as level
a plane as was considered practicable for the working of the locomotive engine. In some places, the high grounds were passed in
open cuttings, while in others it was necessary to bore through
them in tunnels with deep cuttings at each end.

The most formidable excavations on the line are those at Tring,
Denbigh Hall, and Blisworth. The Tring cutting is an immense
chasm across the great chalk ridge of Ivinghoe. It is $2\frac{1}{2}$ miles long,
and for $\frac{1}{4}$ of a mile is 57 feet deep. A million and a half cubic yards
of chalk and earth were taken out of this cutting by means of
horse-runs and deposited in spoil banks; besides the immense
quantity run into the embankment north of the cutting, forming
a solid mound nearly 6 miles long and about 30 feet high. Passing
over the Denbigh Hall cutting, and the Wolverton embankment of
$1\frac{1}{2}$ mile in length across the valley of the Ouse, we come to the
excavation at Blisworth, a brief description of which will give the
reader an idea of one of the most difficult kinds of railway work.

The Blisworth Cutting is one of the longest and deepest grooves
cut in the solid earth. It is $1\frac{1}{2}$ mile long, in some places 54 feet deep,

passing through earth, stiff clay, and hard rock. Not less than a million cubic yards of these materials were dug, quarried, and blasted out of it. One-third of the cutting was stone, and beneath the stone lay a thick bed of clay, under which were found beds of loose shale so full of water that almost constant pumping was necessary at many points to enable the works to proceed. For a year and a half the contractor went on fruitlessly contending with these difficulties, and at length he was compelled to abandon the adventure. The engineer then took the works in hand for the Company, and they were vigorously proceeded with. Steam-engines were set to work to pump out the water; two locomotives were put on, one at each end of the cutting, to drag away the excavated rock and clay; and 800 men and boys were employed along the work, in digging, wheeling, and blasting, besides a large number of horses. Some idea of the extent of the blasting operations may be formed from the fact that twenty-five barrels of gunpowder were used weekly; the total quantity exploded in forming this one cutting being about 3,000 barrels. Considerable difficulty was experienced in supporting the bed of rock cut through, which overlaid the clay and shale along each side of the cutting. It was found necessary to hold it up by strong retaining walls, to prevent the clay bed from bulging out, and these walls were further supported by a strong invert, that is, an arch placed in an inverted position under the road, thus binding together the walls on both sides. Behind the retaining walls, a drift or horizontal drain was provided to enable the water to run off, and occasional openings were left in the walls themselves for the same purpose. The work was at length brought to a successful completion, but the extraordinary difficulties encountered in forming the cutting had the effect of greatly increasing the cost of this portion of the railway.

The Tunnels on the line are eight in number, their total length being 7,336 yards. The first high ground encountered was Primrose Hill, where the stiff London clay was passed through for a distance of about 1,164 yards. The clay was close, compact, and dry, more difficult to work than stone itself. It was entirely free from water; but the absorbing properties of the clay were such that when exposed to the air it swelled out rapidly. Hence an unusual thickness of brick lining was found necessary; and the engineer afterwards informed the author that for some time he entertained an apprehension lest the pressure should force in the brickwork altogether. It was so great that it made the face of the bricks to fly off in minute chips which covered his clothes while he was inspecting the work. The materials used in the building were, however, of excellent quality; and the tunnel was happily brought to a completion without any accident.

At Watford the chalk ridge was penetrated by a tunnel about 1,800 yards long; and at Northchurch, Lindslade, and Stowe Hill, there were other tunnels of minor extent. But the chief difficulty of the undertaking was the execution of that under the Kilsby ridge. Though not the largest, this is in many respects one of the most interesting works of the kind in England. It is about 2,400 yards long, and runs at an average depth of about 160 feet below the surface. The ridge under which it extends is of considerable extent, the famous battle of Naseby having been fought upon one of the spurs of the same high ground about seven miles to the eastward.

Previous to the letting of the contract, the character of the underground soil was examined by trial-shafts. The tests indicated that it consisted of shale of the lower oolite, and the works were let accordingly. But they had scarcely been commenced when it was discovered that, at an interval between the two trial shafts which had been sunk, about 200 yards from the south end of the tunnel, there existed an extensive quicksand under a bed of clay 40 feet thick, which the borings had escaped in the most singular manner. At the bottom of one of these shafts the excavation and building of the tunnel were proceeding, when the roof at one part suddenly gave way, a deluge of water burst in, and the party of workmen with the utmost difficulty escaped with their lives. They were only saved by means of a raft, on which they were towed by one of the engineers swimming with the rope in his mouth to the lower end of the shaft, out of which they were safely lifted to the daylight. The works were of course at that point immediately stopped. The contractor, who had undertaken the construction of the tunnel, was so overwhelmed by the calamity, that, though he was relieved by the Company from his engagement, he took to his bed and shortly after died. Pumping-engines were then erected for the purpose of draining off the water, but for a long time it prevailed, and sometimes even rose in the shaft. The question then presented itself, whether in the face of so formidable a difficulty, the works should be proceeded with or abandoned. Robert Stephenson sent over to Alton Grange for his father, and the two took serious counsel together. George was in favour of pumping out the water from the top by powerful engines erected over each shaft, until the water was mastered. Robert concurred in that view, and although other engineers pronounced strongly against the practicability of the scheme and advised its abandonment, the directors authorized him to proceed; and powerful steam-engines were ordered to be constructed and delivered without loss of time.

In the mean time, Robert suggested to his father the expediency of running a drift along the heading from the south end of the tunnel, with the view of draining off the water in that way. George said he thought it would scarcely answer, but that it was worth a trial, at all events until the pumping-engines were got ready. Robert accordingly gave orders for the drift to be proceeded with. The excavators were immediately set to work; and they were very soon close upon the sand bed. One day, when the engineer, his assistants, and the workmen were clustered about the open entrance of the drift-way, they heard a sudden roar as of distant thunder. It was hoped that the water had burst in – for all the workmen were out of the drift – and that the sand bed would now drain itself off in a natural way. Instead of which, very little water made its appearance; and on examining the inner end of the drift, it was found that the loud noise had been caused by the sudden discharge into it of an immense mass of sand, which had completely choked up the passage, and prevented the water from flowing away.

The engineer now found that there was nothing for it but to sink numerous additional shafts over the line of the tunnel at the points at which it crossed the quicksand, and endeavour to master the water by sheer force of engines and pumps. The engines erected, possessed an aggregate power of 160 horses; and they went on pumping for eight successive months, emptying out an almost incredible quantity of water. It was found that the water, with which the bed of sand extending over many miles was charged, was to a certain degree held back by the particles of the sand itself, and that it could only percolate through at a certain average rate. It appeared in its flow to take a slanting direction to the suction of the pumps, the angle of inclination depending upon the coarseness or fineness of the sand, and regulating the time of the flow. Hence the distribution of the pumping power at short intervals along the line of the tunnel had a much greater effect than the concentration of that power at any one spot. It soon appeared that the water had found its master. Protected by the pumps, which cleared a space for the engineering operations – carried on in the midst, as it were, of two almost perpendicular walls of water and sand on either side – the workmen proceeded with the building of the tunnel at numerous points. Every exertion was used to wall in the dangerous parts as quickly as possible; the excavators and bricklayers labouring night and day until the work was finished. Even while under the protection of the immense pumping power above described, it often happened that the bricks were scarcely covered with cement ready for the setting, ere they were washed quite clean by the streams of water which poured from overhead. The men were accordingly under the necessity of holding over their work large whisks of straw and other appliances to protect the bricks and cement at the moment of setting.

The quantity of water pumped out of the sand bed during eight months of incessant pumping, averaged 2,000 gallons per minute, raised from an average depth of 120 feet. It is difficult to form an adequate idea of the bulk of the water thus raised, but it may be stated that if allowed to flow for three hours only, it would fill a lake one acre square to the depth of one foot, and if allowed to flow for one entire day it would fill the lake to over eight feet in depth, or sufficient to float vessels of 100 tons' burden. The water pumped out of the tunnel while the work was in progress would be nearly equivalent to the contents of the Thames at high water, between London and Woolwich. It is a curious circumstance, that notwithstanding the quantity thus removed, the level of the surface of the water in the tunnel was only lowered about $2\frac{1}{2}$ to 3 inches per week, proving the vast area of the quicksand, which probably extended along the entire ridge of land under which the railway passed.

The cost of the line was greatly increased by the difficulties encountered at Kilsby. The original estimate for the tunnel was only £99,000; but before it was finished it had cost more than £100 per lineal yard forward, or a total of nearly £300,000. The expenditure on the other parts of the line also greatly exceeded the amount first set down by the engineer; and before the works were finished it was more than doubled. The land cost three times more than the estimate; and the claims for compensation were enormous. Although the contracts were let within the estimates, very few of the contractors were able to complete them without the assistance of the Company, and many became bankrupt.

The magnitude of the works, which were unprecedented in England, was one of the most remarkable features in the undertaking. The following striking comparison has been made between this railway and one of the greatest works of ancient times. The Great Pyramid of Egypt was, according to Diodorus Siculus, constructed by 300,000 – according to Herodotus, by 100,000 – men. It required for its execution twenty years, and the labour expended upon it has been estimated as equivalent to lifting 15,733,000,000 of cubic feet of stone one foot high. Whereas, if the labour expended in constructing the London and Birmingham Railway be in like manner reduced to one common denomination the result is 25,000,000,000 of cubic feet *more* than was lifted for the Great Pyramid; and yet the English work was performed by about 20,000 men in less than five years. And while the Egyptian work was executed by a powerful monarch concentrating upon it the labour and capital of a great nation, the English railway was constructed, in the face of every conceivable obstruction and difficulty, by a company of private individuals out of their own resources, without the aid of Government or the contribution of one farthing of public money.

The labourers who executed this formidable work were in many respects a remarkable class. The 'railway navvies', as they are called, were men drawn by the attraction of good wages from all parts of the kingdom; and they were ready for any sort of hard work. Some of the best came from the fen districts of Lincoln and Cambridge, where they had been trained to execute works of excavation and embankment. These old practitioners formed a nucleus of skilled manipulation and aptitude, which rendered them of indispensable utility in the immense undertakings of the period. Their expertness in all sorts of earthwork, in embanking, boring, and well-sinking – their practical knowledge of the nature of soils and rocks, the tenacity of clays, and the porosity of certain stratifications – were very great; and, rough-looking though they were, many of them were as important in their own department as the contractor or the engineer.

During the railway-making period the navvy wandered about from one public work to another – apparently belonging to no country and having no home. He usually wore a white felt hat with the brim turned up, a velveteen or jean square-tailed coat, a scarlet plush waistcoat with little black spots, and a bright-coloured kerchief round his herculean neck, when, as often happened, it was not left entirely bare. His corduroy breeches were retained in position by a leathern strap round the waist, and were tied and buttoned at the knee, displaying beneath a solid calf and foot encased in strong high-laced boots. Joining together in a 'butty gang', some ten or twelve of these men would take a contract to cut out and remove so much 'dirt' – as they denominated earth-cutting – fixing

their price according to the character of the 'stuff', and the distance to which it had to be wheeled and tipped. The contract
taken, every man put himself on his mettle; if any was found
skulking, or not putting forth his full working power, he was
ejected from the gang. Their powers of endurance were extraordinary. In times of emergency they would work for twelve and
even sixteen hours, with only short intervals for meals. The
quantity of flesh-meat which they consumed was something enormous; but it was to their bones and muscles what coke is to the
locomotive – the means of keeping up the steam. They displayed
great pluck, and seemed to disregard peril. Indeed the most
dangerous sort of labour – such as working horse-barrow runs, in
which accidents are of constant occurrence – has always been most
in request among them, the danger seeming to be one of its chief
recommendations.

Working, eating, drinking, and sleeping together, and daily
exposed to the same influences, these railway labourers soon presented a distinct and well-defined character, strongly marking
them from the population of the districts in which they laboured.
Reckless alike of their lives as of their earnings, the navvies worked
hard and lived hard. For their lodging, a hut of turf would content
them; and, in their hours of leisure, the meanest public-house
would serve for their parlour. Unburdened, as they usually were,
by domestic ties, unsoftened by family affection, and without
much moral or religious training, the navvies came to be distinguished by a sort of savage manners, which contrasted strangely
with those of the surrounding population. Yet, ignorant and violent though they may be, they were usually good-hearted fellows
in the main – frank and open-handed with their comrades, and
ready to share their last penny with those in distress. Their pay-
nights were often a saturnalia of riot and disorder, dreaded by the
inhabitants of the villages along the line of works. The irruption of
such men into the quiet hamlet of Kilsby must, indeed, have produced a very startling effect on the recluse inhabitants of the place.
Robert Stephenson used to tell a story of the clergyman of the
parish waiting upon the foreman of one of the gangs to expostulate
with him as to the shocking impropriety of his men working during
Sunday. But the head navvy merely hitched up his trousers, and
said, 'Why, Soondays hain't cropt out here yet!' In short, the
navvies were little better than heathens, and the village of Kilsby
was not restored to its wonted quiet until the tunnel-works were
finished, and the engines and scaffoldings removed, leaving only

Great Ventilating Shaft: West Kilsby Tunnel

the immense masses of *débris* around the line of shafts which extend along the top of the tunnel.

In illustration of the extraordinary working energy and powers of endurance of the English navvies, we may mention that when railway-making extended to France, the English contractors for the works took with them gangs of English navvies, with the usual plant, which included wheelbarrows. These the English navvy was accustomed to run out rapidly and continuously, piled so high with 'stuff' that he could barely see, over the summit of his load, the gang-board along which he wheeled his barrow. While he thus easily ran out some 3 or 4 cwt at a time, the French navvy was contented with half the weight. Indeed, the French navvies on one occasion struck work because of the size of the English barrows, and there was an *émeute* on the Rouen Railway, which was only quelled by the aid of the military. The consequence was that the big barrows were abandoned to the English workmen, who earned nearly double the wages of the Frenchmen. The manner in which they stood to their work was matter of great surprise and wonderment to the French country people, who came crowding round them in their blouses, and, after gazing admiringly at their expert handling of the pick and mattock, and the immense loads of 'dirt' which they wheeled out, would exclaim to each other, '*Mon Dieu, voila! voilà ces Anglais, comme ils travaillent!*'

CHAPTER XIV — MANCHESTER AND LEEDS, AND
MIDLAND RAILWAYS — STEPHENSON'S LIFE AT
ALTON — VISIT TO BELGIUM — GENERAL EXTENSION
OF RAILWAYS AND THEIR RESULTS

THE rapidity with which railways were carried out, when the
spirit of the country became roused, was indeed remarkable.
This was doubtless in some measure owing to the increased force
of the current of speculation at the time, but chiefly to the desire
which the public began to entertain for the general extension of
the system. It was even proposed to fill up the canals, and convert
them into railways. The new roads became the topic of conversation in all circles; they were felt to give a new value to time; their
vast capabilities for 'business' peculiarly recommended them to
the trading classes; while the friends of 'progress' dilated on the
great benefits they would eventually confer upon mankind at
large. It began to be seen that Edward Pease had not been exag-
gerating when he said, 'Let the country but make the railroads,
and the railroads will make the country!' They also came to be
regarded as inviting objects of investment to the thrifty, and a
safe outlet for the accumulations of inert men of capital. Thus new
avenues of iron road were soon in course of formation, branching in
all directions, so that the country promised in a wonderfully short
time to become wrapped in one vast network of iron.

In 1836 the Grand Junction Railway was under construction

between Warrington and Birmingham – the northern part by Mr
Stephenson, and the southern by Mr Rastrick. The works on that
line embraced heavy cuttings, long embankments, and numerous
viaducts; but none of these are worthy of any special description.
Perhaps the finest piece of masonry on the railway is the Dutton
Viaduct across the valley of the Weaver. It consists of twenty
arches of 60 feet span, springing 16 feet from the perpendicular
shaft of each pier, and 60 feet in height from the crown of the
arches to the level of the river. The foundations of the piers were
built on piles driven 20 feet deep. The structure has a solid and
majestic appearance, and is perhaps the finest of George Stephenson's viaducts.

The Manchester and Leeds line was in progress at the same time
– an important railway connecting the principal manufacturing
towns of Yorkshire and Lancashire. An attempt was made to obtain the Act as early as 1831; but its promoters were defeated by
the powerful opposition of the landowners aided by the canal companies, and the project was not revived for several years. The line
was somewhat circuitous, and the works were heavy; but on the
whole the gradients were favourable, and it had the advantage of
passing through a district full of manufacturing towns and villages,
teeming hives of population, industry, and enterprise. The Act
authorizing the construction of the railway was obtained in 1836;
it was greatly amended in the succeeding year, and the first ground
was broken on 18 August 1837.

In conducting this project to an issue, the engineer had the usual
opposition and prejudices to encounter. Predictions were confidently made in many quarters that the line could never succeed.
It was declared that the utmost engineering skill could not construct a railway through such a country of hills and hard rocks;
and it was maintained that, even if the railroad were practicable,
it could only be made at a ruinous cost.

During the progress of the works, as the Summit Tunnel, near
Littleborough, was approaching completion, the rumour was
spread abroad in Manchester that the tunnel had fallen in and
buried a number of the workmen. The last arch had been keyed
in, and the work was all but finished, when the accident occurred
which was thus exaggerated by the lying tongue of rumour. An
invert had given way through the irregular pressure of the surrounding earth and rock at a part of the tunnel where a 'fault' had
occurred in the strata. A party of the directors accompanied the
engineer to inspect the scene of the accident. They entered the

tunnel's mouth preceded by upwards of fifty navvies, each bearing a torch.

After walking a distance of about half a mile, the inspecting party arrived at the scene of the 'frightful accident', about which so much alarm had been spread. All that was visible was a certain unevenness of the ground, which had been forced up by the invert under it giving way; thus the ballast had been loosened, the drain running along the centre of the road had been displaced, and small pools of water stood about. But the whole of the walls and the roof were still as perfect as at any other part of the tunnel. The engineer explained the cause of the accident, the blue shale, he said, through which the excavation passed at that point, was considered so hard and firm, as to render it unnecessary to build the invert very strong there. But shale is always a deceptive material. Subjected to the influence of the atmosphere, it gives but a treacherous support. In this case, falling away like quicklime, it had left the lip of the invert alone to support the pressure of the arch above, and hence its springing inwards and upwards. Mr Stephenson directed the attention of the visitors to the completeness of the arch overhead, where not the slightest fracture or yielding could be detected. Speaking of the work, in the course of the same day, he said, 'I will stake my character and my head, if that tunnel ever give way, so as to cause danger to any of the public passing through it. Taking it as a whole, I don't think there is such another piece of work in the world. It is the greatest work that has yet been done of this kind, and there has been less repairing than is usual, though an engineer might well be beaten in his calculations, for he cannot beforehand see into those little fractured parts of the earth he may meet with.' As Stephenson had promised, the invert was put in; and the tunnel was made perfectly safe.

The construction of this subterranean road employed the labour of above a thousand men for nearly four years. Besides excavating the arch out of a solid rock, they used 23,000,000 of bricks, and 8,000 tons of Roman cement in the building of the tunnel. Thirteen stationary engines, and about 100 horses, were also employed in drawing the earth and stone out of the shafts. Its entire length is 2,869 yards, or nearly $1\frac{3}{4}$ mile – exceeding the famous Kilsby Tunnel by 471 yards.

The Midland Railway was a favourite line of Mr Stephenson's for several reasons. It passed through a rich mining district, in which it opened up many valuable coal-fields, and it formed part of the great main line of communication between London and Edinburgh. The Act was obtained in 1836, and the first ground was broken in February 1837.

Although the Midland Railway was only one of the many great works of the same kind executed at that time, it was almost enough of itself to be the achievement of a life. Compare it, for example, with Napoleon's military road over the Simplon, and it will at once be seen how greatly it excels that work, not only in the constructive skill displayed in it, but also in its cost and magnitude, and the amount of labour employed in its formation. The road of the Simplon is 45 miles in length; the North Midland Railway is $72\frac{1}{2}$ miles. The former has 50 bridges and 5 tunnels, measuring together 1,338 feet in length; the latter has 200 bridges and 7 tunnels, measuring together 11,400 feet, or about $2\frac{1}{4}$ miles. The former cost about £720,000 sterling, the latter above £3,000,000. Napoleon's grand military road was constructed in six years, at the public cost of the two great kingdoms of France and Italy; while Stephenson's railway was formed in about three years, by a company of private merchants and capitalists out of their own funds, and under their own superintendence.

It is scarcely necessary that we should give any account in detail of the North Midland works. The making of one tunnel so much resembles the making of another, the building of bridges and viaducts, no matter how extensive, so much resembles the building of others, the cutting out of 'dirt', the blasting of rocks, and the wheeling of excavation into embankments, is so much a matter of mere time and hard work, that is quite unnecessary for us to detain the reader by any attempt at their description. Of course there were the usual difficulties to encounter and overcome, but the railway engineer regarded these as mere matters of course, and would probably have been disappointed if they had not presented themselves.

On the Midlands, as on other lines, water was the great enemy to be fought against, water in the Claycross and other tunnels, water in the boggy or sandy foundations of bridges, and water in cuttings and embankments. As an illustration of the difficulties of bridge building, we may mention the case of the five-arch bridge over the Derwent, where it took two years' work, night and day, to get in the foundations of the piers alone. Another curious illustration of the mischief done by water in cuttings may be briefly mentioned. At a part of the North Midland Line, near Ambergate, it was necessary to pass along a hillside in a cutting a few yards deep. As the cutting proceeded, a seam of shale was cut across, laying at an inclination of 6 to 1; and shortly after, the water getting behind the bed of shale, the whole mass of earth along the hill above began to move down across the line of excavation. The accident completely upset the estimates of the contractor, who, instead of 50,000 cubic yards, found that he had about 500,000 to remove; the execution of this part of the railway occupying fifteen months instead of two.

The Oakenshaw cutting near Wakefield was also of a very formidable character. About 600,000 yards of rock shale and bind were quarried out of it, and led to form the adjoining Oakenshaw embankment. The Normanton cutting was almost as heavy, requiring the removal of 400,000 yards of the same kind of excavation into embankment and spoil. But the progress of the works on the line was so rapid in 1839, that not less than 450,000 cubic yards of excavation were removed monthly.

As a curiosity in construction, we may also mention a very delicate piece of work executed on the same railway at Bullbridge in Derbyshire, where the line at the same point passes *over* a bridge which here spans the river Amber, and *under* the bed of the Cromford Canal. Water, bridge, railway, and canal, were thus piled one above the other, four storeys high; such another curious complication probably not existing. In order to prevent the possibility of the waters of the canal breaking in upon the works of the railroad, Mr Stephenson had an iron trough made, 150 feet long, of the width of the canal, and exactly fitting the bottom. It was brought to the spot in three pieces, which were firmly welded together, and the trough was then floated into its place and sunk; the whole operation being completed without in the least interfering with the navigation of the canal. The railway works underneath were then proceeded with and finished.

Another line of the same series constructed by George Stephenson, was the York and North Midland, extending from Normanton – a point on the Midland Railway – to York; but it was a line of easy formation, traversing a comparatively level country.

During the time that our engineer was engaged in superintending the execution of these undertakings, he was occupied upon other projected railways in various parts of the country. He surveyed several lines in the neighbourhood of Glasgow, and afterwards routes along the east coast from Newcastle to Edinburgh, with the view of completing the main line of communication with London. When out on foot in the fields, on these occasions, he was ever foremost in the march; and he delighted to test the prowess of his companions by a good jump at any hedge or ditch that lay in their way. His companions used to remark his singular quickness of observation. Nothing escaped his attention – the trees, the crops, the birds, or the farmer's stock; and he was usually full of lively conversation, everything in nature affording him an opportunity for making some striking remark, or propounding some ingenious theory. When taking a flying survey of a new line, his keen observation proved very useful to him, for he rapidly noted the general configuration of the country, and inferred its geological structure. He afterwards remarked to a friend, 'I have planned many a railway travelling along in a postchaise, and following the natural line of the country.' And it was remarkable that his first impressions of the direction to be taken almost invariably proved correct; and there are few of the lines surveyed and recommended by him which have not been executed, either during his lifetime or since. As an illustration of his quick and shrewd observation on such occasions, we may mention that when employed to lay out a line to connect Manchester, through Macclesfield, with the Potteries, the gentleman who accompanied him on the journey of inspection cautioned him to provide large accommodation for carrying off the water, observing: 'You must not judge by the appearance of the brooks; for after heavy rains these hills pour down volumes of water, of which you can have no conception.' 'Pooh! pooh! *don't I see your bridges?*' replied the engineer. He had noted the details of each as he passed along.

Among the other projects which occupied his attention about the same time, were the projected lines between Chester and Holyhead, between Leeds and Bradford, and between Lancaster and Maryport by the western coast. This latter was intended to form part of a west-coast line to Scotland; Stephenson favouring it partly because of the flatness of the gradients, and also because it could be formed at comparatively small cost, while it would open out a valuable iron-mining district, from which a large traffic in ironstone was expected. One of its collateral advantages, in the engineer's opinion, was, that by forming the railway directly across Morecambe Bay, on the north-west coast of Lancashire, a large tract of valuable land might be reclaimed from the sea, the sale of which would considerably reduce the cost of the works. He estimated that by means of a solid embankment across the bay, not less than 40,000 acres of rich alluvial land would be gained. He proposed to carry the road across the ten miles of sands which lie between Poulton, near Lancaster, and Humphrey Head on the opposite coast, forming the line in a segment of a circle of five miles' radius. His plan was to drive in piles across the entire length, forming a solid fence of stone blocks on the land side for the purpose of retaining the sand and silt brought down by the rivers from the interior. The embankment would then be raised from time to time as the deposit accumulated, until the land was filled up to high-water mark; provision being made by means of sufficient arches, for the flow of the river waters into the bay. The execution of the railway after this plan would, however, have occupied more years than the promoters of the West Coast line were disposed to wait; and eventually Mr Locke's more direct but uneven line by Shap Fell was adopted. A railway has since been carried across the head of the bay; and it is not improbable that Stephenson's larger scheme of reclaiming the vast tract of land now left bare at each receding tide, may yet be carried out.

While occupied in carrying out the great railway undertakings which we have above so briefly described, Mr Stephenson's home continued, for the greater part of the time, to be at Alton Grange, near Leicester. But he was so much occupied in travelling about from one committee of directors to another – one week in England, another in Scotland, and probably the next in Ireland – that he often did not see his home for weeks together. He had also to make frequent inspections of the various important and difficult works in progress, especially on the Midland and Manchester and Leeds lines; besides occasionally going to Newcastle to see how the locomotive works were going on there. During the three years ending in 1837 – perhaps the busiest years of his life* – he travelled by postchaise alone upwards of 20,000 miles, and yet not less than six months out of the three years were spent in London. Hence there is comparatively little to record of Mr Stephenson's private life at this period; during which he had scarcely a moment that he could call his own.

His correspondence increased so much, that he found it necessary to engage a private secretary, who accompanied him on his

* During this period he was engaged on the North Midland, extending from Derby to Leeds; the York and North Midland, from Normanton to York; the Manchester and Leeds; the Birmingham and Derby, and the Sheffield and Rotherham Railways; the whole of these, of which he was principal engineer, having been authorized in 1836. In that session alone, powers were obtained for the construction of 214 miles of new railways under his direction, at an expenditure of upwards of five millions sterling.

journeys. He was himself exceedingly averse to writing letters. The comparatively advanced age at which he learnt the art of writing, and the nature of his duties while engaged at the Killingworth colliery, precluded that facility in correspondence which only constant practice can give. He gradually, however, acquired great facility in dictation, and possessed the power of labouring continuously at this work; the gentleman who acted as his secretary in 1835, having informed us that during his busy season he one day dictated not fewer than thirty-seven letters, several of them embodying the results of much close thinking and calculation. On another occasion, he dictated reports and letters for twelve continuous hours, until his secretary was ready to drop off his chair from sheer exhaustion, and at length he pleaded for a suspension of the labour. This great mass of correspondence, although closely bearing on the subjects under discussion, was not, however, of a kind to supply the biographer with matter for quotation, or give that insight into the life and character of the writer which the letters of literary men so often furnish. They were, for the most part, letters of mere business, relating to works in progress, parliamentary contests, new surveys, estimates of cost, and railway policy, curt, and to the point; in short, the letters of a man every moment of whose time was precious. He was also frequently called upon to inspect and report upon colliery works, salt works, brass and copper works, and such like, in addition to his own colliery and railway business. And occasionally he would run up to London, for the purpose of attending in person to the preparation and deposit of the plans and sections of the projected undertakings of which he had been appointed engineer.

Fortunately Stephenson possessed a facility of sleeping, which enabled him to pass through this enormous amount of fatigue and labour without injury to his health. He had been trained in a hard school, and could bear with ease conditions which, to men more softly nurtured, would have been the extreme of physical discomfort. Many, many nights he snatched his sleep while travelling in his chaise; and at break of day he would be at work, surveying until dark, and this for weeks in succession. His whole powers seemed to be under the control of his will, for he could wake at any hour, and go to work at once. It was difficult for secretaries and assistants to keep up with such a man.

It is pleasant to record that in the midst of these engrossing occupations, his heart remained as soft and loving as ever. In springtime he would not be debarred of his boyish pursuit of birdnesting; but would go rambling along the hedges spying for nests. In the autumn he went nutting, and when he could snatch a few minutes he indulged in his old love of gardening. His uniform kindness and good temper, and his communicative, intelligent disposition, made him a great favourite with the neighbouring farmers, to whom he could volunteer much valuable advice on agricultural operations, drainage, ploughing, and labour-saving processes. Sometimes he took a long rural ride on his favourite 'Bobby', now growing old, but as fond of his master as ever. Towards the end of his life, 'Bobby' lived in clover, its master's pet, doing no work; and he died at Tapton, in 1845, more than twenty years old.

During one of George's brief sojourns at the Grange, he found time to write to his son a touching account of a pair of robins that had built their nest within one of the upper chambers of the house. One day he observed a robin fluttering outside the windows, and beating its wings against the panes, as if eager to gain admission. He went upstairs, and there found, in a retired part of one of the rooms, a robin's nest, with one of the parent birds sitting over three or four young – all dead. The excluded bird outside still beat against the panes; and on the window being let down, it flew into the room, but was so exhausted that it dropped upon the floor. Mr Stephenson took up the bird, carried it downstairs, had it warmed and fed. The poor robin revived, and for a time was one of his pets. But it shortly died too, as if unable to recover from the privations it had endured during its three days' fluttering and beating at the windows. It appeared that the room had been unoccupied, and, the sash having been let down, the robins had taken the opportunity of building their nest within it; but the servant having closed the window again, the calamity befell the birds which so strongly excited Mr Stephenson's sympathies. An incident such as this, trifling though it may seem, gives the true key to the heart of the man.

The amount of their Parliamentary business having greatly increased with the projection of new lines of railway, the Stephensons found it necessary to set up an office in London in 1836. George's first office was at 9 Duke Street, Westminster, from whence he removed in the following year to 30½ Great George Street. That office was the busy scene of railway politics for several years. There consultations were held, schemes were matured, deputations were received, and many projectors called upon our engineer for the purpose of submitting to him their plans of railways and railway working. His private secretary at the time has informed us that at the end of the first Parliamentary session in which he had been engaged as engineer for more companies than one, it became necessary for him to give instructions as to the preparation of the accounts to be rendered to the respective companies. In the simplicity of his heart, he directed Mr Binns to take his full time at the rate of ten guineas a day, and charge the railway companies in the proportion in which he had been actually employed on their respective business during each day. When Robert heard of this instruction, he went directly to his father and expostulated with him against this unprofessional course; and, other influences being brought to bear upon him, George at length reluctantly consented to charge as other engineers did, an entire day's fee to each of the Companies for which he was concerned while their business was going forward; but he cut down the number of days charged for and reduced the daily amount from ten to seven guineas.

Besides his journeys at home, Mr Stephenson was on more than one occasion called abroad on railway business. Thus, at the desire of King Leopold, he made several visits to Belgium to assist the Belgian engineers in laying out the national lines of that kingdom. That enlightened monarch at an early period discerned the powerful instrumentality of railways in developing a country's resources, and he determined at the earliest possible period to adopt them as the great high-roads of the nation. The country, being rich in coal and minerals, had great manufacturing capabilities. It had good ports, fine navigable rivers, abundant canals, and a teeming, industrious population. Leopold perceived that railways were eminently calculated to bring the industry of the country into full play, and to render the riches of the provinces available to the rest of the kingdom. He therefore openly declared himself the promoter of public railways throughout Belgium. A system of lines was projected, at his instance, connecting Brussels with the chief towns and cities of the kingdom; extending from Ostend eastward to the Prussian frontier, and from Antwerp southward to the French frontier.

Mr Stephenson and his son, as the leading railway engineers of England, were consulted by the King on the best mode of carrying out his important plans, as early as 1835. In the course of that year they visited Belgium, and had several interesting conferences with Leopold and his ministers on the subject of the proposed railways. The King then appointed George Stephenson by royal ordinance a Knight of the Order of Leopold. At the invitation of the monarch, Mr Stephenson made a second visit to Belgium in 1837, on the occasion of the public opening of the line from Brussels to Ghent. At Brussels there was a public procession, and another at Ghent on the arrival of the train. Stephenson and his party accompanied it to the Public Hall, there to dine with the chief Ministers of State, the municipal authorities, and about five hundred of the principal inhabitants of the city; the English Ambassador being also present. After the King's health and a few others had been drunk, that of Mr Stephenson was proposed; on which the whole assembly rose up, amidst great excitement and loud applause, and made their way to where he sat, in order to jingle glasses with him, greatly to his own amazement. On the day following, our engineer dined with the King and Queen at their own table at Laaken, by special invitation; afterwards accompanying his Majesty and suite to a public ball given by the municipality of Brussels, in honour of the opening of the line to Ghent, as well as of their distinguished English guest. On entering the room, the general and excited inquiry was, 'Which is Stephenson?' The English engineer had not before imagined that he was esteemed to be so great a man.

The London and Birmingham Railway having been completed in September 1838, after being about five years in progress, the great main system of railway communication between London, Liverpool, and Manchester was then opened to the public. For some months previously, the line had been partially opened, coaches performing the journey between Denbigh Hall (near Wolverton) and Rugby, the works of the Kilsby tunnel being still incomplete. It was already amusing to hear the complaints of the travellers about the slowness of the coaches as compared with the railway, though the coaches travelled at the speed of eleven miles an hour. The comparison of comfort was also greatly to the disparagement of the coaches. Then the railway train could accommodate any quantity, while the road conveyances were limited; and when a press of travellers occurred – as on the occasion of the Queen's coronation – the greatest inconvenience was experienced, and as much as £10 was paid for a seat on a donkey-chaise between Rugby and Denbigh. On the opening of the railway throughout, of course all this inconvenience and delay was brought to an end.

Numerous other openings of railways constructed by Mr Stephenson took place about the same time. The Birmingham and Derby line was opened for traffic in August 1839; the Sheffield and Rotherham in November 1839; and in the course of the following

year, the Midland, the York and North Midland, the Chester and
Crewe, the Chester and Birkenhead, the Manchester and Birmingham, the Manchester and Leeds, and the Maryport and Carlisle
railways, were all publicly opened in whole or in part. Thus 321
miles of railway (exclusive of the London and Birmingham)
constructed under Mr Stephenson's superintendence, at a
cost of upwards of eleven millions sterling, were, in the course
of about two years, added to the traffic accommodation of the
country.

The ceremonies which accompanied the public opening of these
lines were often of an interesting character. The adjoining population held general holiday; bands played, banners waved, and
assembled thousands cheered the passing trains amidst the occasional booming of cannon. The proceedings were usually wound
up by a public dinner; and in the course of the speeches which
followed, Mr Stephenson would revert to his favourite topic – the
difficulties which he had early encountered in the promotion of the
railway system, and in establishing the superiority of the locomotive.
On such occasions he always took great pleasure in alluding to the
services rendered to himself and the public by the young men
brought up under his eye – his pupils at first, and afterwards his
assistants. No great master ever possessed a more devoted band of
assistants and fellow-workers than he did. It was one of the most
marked evidences of his own admirable tact and judgement that
he selected, with such undeviating correctness, the men best fitted
to carry out his plans. Indeed, the ability to accomplish great
things, and to carry grand ideas into practical effect, depends in no
small measure on that intuitive knowledge of character, which
Stephenson possessed in so remarkable a degree.

At the dinner in York, which followed the partial opening of the
York and North Midland Railway, Mr Stephenson said, 'he was
sure they would appreciate his feelings when he told them, that
when he first began railway business his hair was black, although
it was now grey; and that he began his life's labour as but a poor
ploughboy. About thirty years since, he had applied himself to the
study of how to generate high velocities by mechanical means. He
thought he had solved that problem; and they had for themselves
seen, that day, what perseverance had brought him too. He was,
on that occasion, only too happy to have an opportunity of
acknowleding that he had, in the latter portion of his career,
received much most valuable assistance, particularly from young
men brought up in his manufactory. Whenever talent showed itself

in a young man he had always given that talent encouragement where he could, and he would continue to do so.'

That this was no exaggerated statement is amply proved by many facts which redound to Mr Stephenson's credit. He was no niggard of encouragement and praise when he saw honest industry struggling for a footing. Many were the young men whom, in the course of his useful career, he took by the hand and led steadily up to honour and emolument, simply because he had noted their zeal, diligence, and integrity. One youth excited his interest while working as a common carpenter on the Liverpool and Manchester line; and before many years had passed, he was recognized as an engineer of distinction. Another young man he found industriously working away at his bye-hours, and, admiring his diligence, engaged him for his private secretary, the gentleman shortly after rising to a position of eminent influence and usefulness. Indeed, nothing gave Mr Stephenson greater pleasure than in this way to help on any deserving youth who came under his observation, and, in his own expressive phrase, to 'make a man of him'.

The openings of the great main lines of railroad communication shortly proved the fallaciousness of the numerous rash prophecies which had been promulgated by the opponents of railways. The proprietors of the canals were astounded by the fact that, notwithstanding the immense traffic conveyed by rail, their own traffic and receipts continued to increase; and that, in common with other interests, they fully shared in the expansion of trade and commerce which had been so effectually promoted by the extension of the railway system. The cattle-owners were equally amazed to find the price of horse-flesh increasing with the extension of railways, and that the number of coaches running to and from the new railway-stations gave employment to a greater number of horses than under the old stage-coach system. Those who had prophesied the decay of the metropolis, and the ruin of the suburban cabbage-growers, in consequence of the approach of railways to London, were also disappointed; for, while the new roads let citizens out of London, they let country people in. Their action, in this respect, was centripetal as well as centrifugal. Tens of thousands who had never seen the metropolis could now visit it expeditiously and cheaply; and Londoners who had never visited the country, or but rarely, were enabled, at little cost of time or money, to see green fields and clear blue skies, far from the smoke and bustle of town. If the dear suburban-grown cabbages became depreciated in value, there were truck-loads of fresh-grown country cabbages to make amends for the loss: in this case, the 'partial evil' was a far more general good. The food of the metropolis became rapidly improved, especially in the supply of wholesome meat and vegetables. And then the price of coals – an article which, in this country, is as indispensable as daily food to all classes – was greatly reduced. What a blessing to the metropolitan poor is described in this single fact!

The prophecies of ruin and disaster to landlords and farmers were equally confounded by the openings of the railways. The agricultural communications, so far from being 'destroyed', as had been predicted, were immensely improved. The farmers were enabled to buy their coals, lime, and manure for less money, while they obtained a readier access to the best markets for their stock and farm-produce. Notwithstanding the predictions to the contrary, their cows gave milk as before, their sheep fed and fattened, and even skittish horses ceased to shy at the passing locomotive. The smoke of the engines did not obscure the sky, nor were farm-yards burnt up by the fire thrown from the locomotives. The farming classes were not reduced to beggary; on the contrary, they soon felt that, so far from having anything to dread, they had very much good to expect from the extension of railways.

Landlords also found that they could get higher rents for farms situated near a railway than at a distance from one. Hence they became clamorous for 'sidings'. They felt it to be a grievance to be placed at a distance from a station. After a railway had been once opened, not a landlord would consent to have the line taken from him. Owners who had fought the promoters before Parliament, and compelled them to pass their domains at a distance, at a vastly-increased expense in tunnels and deviations, now petitioned for branches and nearer station accommodation. Those who held property near towns, and had extorted large sums as compensation for the anticipated deterioration in the value of their building land, found a new demand for it springing up at greatly advanced prices. Land was now advertised for sale, with the attraction of being 'near a railway station'.

The prediction that, even if railways were made, the public would not use them, was also completely falsified by the results. The ordinary mode of fast travelling for the middle classes had heretofore been by mail-coach and stage-coach. Those who could not afford to pay the high prices charged for such conveyances went by waggon, and the poorer classes trudged on foot. George Stephenson was wont to say that he hoped to see the day when it would be cheaper for a poor man to travel by railway than to walk, and not many years passed before his expectation was fulfilled. In no country in the world is time worth more money than in England; and by saving time – the criterion of distance – the railway proved a great benefactor to men of industry in all classes.

It was some time before the more opulent, who could afford to post to town in aristocratic style, became reconciled to railway travelling. In the opinion of many, it was only another illustration of the levelling tendencies of the age. It put an end to that gradation of rank in travelling which was one of the few things left by which the nobleman could be distinguished from the Manchester manufacturer and bagman. But to younger sons of noble families the convenience and cheapness of the railway did not fail to recommend itself. One of these, whose eldest brother had just succeeded to an earldom, said one day to a railway manager: 'I like railways – they just suit young fellows like me with "nothing per annum paid quarterly". You know we can't afford to post, and it used to be deuced annoying to me, as I was jogging along on the box-seat of the stage-coach, to see the little Earl go by drawn by his four posters, and just look up at me and give me a nod. But now, with railways, it's different. It's true, he may take a first-class ticket, while I can only afford a second-class one, but *we both go the same pace.*'

For a time, however, many of the old families sent forward their servants and luggage by railroad, and condemned themselves to jog along the old highway in the accustomed family chariot, dragged by country post-horses. But the superior comfort of the railway shortly recommended itself to even the oldest families; posting went out of date; post-horses were with difficulty to be had along even the great high-roads; and nobles and servants, manufacturers and peasants, alike shared in the comfort, the convenience, and the despatch of railway travelling. The late Dr Arnold, of Rugby, regarded the opening of the London and Birmingham line as another great step accomplished in the march of civilization. 'I rejoice to see it,' he said, as he stood on one of the bridges over the railway, and watched the train flashing along under him, and away through the distant hedgerows: 'I rejoice to see it, and to think that feudality is gone for ever: it is so great a blessing to think that any one evil is really extinct.'

It was long before the late Duke of Wellington would trust himself behind a locomotive. The fatal accident to Mr Huskisson, which had happened before his eyes, contributed to prejudice him

strongly against railways, and it was not until the year 1843 that
he performed his first trip on the South-Western Railway, in
attendance upon her Majesty. Prince Albert had for some time
been accustomed to travel by railway alone, but in 1842 the Queen
began to make use of the same mode of conveyance between
Windsor and London. Even Colonel Sibthorpe was eventually compelled to acknowledge its utility. For a time he continued to post
to and from the country as before. Then he compromised the
matter by taking a railway ticket for the long journey, and posting
only a stage or two nearest town; until, at length, he undisguisedly
committed himself, like other people, to the express train, and
performed the journey throughout upon what he had formerly
denounced as 'the infernal railroad'.

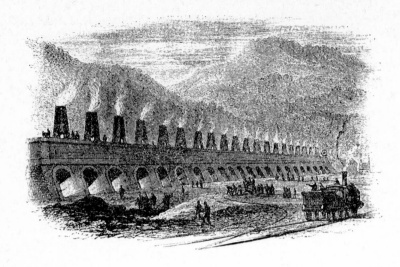

CHAPTER XV — GEORGE STEPHENSON'S COAL MINES — APPEARS AT MECHANICS' INSTITUTES — HIS OPINION ON RAILWAY SPEEDS — ATMOSPHERIC SYSTEM — RAILWAY MANIA — VISITS TO BELGIUM AND SPAIN

WHILE George Stephenson was engaged in carrying on the works of the Midland Railway in the neighbourhood of Chesterfield, several seams of coal were cut through in the Clay-cross Tunnel, and it occurred to him that if mines were opened out there, the railway would provide the means of a ready sale for the article in the Midland counties, and as far south as even the metropolis itself.

At a time when everybody else was sceptical as to the possibility of coals being carried from the Midland counties to London, and sold there at a price to compete with those which were sea-borne, he declared his firm conviction that the time was fast approaching when the London market would be regularly supplied with north-country coals led by railway. One of the greatest advantages of railways, in his opinion, was that they would bring iron and coal, the staple products of the country, to the doors of all England. 'The strength of Britain,' he would say, 'lies in her iron and coal beds; and the locomotive is destined, above all other agencies, to bring it forth. The Lord Chancellor now sits upon a bag of wool; but wool has long ceased to be emblematical of the staple commodity of England. He ought rather to sit upon a bag of coals,

though it might not prove quite so comfortable a seat. Then think
of the Lord Chancellor being addressed as the noble and learned
lord *on the coal-sack!* I am afraid it wouldn't answer, after all.'

To one gentleman he said: 'We want from the coal-mining, the
iron-producing and manufacturing districts, a great railway for
the carriage of these valuable products. We want, if I may so say,
a stream of steam running directly through the country, from the
North to London, and from other similar districts to London.
Speed is not so much an object as utility and cheapness. It will not
do to mix up the heavy merchandise and coal trains with the
passenger trains. Coal and most kinds of goods can wait; but passengers will not. A less perfect road and less expensive works will do
well enough for coal trains, if run at a low speed; and if the line be
flat, it is not of much consequence whether it be direct or not.
Whenever you put passenger trains on a line, all the other trains
must be run at high speeds to keep out of their way. But coal
trains run at high speeds pull the road to pieces, besides causing
large expenditure in locomotive power; and I doubt very much
whether they will pay after all; but a succession of long coal trains, if
run at from ten to fourteen miles an hour, would pay very well. Thus
the Stockton and Darlington Company made a larger profit when
running coal at low speeds at a halfpenny a ton per mile, than they
have been able to do since they put on their fast passenger
trains, when everything must needs be run faster, and a much larger
proportion of the gross receipts is absorbed by working expenses.'

In advocating these views, Mr Stephenson was considerably
ahead of his time; and although he did not live to see his anticipations fully realized as to the supply of the London coal-market, he
was nevertheless the first to point out, and to some extent to prove,
the practicability of establishing a profitable coal trade by railway
between the northern counties and the metropolis. So long, however, as the traffic was conducted on main passenger lines at
comparatively high speeds, it was found that the expenditure on
tear and wear of road and locomotive power, not to mention the
increased risk of carrying on the first-class passenger traffic with
which it was mixed up, necessarily left a very small margin of
profit; and hence Mr Stephenson was in the habit of urging the
propriety of constructing a railway which should be exclusively
devoted to goods and mineral traffic run at low speeds as the only
condition on which large railway traffic of that sort could be
profitably conducted.

Having induced some of his Liverpool friends to join him in a coal-mining adventure at Chesterfield, a lease was taken of the Claycross estate, then for sale, and operations were shortly after begun. At a subsequent period Mr Stephenson extended his coal-mining operations in the same neighbourhood; and in 1841 he himself entered into a contract with owners of land in adjoining town-ships for the working of the coal thereunder; and pits were opened on the Tapton estate on an extensive scale. About the same time he erected great lime-works, close to the Ambergate station of the Midland Railway, from which, when in full operation he was able to turn out upwards of 200 tons a day. The limestone was brought on a tramway from the village of Crich, two or three miles distant, the coal being supplied from his adjoining Claycross colliery. The works were on a scale such as had not before been attempted by any private individual engaged in a similar trade; and we believe they proved very successful.

Tapton House was included in the lease of one of the collieries, and as it was conveniently situated – being, as it were, a central point on the Midland Railway, from which he could readily pro-ceed north or south, on his journeys of inspection of the various lines then under construction in the Midland and northern coun-ties – he took up his residence there, and it continued his home until the close of his life.

Tapton House is a large roomy brick mansion, beautifully situated amidst woods, upon a commanding eminence, about a mile to the north-east of the town of Chesterfield. Green fields dotted with fine trees slope away from the house in all directions. The surrounding country is undulating and highly picturesque. North and south the eye ranges over a vast extent of lovely scenery; and on the west, looking over the town of Chesterfield, with its church and crooked spire, the extensive range of the Derbyshire hills bounds the distance. The Midland Railway skirts the western edge of the park in a deep rock cutting, and the shrill whistle of the locomotive sounds near at hand as the trains speed past. The gardens and pleasure-grounds adjoining the house were in a very neglected state when Mr Stephenson first went to Tapton; and he promised himself, when he had secured rest and leisure from business, that he would put a new face upon both. The first im-provement he made was cutting a woodland footpath up the hillside, by which he at the same time added a beautiful feature to the park, and secured a shorter road to the Chesterfield station. But it was some years before he found time to carry into effect his contemplated improvements in the adjoining gardens and pleasure-grounds. He had so long been accustomed to laborious pursuits, and felt himself still so full of work, that he could not at once settle down into the habit of quietly enjoying the fruits of his industry.

He had no difficulty in usefully employing his time. Besides directing the mining operations at Claycross, the establishment of the lime-kilns at Ambergate, and the construction of the extensive railways still in progress, he occasionally paid visits to Newcastle, where his locomotive manufactory was now in full work, and the proprietors were reaping the advantages of his early foresight in an abundant measure of prosperity. One of his most interesting visits to the place was in 1838, on the occasion of the meeting of the British Association there, when he acted as one of the Vice-Presidents in the section of Mechanical Science. Extraordinary changes had occurred in his own fortunes, as well as in the face of the country, since he had first appeared before a scientific body in Newcastle – the members of the Literary and Philosophical Institute – to submit his safety-lamp for their examination. Twenty-three years had passed over his head, full of honest work, of manful struggle; and the humble 'colliery engine-wright of the name of Stephenson' had achieved an almost world-wide reputation as a public benefactor. His fellow-townsmen, therefore, could not hesitate to recognize his merits and do honour to his name. During the sittings of the Association, Mr Stephenson took the opportunity of paying a visit to Killingworth, accompanied by some of the distinguished *savans* whom he numbered among his friends. He there pointed out to them, with a degree of honest pride, the cottage in which he had lived for so many years, showed what parts of it had been his own handiwork, and told them the story of the sundial over the door, describing the study and the labour it had cost him and his son to calculate its dimensions, and fix it in its place. The dial had been serenely numbering the hours through the busy years that had elapsed since that humble dwelling had been his home; during which the Killingworth locomotive had become a great working power, and its contriver had established the railway system, which was now rapidly becoming extended in all parts of the world.

About the same time, his services were very much in request at the meetings of Mechanics' Institutes held throughout the northern counties. From an early period in his history, he had taken an active interest in these institutions. While residing at Newcastle in 1824, shortly after his locomotive foundry had been started in Forth Street, he presided at a public meeting held in that town for

the purpose of establishing a Mechanics' Institute. The meeting
was held; but as George Stephenson was a man comparatively
unknown even in Newcastle at that time, his name failed to secure
'an influential attendance'. Among those who addressed the meeting on the occasion was Joseph Locke, then his pupil, and afterwards his rival as an engineer. The local papers scarcely noticed
the proceedings; yet the Mechanics' Institute was founded, and
struggled into existence. Years passed, and it was now felt to be an
honour to secure Mr Stephenson's presence at any public meetings
held for the promotion of popular education. Among the Mechanics' Institutes in his immediate neighbourhood at Tapton, were
those of Belper and Chesterfield; and at their soirées he was a frequent and a welcome visitor. On these occasions he loved to tell his
auditors of the difficulties which had early beset him through want
of knowledge, and of the means by which he had overcome them.
His grand text was PERSEVERE; and there was manhood in the
very word.

On more than one occasion, the author had the pleasure of
listening to George Stephenson's homely but forcible addresses at
the annual soirées of the Leeds Mechanics' Institute. He was
always an immense favourite with his audiences there. His personal
appearance was greatly in his favour. A handsome, ruddy, expressive face, lit up by bright dark-blue eyes, prepared one for his
earnest words when he stood up to speak and the cheers had subsided which invariably hailed his rising. He was not glib, but he
was very impressive. And who, so well as he, could serve as a guide
to the working man in his endeavours after higher knowledge? His
early life had been all struggle – encounter with difficulty – groping
in the dark after greater light, but always earnestly and perse-
veringly. His words were therefore all the more weighty, since he
spoke from the fulness of his own experience.

Nor did he remain a mere inactive spectator of the improvements in railway working which increasing experience from day to
day suggested. He continued to contrive improvements in the locomotive, and to mature his invention of the carriage-brake. When
examined before the Select Committee on Railways in 1841, his
mind seems principally to have been impressed with the necessity
which existed for adopting a system of self-acting brakes; stating
that, in his opinion, this was the most important arrangement that
could be provided for increasing the safety of railway travelling.
'I believe,' he said, 'that if self-acting brakes were put upon every
carriage, scarcely any accident could take place.' His plan con-

sisted in employing the momentum of the running train to throw
his proposed brakes into action, immediately on the moving power
of the engine being checked. He would also have these brakes under
the control of the guard, by means of a connecting line running
along the whole length of the train, by which they should at once
be thrown out of gear when necessary. At the same time he suggested, as an additional means of safety, that the signals of the line
should be self-acting, and worked by the locomotives as they
passed along the railway. He considered the adoption of this plan
of so much importance, that, with a view to the public safety, he
would even have it enforced upon railway companies by the legislature. At the same time he was of opinion that it was the interest
of the companies themselves to adopt the plan, as it would save
great tear and wear of engines, carriages, tenders, and brake-vans,
besides greatly diminishing the risk of accidents upon railways.

While before the same Committee, he took the opportunity of
stating his views with reference to railway speed, about which
wild ideas were then afloat – one gentleman of celebrity having
publicly expressed the opinion that a speed of 100 miles an hour
was practicable in railway travelling! Not many years had passed
since George Stephenson had been pronounced insane for stating
his conviction that 12 miles an hour could be performed by the
locomotive; but now that he had established the fact, and greatly
exceeded that speed, he was thought behind the age because he
recommended the rate to be limited to 40 miles an hour. He said:
'I do not like either 40 or 50 miles an hour upon any line – I think
it is an unnecessary speed; and if there is danger upon a railway,
it is high velocity that creates it. I should say no railway ought to
exceed 40 miles an hour on the most favourable gradient; but upon
a curved line the speed ought not to exceed 24 or 25 miles an hour.'
He had, indeed, constructed for the Great Western Railway an
engine capable of running 50 miles an hour with a load, and 80
miles without one. But he never was in favour of a hurricane speed
of this sort, believing it could only be accomplished at an unnecessary increase both of danger and expense.

'It is true,' he observed on other occasions, 'I have said the
locomotive engine *might* be made to travel 100 miles an hour; but
I always put a qualification on this, namely, as to what speed
would best suit the public. The public may, however, be unreasonable; and 50 or 60 miles an hour *is* an unreasonable speed.
Long before railway travelling became general, I said to my friends
that there was no limit to the speed of the locomotive, *provided the*

works could be made to stand. But there are limits to the strength of iron, whether it be manufactured into rails or locomotives; and there is a point at which both rails and tyres must break. Every increase of speed, by increasing the strain upon the road and the rolling-stock, brings us nearer to that point. At 30 miles a slighter road will do, and less perfect rolling-stock may be run upon it with safety. But if you increase the speed by say 10 miles, then everything must be greatly strengthened. You must have heavier engines, heavier and better-fastened rails, and all your working expenses will be immediately increased. I think I know enough of mechanics to know where to stop. I know that a pound will weigh a pound, and that no more should be put upon an iron rail than it will bear. If you could ensure perfect iron, perfect rails, and perfect locomotives, I grant 50 miles an hour or more might be run with safety on a level railway. But then you must not forget that iron, even the best, will "tire", and with constant use will become more and more liable to break at the weakest point – perhaps where there is a secret flaw that the eye cannot detect. Then look at the rubbishy rails now manufactured on the contract system – some of them little better than cast metal: indeed, I have seen rails break merely on being thrown from the truck on to the ground. How is it possible for such rails to stand a 20- or 30-ton engine dashing over them at the speed of 50 miles an hour? No, no,' he would conclude, 'I am in favour of low speeds because they are safe, and because they are economical; and you may rely upon it that, beyond a certain point, with every increase of speed there is an increase in the element of danger.'

When railways became the subject of popular discussion, many new and unsound theories were started with reference to them, which Stephenson opposed as calculated, in his opinion, to bring discredit on the locomotive system. One of these was with reference to what were called 'undulating lines'. Among others, Dr Lardner, who had originally been somewhat sceptical about the powers of the locomotive, now promulgated the idea that a railway constructed with rising and falling gradients would be practically as easy to work as a line perfectly level. Mr Badnell went even beyond him, for he held that an undulating railway was much better than a level one for purposes of working. For a time, this theory found favour, and the 'undulating system' was extensively adopted; but Mr Stephenson never ceased to inveigh against it; and experience has amply proved that his judgement was correct. His practice, from the beginning of his career until the end of it,

was to secure a road as nearly as possible on a level, following the
course of the valleys and the natural line of the country: preferring
to go round a hill rather than to tunnel under it or carry his railway
over it, and often making a considerable circuit to secure good,
workable gradients. He studied to lay out his lines so that long
trains of minerals and merchandise, as well as passengers, might be
hauled along them at the least possible expenditure of locomotive
power. He had long before ascertained, by careful experiments at
Killingworth, that the engine expends half of its power in overcoming a rising gradient of 1 in 260, which is about 20 feet in the
mile; and that when the gradient is so steep as 1 in 100, not less
than three-fourths of its power is sacrificed in ascending the
acclivity. He never forgot the valuable practical lesson taught him
by the early trials which he had made and registered long before
the advantages of railways had been recognized. He saw clearly
that the longer flat line must eventually prove superior to the
shorter line of steep gradients as respected its paying qualities. He
urged that, after all, the power of the locomotive was but limited;
and, although he and his son had done more than any other men
to increase its working capacity, it provoked him to find that every
improvement made in it was neutralized by the steep gradients
which the new school of engineers were setting it to overcome. On
one occasion, when Robert Stephenson stated before a Parliamentary Committee that every successive improvement in the
locomotive was being rendered virtually nugatory by the difficult and
almost impracticable gradients proposed on many of the new lines,
his father, on his leaving the witness-box, went up to him, and said,
'Robert, you never spoke truer words than those in all your life.'

To this it must be added, that in urging these views Mr Stephenson was strongly influenced by commercial considerations. He had
no desire to build up his reputation at the expense of railway
shareholders, nor to obtain engineering éclat by making 'ducks and
drakes' of their money. He was persuaded that, in order to secure
the practical success of railways, they must be so laid out as not
only to prove of decided public utility, but also to be worked
economically and to the advantage of their proprietors. They were
not government roads, but private ventures – in fact, commercial
speculations. He therefore endeavoured to render them financially
profitable; and he repeatedly declared that if he did not believe
they could be 'made to pay', he would have nothing to do with
them. He was not influenced by the sordid consideration of what
he could *make* out of any company that employed him; indeed, in

many cases he voluntarily gave up his claim to remuneration where the promoters of schemes which he thought praiseworthy had suffered serious loss. Thus, when the first application was made to Parliament for the Chester and Birkenhead Railway Bill, the promoters were defeated. They repeated their application, on the understanding that in event of their succeeding, the engineer and surveyor were to be paid their costs in respect of the defeated measure. The Bill was successful, and to several parties their costs were paid. Mr Stephenson's amounted to £800, and he very nobly said, 'You have had an expensive career in Parliament; you have had a great struggle; you are a young Company; you cannot afford to pay this amount of money. I will reduce it to £200, and I will not ask you for that £200 until your shares are at £20 premium: for whatever may be the reverses you will go through, I am satisfied I shall live to see the day when your shares will be at £20 premium, and when I can legally and honourably claim that £200.' We may add that the shares did eventually rise to the premium specified, and the engineer was no loser by his generous conduct in the transaction.

Another novelty of the time, with which George Stephenson had to contend, was the substitution of atmospheric pressure for locomotive steam-power in the working of railways. The idea of obtaining motion by means of atmospheric pressure is said to have originated with Denis Papin, more than 150 years ago; but it slept until revived in 1810 by Mr Medhurst, who published a pamphlet to prove the practicability of carrying letters and goods by air. In 1824, Mr Vallance of Brighton took out a patent for projecting passengers through a tube large enough to contain a train of carriages; the tube being previously exhausted of its atmospheric air. The same idea was afterwards taken up, in 1835, by Mr Pinkus, an ingenious American. Scientific gentlemen, Dr Lardner and Mr Clegg among others, advocated the plan; and an association was formed to carry it into effect. Shares were created, and £18,000 raised: and a model apparatus was exhibited in London. Mr Vignolles took his friend Stephenson to see the model; and after carefully examining it, he observed emphatically, 'It won't do: it is only the fixed engines and ropes over again, in another form; and, to tell you the truth, I don't think this rope of wind will answer so well as the rope of wire did.' He did not think the principle would stand the test of practice, and he objected to the mode of applying the principle. After all, it was only a modification of the stationary-engine plan; and every day's experience was proving that fixed

engines could not compete with locomotives in point of efficiency
and economy. He stood by the locomotive engine; and subsequent
experience proved that he was right.

Messrs. Clegg and Samuda afterwards, in 1840, patented their
plan of an atmospheric railway; and they publicly tested its working on an unfinished portion of the West London Railway. The
results of the experiment were so satisfactory, that the directors of
the Dublin and Kingstown line adopted it between Kingstown and
Dalkey. The London and Croydon Company also adopted the
atmospheric principle; and their line was opened in 1845. The
ordinary mode of applying the power was to lay between the line
of rails a pipe, in which a large piston was inserted, and attached
by a shaft to the framework of a carriage. The propelling power
was the ordinary pressure of the atmosphere acting against the
piston in the tube on one side, a vacuum being created in the tube
on the other side of the piston by the working of a stationary
engine. Great was the popularity of the atmospheric system; and
still George Stephenson said 'It won't do: it's but a gimcrack.'
Engineers of distinction said he was prejudiced, and that he looked
upon the locomotive as a pet child of his own. 'Wait a little,' he
replied, 'and you will see that I am right.' It was generally supposed that the locomotive system was about to be snuffed out.
'Not so fast,' said Stephenson. 'Let us wait to see if it will pay.' He
never believed it would. It was ingenious, clever, scientific, and all
that; but railways were commercial enterprises, not toys; and if
the atmospheric railway could not work to a profit, it would not do.
Considered in this light, he even went so far as to call it 'a great
humbug'. 'Nothing will beat the locomotive,' said he, 'for
efficiency in all weathers, for economy in drawing loads of average
weight, and for power and speed as occasion may require.'

The atmospheric system was fairly and fully tried, and it was
found wanting. It was admitted to be an exceedingly elegant mode
of applying power; its devices were very skilful, and its mechanism
was most ingenious. But it was costly, irregular in action, and, in
particular kinds of weather, not to be depended upon. At best, it
was but a modification of the stationary-engine system, and experience prove it to be so expensive that it was shortly after entirely
abandoned in favour of locomotive power.*

* The question of the specific merits of the atmospheric as compared with
the fixed engine and locomotive systems, will be found fully discussed in
Robert Stephenson's able *Report on the Atmospheric Railway System*, 1844,
in which he gives the result of numerous observations and experiments

One of the remarkable results of the system of railway locomotion which George Stephenson had by his persevering labours
mainly contributed to establish, was the outbreak of the railway
mania towards the close of his professional career. The success of
the first main lines of railway naturally led to their extension into
many new districts; but a strongly speculative tendency soon
began to display itself, which contained in it the elements of great
danger.

The extension of railways had, up to the year 1844, been mainly
effected by men of the commercial classes, and the shareholders in
them principally belonged to the manufacturing districts, the
capitalists of the metropolis as yet holding aloof, and prophesying
disaster to all concerned in railway projects. But when the
lugubrious anticipations of the City men were found to be so
entirely falsified by the results – when, after the lapse of years, it
was ascertained that railway traffic rapidly increased and dividends steadily improved – a change came over the spirit of the
London capitalists. They then invested largely in railways, the
shares in which became a leading branch of business on the Stock
Exchange, and the prices of some rose to nearly double their
original value.

A stimulus was thus given to the projection of further lines, the
shares in most of which came out at a premium, and became the
subject of immediate traffic. A reckless spirit of gambling set in,
which completely changed the character and objects of railway
enterprise. The public outside the Stock Exchange became also
infected, and many persons utterly ignorant of railways, knowing
and caring nothing about their national uses, but hungering and
thirsting after premiums, rushed eagerly into the vortex. They
applied for allotments, and subscribed for shares in lines, of the
engineering character or probable traffic of which they knew
nothing. Provided they could but obtain allotments which they
could sell at a premium, and put the profit – in many cases the
only capital they possessed* – into their pocket, it was enough for

* The Marquis of Clanricarde brought under the notice of the House of
Lords, in 1845, that one Charles Guernsey, the son of a charwoman, and a
clerk in a broker's office, at 12s. a week, had his name down as a subscriber
for shares in the London and York line, for £52,000. Doubtless he had been
made useful for the purpose by the brokers, his employers.

made by him on the Kingstown Atmospheric Railway, with the object of
ascertaining whether the new power would be applicable for the working of
the Chester and Holyhead Railway, then under construction. His opinion
was decidedly against the atmospheric system.

them. The mania was not confined to the precincts of the Stock Exchange, but infected all ranks. It embraced merchants and manufacturers, gentry and shopkeepers, clerks in public offices, and loungers at the clubs. Noble lords were pointed at as 'stags'; there were even clergymen who were characterized as 'bulls'; and amiable ladies who had the reputation of 'bears', in the share markets. The few quiet men who remained uninfluenced by the speculation of the time were, in not a few cases, even reproached for doing injustice to their families, in declining to help themselves from the stores of wealth that were poured out on all sides.

Folly and knavery were, for a time, completely in the ascendant. The sharpers of society were let loose, and jobbers and schemers became more and more plentiful. They threw out railway schemes as lures to catch the unwary. They fed the mania with a constant succession of new projects. The railway papers became loaded with their advertisements. The post-office was scarcely able to distribute the multitude of prospectuses and circulars which they issued. For a time their popularity was immense. They rose like froth into the upper heights of society, and the flunkey FitzPlushe, by virtue of his supposed wealth, sat among peers and was idolized. Then was the harvest-time of scheming lawyers, parliamentary agents, engineers, surveyors, and traffic-takers, who were ready to take up any railway scheme however desperate, and to prove any amount of traffic even where none existed. The traffic in the credulity of their dupes was, however, the great fact that mainly concerned them, and of the profitable character of which there could be no doubt.

Mr Stephenson was anxiously entreated to lend his name to prospectuses during the railway mania; but he invariably refused. He held aloof from the headlong folly of the hour, and endeavoured to check it, but in vain. Had he been less scrupulous, and given his countenance to the numerous projects about which he was consulted, he might, without any trouble, have thus secured enormous gains; but he had no desire to accumulate a fortune without labour and without honour. He himself never speculated in shares. When he was satisfied as to the merits of any undertaking, he subscribed for a certain amount of capital in it, and held on, neither buying nor selling. At a dinner of the Leeds and Bradford directors at Ben Rydding in October 1844, before the mania had reached its height, he warned those present against the prevalent disposition towards railway speculation. It was, he said, like walking upon a piece of ice with shallows and deeps; the shallows were frozen over, and they would carry, but it required great caution to get over the deeps. He was satisfied that in the course of the next year many would step on to places not strong enough to carry them, and would get into the deeps; they would be taking shares, and afterwards be unable to pay the calls upon them. Yorkshiremen were reckoned clever men, and his advice to them was, to stick together and promote communication in their own neighbourhood, not to go abroad with their speculations. If any had done so, he advised them to get their money back as fast as they could, for if they did not they would not get it at all. He informed the company, at the same time, of his earliest holding of railway shares; it was in the Stockton and Darlington Railway, and the number he held was *three* – 'a very large capital for him to possess at the time'. But a Stockton friend was anxious to possess a share, and he sold him *one* at a premium of 33*s.*; he supposed he had been about the first man in England to sell a railway share at a premium.

During 1845, his son's offices in Great George Street, Westminster, were crowded with persons of various conditions seeking interviews, presenting very much the appearance of the levee of a minister of state. The burly figure of Mr Hudson, the 'Railway King', surrounded by an admiring group of followers, was often to be seen there; and a still more interesting person, in the estimation of many, was George Stephenson, dressed in black, his coat of somewhat old-fashioned cut, with square pockets in the tails. He wore a white neckcloth, and a large bunch of seals was suspended from his watch-ribbon. Altogether, he presented an appearance of health, intelligence, and good humour, that rejoiced one to look upon in that sordid, selfish, and eventually ruinous saturnalia of railway speculation.

Powers were granted by Parliament, in 1845, to construct not less than 2,883 miles of new railways in Britain, at an expenditure of about forty-four millions sterling! Yet the mania was not appeased; for in the following session of 1846, applications were made to Parliament for powers to raise £389,000,000 sterling for the construction of further lines; and powers were actually conceded for forming 4,790 miles (including 60 miles of tunnels), at a cost of about £120,000,000 sterling. During this session, Mr Stephenson appeared as engineer for only one new line, the Buxton, Macclesfield, Congleton, and Crewe Railway – a line in which, as a coal-owner, he was personally interested; and of three branch-lines in connection with existing companies for which he had long acted as engineer. At the same time, all the leading professional men were fully occupied, some of them appearing as consulting engineers for upwards of thirty lines each!

One of the features of the mania was the rage for 'direct lines' which everywhere displayed itself. There were 'Direct Manchester', 'Direct Exeter', 'Direct York', and, indeed, new direct lines between most of the large towns. The Marquis of Bristol, speaking in favour of the 'Direct Norwich and London' project, at a public meeting at Haverhill, said, 'If necessary, they might *make a tunnel beneath his very drawing-room*, rather than be defeated in their undertaking!' And the Rev. F. Litchfield, at a meeting in Banbury, on the subject of a line to that town, said 'He had laid down for himself a limit to his approbation of railways, at least of such as approached the neighbourhood with which he was connected, and that limit was, that he did not wish them to approach any nearer to him than *to run through his bedroom, with the bedposts for a station!*' How different was the spirit which influenced these noble lords and gentlemen but a few years before!

The House of Commons became thoroughly influenced by the prevailing excitement. Even the Board of Trade began to favour the views of the fast school of engineers. In their 'Report on the Lines projected in the Manchester and Leeds District', they promulgated some remarkable views respecting gradients, declaring themselves in favour of the 'undulating system'. They there stated that lines of an undulating character 'which have gradients of 1 in 70 or 1 in 80 distributed over them in short lengths, may be positively *better* lines, *i.e. more susceptible of cheap and expeditious working*, than others which have nothing steeper than 1 in 100 or 1 in 120!' They concluded by reporting in favour of the line which exhibited the worst gradients and the sharpest curves, chiefly on the ground that it could be constructed for less money.

Sir Robert Peel took occasion to advert to this Report in the House of Commons on 4 March following, as containing 'a novel and highly important view on the subject of gradients, which, he was certain, never could have been taken by any Committee of the House of Commons, however intelligent'; and he might have added, that the more intelligent, the less likely they were to arrive at any such conclusion. When Mr Stephenson saw this report of the Premier's speech in the newspapers of the following morning, he went forthwith to his son, and asked him to write a letter to Sir Robert Peel on the subject. He saw clearly that if these views were adopted, the utility and economy of railways would be seriously curtailed. 'These members of Parliament,' said he, 'are now as much disposed to exaggerate the powers of the locomotive, as they were to under-estimate them but a few years ago.' Robert accordingly wrote a letter for his father's signature, embodying the views which he so strongly entertained as to the importance of flat gradients, and referring to the experiments conducted by him many years before, in proof of the great loss of working power which was incurred on a line of steep as compared with easy gradients. It was clear, from the tone of Sir Robert Peel's speech in a subsequent debate, that he had carefully read and considered Mr Stephenson's practical observations on the subject; though it did not appear that he had come to any definite conclusion thereon, further than that he strongly approved of the Trent Valley Railway, by which Tamworth would be placed upon a direct main line of communication.

The result of the labours of Parliament was a tissue of legislative bungling, involving enormous loss to the public. Railway Bills were granted in heaps. Two hundred and seventy-two additional Acts were passed in 1846. Some authorized the construction of lines running almost parallel to existing railways, in order to afford the public 'the benefits of unrestricted competition'. Locomotive and atmospheric lines, broad-gauge and narrow-gauge lines, were granted without hesitation. Committees decided without judgement and without discrimination; it was a scramble for Bills, in which the most unscrupulous were the most successful.

Among the many ill-effects of the mania, one of the worst was that it introduced a low tone of morality into railway transactions. The bad spirit which had been evoked by it unhappily extended to the commercial classes, and many of the most flagrant swindles of recent times had their origin in the year 1845. Those who had suddenly gained large sums without labour, and also without honour, were too ready to enter upon courses of the wildest extravagance; and a false style of living shortly arose, the poisonous influence of which extended through all classes. Men began to look upon railways as instruments to job with. Persons, sometimes possessing information respecting railways, but more frequently possessing none, got upon boards for the purpose of promoting their individual objects, often in a very unscrupulous manner; landowners, to promote branch lines through their property; speculators in shares, to trade upon the exclusive information which they obtained; while some directors were appointed through the influence mainly of solicitors, contractors, or engineers, who used them as tools to serve their own ends. In this way the unfortunate proprietors were, in many cases, betrayed, and their property was shamefully squandered, much to the discredit of the railway system.

While the mania was at its height in England, railways were also being extended abroad, and George Stephenson was requested on several occasions to give the benefit of his advice to the directors of foreign undertakings. One of the most agreeable of these excursions was to Belgium in 1845. His special object was to examine the proposed line of the Sambre and Meuse Railway, for which a concession had been granted by the Belgian legislature. Arrived on the ground, he went carefully over the entire length of the proposed line, to Couvins, the Forest of Ardennes, and Rocroi, across the French frontier; examining the bearings of the coalfield, the slate and marble quarries, and the numerous iron-mines in existence between the Sambre and the Meuse, as well as carefully exploring the ravines which extended through the district, in order to satisfy himself that the best possible route had been selected. Mr Stephenson was delighted with the novelty of the journey, the beauty of the scenery, and the industry of the population. His companions were entertained by his ample and varied stores of practical information on all subjects, and his conversation was full of reminiscences of his youth, on which he always delighted to dwell in the society of his more intimate friends. The journey was varied by a visit to the coal-mines near Jemappe, where Stephenson examined with interest the mode adopted by the Belgian miners of draining the pits, inspecting their engines and braking machines, so familiar to him in early life.

The engineers of Belgium took the opportunity of Mr Stephenson's visit to their country to invite him to a magnificent banquet at Brussels. The Public Hall, in which they entertained him, was gaily decorated with flags, prominent among which was the Union Jack, in honour of their distinguished guest. A handsome marble pedestal, ornamented with his bust crowned with laurels, occupied one end of the room. The chair was occupied by M. Massui, the Chief Director of the National Railways of Belgium; and the most eminent scientific men of the kingdom were present. Their reception of 'the Father of railways' was of the most enthusiastic description. Mr Stephenson was greatly pleased with the entertainment. Not the least interesting incident of the evening was his observing, when the dinner was about half over, a model of a locomotive engine placed upon the centre table, under a triumphal arch. Turning suddenly to his friend Sopwith, he exclaimed, 'Do you see the "Rocket"?' The compliment thus paid him, was perhaps more prized than all the encomiums of the evening.

The next day (5 April) King Leopold invited him to a private interview at the palace. Accompanied by Mr Sopwith, he proceeded to Laaken, and was very cordially received by His Majesty. The king immediately entered into familiar conversation with him, discussing the railway project which had been the object of his visit to Belgium, and then the structure of the Belgian coalfields, his Majesty expressing his sense of the great importance of economy in a fuel which had become indispensable to the comfort and well-being of society, which was the basis of all manufactures, and the vital power of railway locomotion. The subject was always a favourite one with Mr Stephenson, and, encouraged by the king, he proceeded to describe to him the geological structure of Belgium, the original formation of coal, its subsequent elevation by volcanic forces, and the vast amount of denudation. In describing the coal-beds he used his hat as a sort of model to illustrate his meaning; and the eyes of the king were fixed upon it as he proceeded with his interesting description. The conversation then passed to the rise and progress of trade and manufactures, Mr Stephenson pointing out how closely they everywhere followed the coal, being mainly dependent upon it, as it were, for their very existence.

The king seemed greatly pleased with the interview, and at its close expressed himself obliged by the interesting information which the engineer had communicated. Shaking hands cordially with both the gentlemen, and wishing them success in their important undertakings, he bade them adieu. As they were leaving the palace Mr Stephenson, bethinking him of the model by which he had just been illustrating the Belgian coalfields, said to his friend, 'By the bye, Sopwith, I was afraid the king would see the inside of my hat; it's a shocking bad one!' Little could George Stephenson, when brakesman at a coal-pit, have dreamt that, in the course of his life, he should be admitted to an interview with a monarch, and describe to him the manner in which the geological foundations of his kingdom had been laid!

Mr Stephenson paid a second visit to Belgium in the course of the same year, on the business of the West Flanders Railway; and he had scarcely returned from it ere he made arrangements to proceed to Spain, for the purpose of examining and reporting upon a scheme then on foot for constructing 'the Royal North of Spain Railway'. A concession had been made by the Spanish Government of a line of railway from Madrid to the Bay of Biscay, and a numerous staff of engineers was engaged in surveying it. The directors of the Company had declined making the necessary deposits until more favourable terms had been secured; and Sir Joshua Walmsley, on their part, was about to visit Spain and press the Government on the subject. Mr Stephenson, whom he consulted, was alive to the difficulties of the office which Sir Joshua was induced to undertake, and offered to be his companion and adviser on the occasion, declining to receive any recompense beyond the simple expenses of the journey. He could only arrange to be absent for six weeks, and set out from England about the middle of September 1845.

The party was joined at Paris by Mr Mackenzie, the contractor for the Orleans and Tours Railway, then in course of construction, who took them over the works, and accompanied them as far as Tours. They soon reached the great chain of the Pyrenees, and crossed over into Spain. It was on a Sunday evening, after a long day's toilsome journey through the mountains, that the party suddenly found themselves in one of those beautiful secluded valleys lying amidst the Western Pyrenees. A small hamlet lay before them, consisting of some thirty or forty houses and a fine old church. The sun was low on the horizon, and, under the wide porch, beneath the shadow of the church, were seated nearly all the inhabitants of the place. They were dressed in their holiday attire. The bright bits of red and amber colour in the dresses of the women, and the gay sashes of the men, formed a striking picture, on which the travellers gazed in silent admiration. It was something entirely novel and unexpected. Beside the villagers sat two venerable old men, whose canonical hats indicated their quality as village pastors. Two groups of young women and children were dancing outside the porch to the accompaniment of a simple pipe; and within a hundred yards of them, some of the youths of the village were disporting themselves in athletic exercises; the whole being carried on beneath the fostering care of the old church, and with the sanction of its ministers. It was a beautiful scene, and deeply moved the travellers as they approached the principal group. The villagers greeted them courteously, supplied their present wants, and pressed upon them some fine melons, brought from their adjoining gardens. Mr Stephenson used afterwards to look back upon that simple scene, and speak of it as one of the most charming pastorals he had ever witnessed.

They shortly reached the site of the proposed railway, passing through Irun, St Sebastian, St Andero, and Bilbao, at which places they met deputations of the principal inhabitants who were interested in the subject of their journey. At Raynosa Stephenson carefully examined the mountain passes and ravines through which a railway could be made. He rose at break of day, and surveyed until the darkness set in; and frequently his resting-place at night was the floor of some miserable hovel. He was thus laboriously occupied for ten days, after which he proceeded across the province of Old Castile towards Madrid, surveying as he went. The proposed plan included the purchase of the Castile Canal; and that property was also surveyed. He next proceeded to El Escorial, situated at the foot of the Guadarama mountains, through which he found that it would be necessary to construct two formidable tunnels; added to which he ascertained that the country between El Escorial and Madrid was of a very difficult and expensive character to work through. Taking these circumstances into account, and looking at the expected traffic on the proposed line, Sir Joshua Walmsley, acting under the advice of Mr Stephenson, offered to construct the line from Madrid to the Bay of Biscay, only on condition that the requisite land was given the Company for the purpose; that they should be allowed every facility for cutting such timber belonging the Crown as might be required for the purposes of the railway; and also that the materials required from abroad for the construction of the line should be admitted free of duty. In return for these concessions the Company offered to clothe and feed several thousands of convicts while engaged in the execution of the earthworks. General Narvaez, afterwards Duke of Valencia, received Sir Joshua Walmsley and Mr Stephenson on the subject of their proposition, and expressed his willingness to close with them; but it was necessary that other influential parties should give their concurrence before the scheme could be carried into effect. The deputation waited ten days to receive the answer of the Spanish Government; but no answer of any kind was vouchsafed. The authorities, indeed, invited them to be present at a Spanish bullfight, but that was not quite the business Mr Stephenson had gone all the way to Spain to transact; and the offer was politely declined. The result was, that Mr Stephenson dissuaded his friend from making the necessary deposit at Madrid. Besides, he had by this time formed an unfavourable opinion of the entire project, and considered that the traffic would not amount to one-eighth of the estimate.

Mr Stephenson was now anxious to be in England. During the

journey from Madrid he often spoke with affection of friends and
relatives; and when apparently absorbed by other matters, he
would revert to what he thought might then be passing at home.
Few incidents worthy of notice occurred on the journey homeward, but one may be mentioned. While travelling in an open
conveyance between Madrid and Vittoria, the driver urged his
mules downhill at a dangerous pace. He was requested to slacken
speed; but suspecting his passengers to be afraid, he only flogged
the brutes into a still more furious gallop. Observing this, Mr
Stephenson coolly said, 'Let us try him on the other tack; tell him
to show us the fastest pace at which Spanish mules can go.' The
rogue of a driver, when he found his tricks of no avail, pulled up
and proceeded at a more moderate speed for the rest of the
journey.

Urgent business required Mr Stephenson's presence in London
on the last day of November. They travelled, therefore, almost
continuously, day and night; and the fatigue consequent on the
journey, added to the privations voluntarily endured by the engineer while carrying on the survey among the Spanish mountains,
began to tell seriously on his health. By the time he reached Paris
he was evidently ill, but he nevertheless determined on proceeding.
He reached Havre in time for the Southampton boat; but when
on board, pleurisy developed itself, and it was necessary to bleed
him freely. During the voyage, he spent his time chiefly in dictating
letters and reports to Sir Joshua Walmsley, who never left him,
and whose kindness on the occasion he gratefully remembered. His
friend was struck by the clearness of his dictated composition,
which exhibited a vigour and condensation which to him seemed
marvellous. After a few weeks' rest at home, Mr Stephenson
gradually recovered, though his health remained severely shaken.

CHAPTER XVI – ROBERT STEPHENSON'S CAREER – THE STEPHENSONS AND BRUNEL – EAST COAST ROUTE TO SCOTLAND – ROYAL BORDER BRIDGE, BERWICK – HIGH LEVEL BRIDGE, NEWCASTLE

THE career of George Stephenson was drawing to a close. He had for some time been gradually retiring from the more active pursuit of railway engineering, and confining himself to the promotion of only a few undertakings in which he took a more than ordinary personal interest. In 1840, when the extensive main lines in the Midland districts had been finished and opened for traffic, he publicly expressed his intention of withdrawing from the profession. He had reached sixty, and, having spent the greater part of his life in very hard work, he naturally desired rest and retirement in his old age. There was the less necessity for his continuing 'in harness', as Robert Stephenson was now in full career as a leading railway engineer, and his father had pleasure in handing over to him, with the sanction of the companies concerned, nearly all the railway appointments which he held.

Robert Stephenson amply repaid his father's care. The sound education of which he had laid the foundations at school, improved by his subsequent culture, but more than all by his father's example of application, industry, and thoroughness in all that he undertook, told powerfully in the formation of his character, not less than in the discipline of his intellect. His father had early implanted in him habits of mental activity, familiarized him with the laws of mechanics, and carefully trained and stimulated his inventive faculties, the first great fruits of which, as we have seen, were exhibited in the triumph of the 'Rocket' at Rainhill. 'I am fully conscious in my own mind,' said the son at a meeting of the Mechanical Engineers at Newcastle, in 1858, 'how greatly my civil engineering has been regulated and influenced by the mechanical knowledge which I derived directly from my father; and the more my experience has advanced, the more convinced I have become that it is necessary to educate an engineer in the workshop. That is, emphatically, the education which will render the engineer most intelligent, most useful, and the fullest of resources in times of difficulty.'

Robert Stephenson was but twenty-six years old when the performances of the 'Rocket' established the practicability of steam locomotion on railways. He was shortly after appointed engineer of the Leicester and Swannington Railway; after which, at his father's request, he was made joint engineer with himself in laying out the London and Birmingham Railway, and the execution of that line was afterwards entrusted to him as sole engineer. The stability and excellence of the works of that railway, the difficulties which had been successfully overcome in the course of its construction, and the judgement which was displayed by Robert Stephenson throughout the whole conduct of the undertaking to its completion, established his reputation as an engineer; and his father could now look with confidence and with pride upon his son's achievements. From that time forward, father and son worked together as one man, each jealous of the other's honour; and on the father's retirement, it was generally recognized that, in the sphere of railways, Robert Stephenson was the foremost man, the safest guide, and the most active worker.

Robert Stephenson was subsequently appointed engineer of the Eastern Counties, the Northern and Eastern, and the Blackwall railways, besides many lines in the Midland and southern districts. When the speculation of 1844 set in, his services were, of course, greatly in request. Thus, in one session, we find him engaged as engineer for not fewer than thirty-three new schemes. Projectors thought themselves fortunate who could secure his name, and he had only to propose his terms to obtain them. The work which he performed at this period of his life was indeed enormous, and his income was large beyond any previous instance of engineering gain. But much of his labour was heavy hackwork of a very uninteresting character. During the sittings of the committees of Parliament, almost every moment of his time was occupied in

consultations, and in preparing evidence or in giving it. The
crowded, low-roofed committee-rooms of the old Houses of Parliament were altogether inadequate to accommodate the rush of
perspiring projectors of Bills, and even the lobbies were sometimes
choked with them. To have borne that noisome atmosphere and
heat would have tested the constitutions of salamanders, and
engineers were only human. With brains kept in a state of excitement during the entire day, no wonder their nervous systems became unstrung. Their only chance of refreshment was during an
occasional rush to the bun and sandwich stand in the lobby,
though sometimes even that resource failed them. Then, with mind
and body jaded – probably after undergoing a series of consultations upon many bills after the rising of the committees – the
exhausted engineers would seek to stimulate nature by a late,
perhaps a heavy, dinner. What chance had any ordinary constitution of surviving such an ordeal? The consequence was, that
stomach, brain, and liver were alike irretrievably injured; and
hence the men who bore the brunt of those struggles – Stephenson,
Brunel, Locke, and Errington – have already all died, comparatively young men.

In mentioning the name of Brunel, we are reminded of him as
the principal rival and competitor of Robert Stephenson. Both
were the sons of distinguished men, and both inherited the fame
and followed in the footsteps of their fathers. The Stephensons
were inventive, practical, and sagacious; the Brunels ingenious,
imaginative, and daring. The former were as thoroughly English in
their characteristics as the latter were perhaps as thoroughly
French. The fathers and the sons were alike successful in their
works, though not in the same degree. Measured by practical and
profitable results, the Stephenson were unquestionably the safer
men to follow.

Robert Stephenson and Isambard Kingdom Brunel were destined often to come into collision in the course of their professional
life. Their respective railway districts 'marched' with each other,
and it became their business to invade or defend those districts,
according as the policy of their respective boards might direct. The
gauge of 7 feet fixed by Mr Brunel for the Great Western Railway,
so entirely different from that of 4 ft 8½ in. adopted by the Stephensons on the Northern and Midland lines, was from the first a great
cause of contention. But Mr Brunel had always an aversion to
follow any man's lead; and that another engineer had fixed the
gauge of a railway, or built a bridge, or designed an engine, in one

way, was of itself often a sufficient reason with him for adopting an altogether different course. Robert Stephenson, on his part, though less bold, was more practical, preferring to follow the old routes, and to tread in the safe steps of his father.

Mr Brunel, however, determined that the Great Western should be a giant's road, and that travelling should be conducted upon it at double speed. His ambition was to make the *best* road that imagination could devise; whereas the main object of the Stephensons, both father and son, was to make a road that would *pay*. Although, tried by the Stephenson test, Brunel's magnificent road was a failure so far as the shareholders in the Great Western Company were concerned, the stimulus which his ambitious designs gave to mechanical invention at the time proved a general good. The narrow-gauge engineers exerted themselves to quicken their locomotives to the utmost. They improved and re-improved them; the machinery was simplified and perfected; outside cylinders gave place to inside; the steadier and more rapid and effective action of the engine was secured; and in a few years the highest speed on the narrow-gauge lines went up from 30 to about 50 miles an hour. For this rapidity of progress we are in no small degree indebted to the stimulus imparted to the narrow-gauge engineers by Mr Brunel. And it is well for a country that it should possess men such as he, ready to dare the untried, and to venture boldly into new paths. Individuals may suffer from the cost of the experiments; but the nation, which is an aggregate of individuals, gains, and so does the world at large.

It was one of the characteristics of Brunel to believe in the success of the schemes for which he was professionally engaged as engineer; and he proved this by investing his savings largely in the Great Western Railway, in the South Devon atmospheric line, and in the Great Eastern steamship, with what results are well known. Robert Stephenson, on the contrary, with characteristic caution, towards the latter years of his life avoided holding unguaranteed railway shares; and though he might execute magnificent structures, such as the Victoria Bridge across the St Lawrence, he was careful not to embark any portion of his own fortune in the ordinary capital of these concerns. In 1845, he shrewdly foresaw the inevitable crash that was about to follow the mania of that year; and while shares were still at a premium he took the opportunity of selling out all that he had. He urged his father to do the same thing, but George's reply was characteristic. 'No,' said he; 'I took my shares for an investment, and not to speculate with, and I am not going to sell them now because folks have gone mad about railways.' The consequence was, that he continued to hold the £60,000 which he had invested in the shares of various railways until his death, when they were at once sold out by his son, though at a great depreciation on their original cost.

One of the hardest battles fought between the Stephensons and Brunel was for the railway between Newcastle and Berwick, forming part of the great East Coast route to Scotland. As early as 1836, George Stephenson had surveyed two lines to connect Edinburgh with Newcastle: one by Berwick and Dunbar along the coast, and the other, more inland, by Carter Fell, up the vale of the Gala, to the northern capital; but both projects lay dormant for several years longer, until the completion of the Midland and other main lines as far north as Newcastle, had the effect of again reviving the subject of the extension of the route as far as Edinburgh.

On 18 June 1844, the Newcastle and Darlington line – an important link of the great main highway to the north – was completed and publicly opened, thus connecting the Thames and the Tyne by a continuous line of railway. On that day the Stephensons, with a distinguished party of railwaymen, travelled by express train from London to Newcastle in about nine hours. It was a great event, and was worthily celebrated. The population of Newcastle held holiday; and a banquet given in the Assembly Rooms the same evening assumed the form of an ovation to George Stephenson and his son. Thirty years before, in the capacity of a workman, he had been labouring at the construction of his first locomotive in the immediate neighbourhood. By slow and laborious steps he had worked his way on, dragging the locomotive into notice, and raising himself in public estimation; until at length he had victoriously established the railway system, and went back among his townsmen to receive their greeting.

After the opening of this railway, the project of the East Coast line from Newcastle to Berwick was revived; and George Stephenson, who had already identified himself with the question, and was intimately acquainted with every foot of the ground, was called upon to assist the promoters with his judgement and experience. He again recommended as strongly as before the line he had previously surveyed; and on its being adopted by the local committee, the necessary steps were taken to have the scheme brought before Parliament in the ensuing session. The East Coast line was not, however, to be allowed to pass without a fight. On the contrary, it had to encounter as stout an opposition as the Stephensons had ever experienced.

We have already stated that about this time the plan of substituting atmospheric pressure for locomotive steam-power in the working of railways, had become very popular. Many eminent engineers supported the atmospheric system, and a strong party in Parliament, headed by the Prime Minister, were greatly disposed in its favour. Mr Brunel warmly espoused the atmospheric principle, and his persuasive manner, as well as his admitted scientific ability, unquestionably exercised considerable influence in determining the views of many leading members of both Houses. Among others, Lord Howick, one of the members for Northumberland, adopted the new principle, and, possessing great local influence, he succeeded in forming a powerful confederacy of the landed gentry in favour of Brunel's atmospheric railway through that county.

George Stephenson could not brook the idea of seeing the locomotive, for which he had fought so many stout battles, pushed to one side, and that in the very county in which its great powers had been first developed. Nor did he relish the appearance of Mr Brunel as the engineer of Lord Howick's scheme, in opposition to the line which had occupied his thoughts and been the object of his strenuous advocacy for so many years. When Stephenson first met Brunel in Newcastle, he good-naturedly shook him by the collar, and asked 'What business he had north of the Tyne?' George gave him to understand that they were to have a fair stand-up fight for the ground, and, shaking hands before the battle like Englishmen, they parted in good humour. A public meeting was held at Newcastle in the following December, when, after a full discussion of the merits of the respective plans, Stephenson's line was almost unanimously adopted as the best.

The rival projects went before Parliament in 1845, and a severe contest ensued. The display of ability and tactics on both sides was great. Robert Stephenson was examined at great length as to the merits of the locomotive line, and Brunel at equally great length as to the merits of the atmospheric system. Mr Brunel, in his evidence, said that after numerous experiments, he had arrived at the conclusion that the mechanical contrivance of the atmospheric system was perfectly applicable, and he believed that it would likewise be more economical in most cases than locomotive power. 'In short,' said he, 'rapidity, comfort, safety, and economy, are its chief recommendations.'

But the locomotive again triumphed. The Stephenson Coast Line secured the approval of Parliament; and the shareholders in the Atmospheric Company were happily prevented investing their capital in what would unquestionably have proved a gigantic blunder. For, less than three years later, the whole of the atmospheric tubes which had been laid down on other lines were pulled up and the materials sold – including Mr Brunel's immense tube on the South Devon Railway – to make way for the working of the locomotive engine. George Stephenson's first verdict of 'It won't do', was thus conclusively confirmed.

Robert Stephenson used afterwards to describe with great gusto an interview which took place between Lord Howick and his father, at his office in Great George Street, during the progress of the Bill in Parliament. His father was in the outer office, where he used to spend a good deal of his spare time; occasionally taking a quiet wrestle with a friend when nothing else was stirring.* On the day in question, George was standing with his back to the fire, when Lord Howick called to see Robert. Oh! thought George, he has come to try and talk Robert over about that atmospheric gimcrack; but I'll tackle his Lordship. 'Come in, my Lord,' said he, 'Robert's busy; but I'll answer your purpose quite as well; sit down here, if you please.' George began, 'Now, my Lord, I know very well what you have come about: it's that atmospheric line in the north; I will show you in less than five minutes that it can never answer.' 'If Mr Robert Stephenson is not at liberty, I can call again,' said his Lordship. 'He's certainly occupied on important business just at present,' was George's answer; 'but I can tell you far better than he can what nonsense the atmospheric system is: Robert's good-natured, you see, and if your Lordship were to get alongside of him you might talk him over; so you have been quite lucky in meeting with me. Now, just look at the question of expense' – and then he proceeded in his strong Doric to explain his views in detail, until Lord Howick could stand it no longer, and he rose and walked towards the door. George followed him downstairs, to finish his demolition of the atmospheric system, and

---

* 'When my father came about the office,' said Robert, 'he sometimes did not well know what to do with himself. So he used to invite Bidder to have a wrestle with him, for old acquaintance' sake. And the two wrestled together so often, and had so many "falls" (sometimes I thought they would bring the house down between them), that they broke half the chairs in my outer office. I remember once sending my father in a joiner's bill of about £2 10s. for mending broken chairs.'

his parting words were, 'You may take my word for it, my Lord,
it will never answer.' George afterwards told his son with glee of
'the settler' he had given Lord Howick.

So closely were the Stephensons identified with this measure,
and so great was the personal interest which they were both known
to take in its success, that, on the news of the triumph of the Bill
reaching Newcastle, a sort of general holiday took place, and the
workmen belonging to the Stephenson Locomotive Factory, upwards of 800 in number, walked in procession through the principal
streets of the town, accompanied with music and banners.

It is unnecessary to enter into any description of the works on
the Newcastle and Berwick Railway. There are no fewer than 110
bridges of all sorts on the line – some under and some over it. But
by far the most formidable piece of masonry work on this railway
is at its northern extremity, where it passes across the Tweed into
Scotland, immediately opposite the formerly redoubtable castle of
Berwick. Not many centuries had passed since the district amidst
which this bridge stands was the scene of almost constant warfare.
Berwick was regarded as the key of Scotland, and was fiercely
fought for, sometimes held by a Scotch and sometimes by an
English garrison. Though strongly fortified, it was repeatedly
taken by assault. On its capture by Edward I, Boetius says 17,000
persons were slain, so that its streets 'ran with blood like a river'.
Within sight of the ramparts, a little to the west, is Halidon Hill,
where a famous victory was gained by Edward III, over the
Scottish army under Douglas; and there is scarcely a foot of ground
in the neighbourhood but has been the scene of contention in days
long past. In the reigns of James I and Charles I, a bridge of
fifteen arches was built across the Tweed at Berwick; and in our
own day a railway bridge of twenty-eight arches has been built a
little above the old one, but at a much higher level. The bridge
built by the Kings, out of the national resources, cost £15,000, and
occupied twenty-four years and four months in the building; the
bridge built by the Railway Company, with funds drawn from
private resources, cost £120,000, and was finished in three years
and four months from the day of laying the foundation-stone.

This important viaduct, built after the design of Robert
Stephenson, consists of a series of twenty-eight semicircular arches,
each 61 feet 6 inches in span, the greatest height above the bed of
the river being 126 feet. The whole is built of ashlar, with a heart-
ing of rubble; excepting the river parts of the arches, which are
constructed with bricks laid in cement. The total length of the

work is 2,160 feet. The foundations of the piers were got in by coffer-dams in the ordinary way, Nasmyth's steam-hammer being extensively used in driving the piles. The bearing piles, from which the foundations of the piers were built up, were each capable of carrying 70 tons.

Another bridge, of still greater importance, necessary to complete the continuity of the East Coast route, was the masterwork erected by Robert Stephenson between the north and south banks of the Tyne at Newcastle, commonly known as the High Level Bridge. Mr R. W. Brandling, George Stephenson's early friend, is entitled to the merit of originating the idea of this bridge as it was eventually carried out, with a central terminus for the northern railways in the Castle Garth. The plan was first promulgated by him in 1841; and in the following year it was resolved that George Stephenson should be consulted as to the most advisable site for the proposed structure. A prospectus of a High Level Bridge Company was issued in 1843, the names of George Stephenson and George Hudson appearing on the committee of management, Robert Stephenson being the consulting engineer. The project was eventually taken up by the Newcastle and Darlington Railway Company, and an Act for the construction of the bridge was obtained in 1845.

The rapid extension of railways had given an extraordinary stimulus to the art of bridge-building; the number of such structures erected in Great Britain alone, since 1830, having been above 25,000, or more than all that had before existed in the country. Instead of the erection of a single large bridge constituting, as formerly, an epoch in engineering, hundreds of extensive bridges of novel design were simultaneously constructed. The necessity which existed for carrying rigid roads, capable of bearing heavy railway trains at high speeds, over extensive gaps free of support, rendered it obvious that the methods which had up to that time been employed for bridging space were altogether insufficient. The railway engineer could not, like the ordinary road engineer, divert his road, and make choice of the best point for crossing a river or a valley. He must take such ground as lay in the line of his railway, be it bog, or mud, or shifting sand. Navigable rivers and crowded thoroughfares had to be crossed without interruption to the existing traffic, sometimes by bridges at right angles to the river or road, sometimes by arches more or less oblique. In many cases great difficulty arose from the limited nature of the headway; but, as the level of the original road must generally be preserved, and that of the railway was in a measure fixed and determined, it was necessary to modify the form and structure of the bridge, in almost every case, in order to comply with the public requirements. Novel conditions were met by fresh inventions, and difficulties of the most unusual character were one after another successfully surmounted. In executing these extraordinary works, iron has been throughout the sheet-anchor of the engineer. In its different forms of cast or wrought iron, it offered a valuable resource, where rapidity of execution, great strength, and cheapness of construction in the first instance, were elements of prime importance; and by its skilful use, the railway architect was enabled to achieve results which thirty years ago would scarcely have been thought possible.

In many of the early cast iron bridges the old form of the arch was adopted, the stability of the structure depending wholly on compression, the only novel feature being the use of iron instead of stone. But in a large proportion of cases, the arch, with the railroad over it, was found inapplicable in consequence of the limited headway which it provided. Hence it early occurred to George Stephenson, when constructing the Liverpool and Manchester Railway, to adopt the simple cast iron beam for the crossing of several roads and canals along that line – this beam resembling in some measure the lintel of the early temples – the pressure on the abutments being purely vertical. One of the earliest instances of this kind of bridge was that erected over Water Street, Manchester, in 1829; after which, cast iron girders, with their lower webs considerably larger than their upper, were ordinarily employed where the span was moderate; and wrought iron tie-rods below were added to give increased strength where the span was greater.

The next step was the contrivance of arched beams or bowstring girders, firmly held together by horizontal ties to resist the thrust, instead of abutments. Numerous excellent specimens of this description of bridge were erected by Robert Stephenson on the original London and Birmingham Railway; but by far the grandest work of the kind – perfect as a specimen of modern constructive skill – was the High Level Bridge, which we owe to the genius of the same engineer.

The problem was, to throw a railway bridge across the deep ravine which lies between the towns of Newcastle and Gateshead, at the bottom of which flows the navigable river Tyne. Along and up the sides of the valley – on the Newcastle bank especially – run streets of old-fashioned houses, clustered together in the strange forms peculiar to the older cities. The ravine is of great depth – so deep and so gloomy-looking towards dusk, that local tradition records that when the Duke of Cumberland arrived late in the evening at the brow of the hill overlooking the Tyne, on his way to Culloden, he exclaimed to his attendants, on looking down into the black gorge before him, 'For God's sake, don't think of taking me down that coal-pit at this time of night!' The road down the Gateshead High Street is almost as steep as the roof of a house, and up the Newcastle Side, as the street there is called, it is little better. During many centuries the traffic north and south passed along this dangerous and difficult route, over the old bridge which crosses the river in the bottom of the valley. For about thirty years the Newcastle Corporation had discussed various methods of improving the communication between the towns; and the discussion might have gone on for thirty years more, but for the advent of railways, when the skill and enterprise to which they gave birth speedily solved the difficulty and bridged the ravine. The local authorities adroitly took advantage of the opportunity, and insisted on the provision of a road for ordinary vehicles and foot passengers in addition to the railroad. In this circumstance originated one of the striking peculiarities of the High Level Bridge, which serves two purposes, being a railway above and a carriage roadway underneath.

The breadth of the river at the point of crossing is 515 feet, but the length of the bridge and viaduct between the Gateshead station and the terminus on the Newcastle side is about 4,000 feet. It springs from Pipewell Gate Bank, on the south, directly across to Castle Garth, where, nearly fronting the bridge, stands the fine old Norman keep of the *New* Castle, now nearly 800 years old, and a little beyond it is the spire of St Nicholas Church, with its light and graceful Gothic crown; the whole forming a grand architectural group of unusual historic interest. The bridge passes completely over the roofs of the houses which fill both sides of the valley; and the extraordinary height of the upper parapet, which is about 130 feet above the bed of the river, offers a prospect to the passing traveller the like of which is perhaps nowhere else to be seen. Far below are the queer chares and closes, the wynds and lanes of old Newcastle; the water is crowded with pudgy, black, coal keels; and, when there is a partial dispersion of the great smoke clouds which usually obscure the sky, the funnels of steamers and the masts of shipping may be seen far down the river. The old bridge

Britannia Tubular Bridge

lies so far beneath that the passengers crossing it seem like so
many bees passing to and fro.

The first difficulty encountered in building the bridge was in
securing a solid foundation for the piers. The dimensions of the
piles to be driven were so huge, that the engineer found it necessary
to employ some extraordinary means for the purpose. He called
Nasmyth's Titanic steam-hammer to his aid – the first occasion,
we believe, on which this prodigious power was employed in bridge
pile-driving. A temporary staging was erected for the steam-
engine and hammer apparatus, which rested on two keels, and,
notwithstanding the newness and stiffness of the machinery, the
first pile was driven on 6 October 1846, to a depth of 32 feet, in
four minutes. Two hammers of 30 cwt each were kept in regular
use, making from 60 to 70 strokes a minute; and the results were
astounding to those who had been accustomed to the old style of
pile-driving by means of the ordinary pile-frame, consisting of
slide, ram, and monkey. By the old system, the pile was driven by
a comparatively small mass of iron descending with great velocity
from a considerable height – the velocity being in excess and the
mass deficient, and calculated, like the momentum of a cannon-
ball, rather for destructive than impulsive action. In the case of
the steam pile-driver, on the contrary, the whole weight of a heavy
mass is delivered rapidly upon a driving-block of several tons
weight placed directly over the head of the pile, the weight never
ceasing, and the blows being repeated at the rate of a blow a
second, until the pile is driven home. It is a curious fact, that the
rapid strokes of the steam-hammer evolved so much heat, that on
many occasions the pile-head burst into flames during the process
of driving. The elastic force of steam is the power that lifts the
ram, the escape permitting its entire force to fall upon the head of
the driving block; while the steam above the piston on the upper
part of the cylinder, acting as a buffer or recoil-spring, materially
enhances the effect of the downward blow. As soon as one pile was
driven, the traveller, hovering overhead, presented another, and
down it went into the solid bed of the river, with almost as much
ease as a lady sticks pins into a cushion. By the aid of this powerful
machine, pile-driving, formerly among the most costly and tedious
of engineering operations, became easy, rapid, and comparatively
economical.

When the piles had been driven and the coffer-dams formed and
puddled, the water within the enclosed spaces was pumped out by
the aid of powerful engines, so as, if possible, to lay bare the bed

of the river. Considerable difficulty was experienced in getting in
the foundations of the middle pier, in consequence of the water
forcing itself through the quicksand beneath as fast as it was
removed. This fruitless labour went on for months, and many expedients were tried. Chalk was thrown in in large quantities outside the piling, but without effect. Cement concrete was at last put
within the coffer-dam, until it set, and the bottom was then found
to be secure. A bed of concrete was laid up to the level of the heads
of the piles, the foundation course of stone blocks being commenced about two feet below low water, and the building proceeded without further difficulty. It may serve to give an idea of
the magnitude of the work, when we state that 400,000 cubic feet
of ashlar, rubble, and concrete were worked up in the piers, and
450,000 cubic feet in the land-arches and approaches.

The most novel feature of the structure is the use of cast and
wrought iron in forming the double bridge, which admirably com-
bines the two principles of the arch and suspension; the railway
being carried over the back of the ribbed arches in the usual
manner, while the carriage-road and footpaths, forming a long
gallery or aisle, are suspended from these arches by wrought iron
vertical rods, with horizontal tie-bars to resist the thrust. The
suspension-bolts are enclosed within spandril pillars of cast iron,
which give great stiffness to the superstructure. This system of
longitudinal and vertical bracing has been much admired, for it not
only accomplishes the primary object of securing rigidity in the
roadway, but at the same time, by its graceful arrangement,
heightens the beauty of the structure. The arches consist of four
main ribs, disposed in pairs with a clear distance between the two
inner arches of 20 feet 4 inches, forming the carriage-road, while
between each of the inner and outer ribs there is a space of 6 feet
2 inches, constituting the footpaths. Each arch is cast in five separate lengths or segments, strongly bolted together. The ribs spring
from horizontal plates of cast iron, bedded and secured on the stone
piers. All the abutting joints were carefully executed by machinery, the fitting being of the most perfect kind. In order to provide
for the expansion and contraction of the iron arching, and to preserve the equilibrium of the piers without disturbance or racking of
the other parts of the bridge, it was arranged that the ribs of every
two adjoining arches resting on the same pier should be secured to
the springing-plates by keys and joggles; while on the next piers
on either side, the ribs remained free and were at liberty to expand
or contract according to temperature – a space being left for the

purpose. Hence each arch is complete and independent in itself, the piers having simply to sustain their vertical pressure. There are six arches of 125 feet span each; the two approaches to the bridge being formed of cast iron pillars and bearers in keeping with the arches.

The result is a bridge that for massive solidity may be pronounced unrivalled. It is perhaps the most magnificent and striking of all the bridges to which railways have given birth, and has been worthily styled 'the King of railway structures'. It is a monument of the highest engineering skill of our time, with the impress of power grandly stamped upon it. The bridge was opened on 15 August 1849, and a few days after the royal train passed over it, halting for a few minutes to enable Her Majesty to survey the wonderful scene below. In the course of the following year the Queen opened the extensive stone viaduct across the Tweed, above described, by which the last link was completed of the continuous line of railway between London and Edinburgh. Over the entrance to the Berwick station, occupying the site of the once redoubtable Border fortress, so often the deadly battle-ground of the ancient Scots and English, was erected an arch under which the royal train passed, bearing in large letters of gold the appropriate words, 'The last act of the Union'.

The warders at Berwick no longer look out from the castle walls to descry the glitter of Southron spears. The bell-tower, from which the alarm was sounded of old, though still standing, is deserted; the only bell heard within the precincts of the old castle being the railway porter's bell announcing the arrival and departure of trains. You see the Scotch express pass along the bridge and speed southward on the wings of steam. But no alarm spreads along the border now. Northumbrian beeves are safe. Chevy-Chase and Otterburn are quiet sheep-pastures. The only men at arms on the battlements of Alnwick Castle are of stone. Bamburgh Castle has become an asylum for shipwrecked mariners, and the Norman Keep at Newcastle has been converted into a Museum of Antiquities. The railway has indeed consummated the Union.

CHAPTER XVII – ROBERT STEPHENSON'S TUBULAR BRIDGES AT MENAI AND CONWAY

WE have now to describe briefly another great undertaking, begun by George Stephenson, and taken up and completed by his son, in the course of which the latter carried out some of his greatest works – we mean the Chester and Holyhead Railway, completing the railway connection with Dublin, as the Newcastle and Berwick line completed the connection with Edinburgh. It will thus be seen how closely Telford was followed by the Stephensons in perfecting the highways of their respective epochs; the former by means of turnpike-roads, and the latter by means of railways.

George Stephenson surveyed a line from Chester to Holyhead in 1838, and at the same time reported on the line through North Wales to Port Dynllaen, proposed by the Irish Railway Commissioners. His advice was strongly in favour of adopting the line to Holyhead, as less costly and presenting better gradients. A public meeting was held at Chester, in January 1839, in support of the latter measure, at which he was present to give explanations. Mr Uniacke, the Mayor, in opening the proceedings, said that Mr Stephenson was present, ready to answer any questions which might be put to him on the subject; and it was judiciously remarked that 'it would be better that he should be asked questions than required to make a speech; for, though a very good engineer, he was a bad speaker'. One of the questions then put to Mr Stephenson related to the mode by which he proposed to haul the passenger carriages over the Menai Suspension Bridge by horsepower; and he was asked whether he knew the pressure the bridge was capable of sustaining. His answer was, that 'he had not yet made any calculations; but he proposed getting data which would enable him to arrive at an accurate calculation of the actual strain upon the bridge during the late gale. He had, however, no hesitation in saying that it was more than twenty times as much as the strain of a train of carriages and a locomotive engine. The only reason why he proposed to convey the carriages over by horses, was in order that he might, by distributing the weight, not increase the wavy motion. All the train would be on at once; but distributed. This he thought better than passing them, linked together, by a locomotive engine.' It will thus be observed that the practicability of throwing a rigid railway bridge across the Straits had not yet been contemplated.

The Dublin Chamber of Commerce passed resolutions in favour of Stephenson's line, after hearing his explanation of its essential features. The project, after undergoing much discussion, was at length embodied in an Act passed in 1844; and the work was brought to a successful completion by his son, with several important modifications, including the grand original feature of the tubular bridges across the Menai Straits and the estuary of the Conway. Excepting these great works, the construction of this line presented no unusual features; though the remarkable terrace cut for the accommodation of the railway under the steep slope of Penmaen Mawr is worthy of a passing notice.

About midway between Conway and Bangor, Penmaen Mawr forms a bold and almost precipitous headland, at the base of which, in rough weather, the ocean dashes with great fury. There was not space enough between the mountain and the strand for the passage of the railway; hence in some places the rock had to be blasted to

form a terrace, and in others sea walls had to be built up to the
proper level, on which to form an embankment of sufficient width
to enable the road to be laid. A tunnel 10½ chains in length was cut
through the headland itself; and on its east and west sides the line
was formed by a terrace cut out of the cliff, and by embankments
protected by sea walls; the terrace being three times interrupted
by embankments in its course of about 1¼ mile. The road lies so
close under the steep mountain face, that it was even found necessary at certain places to protect it against possible accidents from
falling stones, by means of a covered way. The terrace on the east
side of the headland was, however, in some measure protected
against the roll of the sea by the mass of stone run out from the
tunnel, and forming a deep shingle bank in front of the wall.

The part of the work which lies on the westward of the headland
penetrated by the tunnel, was exposed to the full force of the sea;
and the formation of the road at that point was attended with
great difficulty. While the sea wall was still in progress, its strength
was severely tried by a strong north-westerly gale, which blew in
October 1846, with a spring tide of 17 feet. On the following
morning it was found that a large portion of the rubble was irre-
parably injured, and 200 yards of the wall were then replaced by
an open viaduct, with the piers placed edgeways to the sea, the
openings between them being spanned by ten cast iron girders each
42 feet long. This accident induced the engineer to alter the con-
tour of the sea wall, so that it should present a diminished resistance to the force of the waves. But the sea repeated its assaults,
and made further havoc with the work; entailing heavy expenses
and a complete reorganization of the contract. Increased solidity
was then given to the masonry, and the face of the wall underwent
further change. At some points outworks were constructed, and
piles were driven into the beach about 15 feet from the base of the
wall, for the purpose of protecting its foundations and breaking
the force of the waves. The work was at length finished after about
three years' anxious labour; but Mr Stephenson confessed that if a
long tunnel had been made in the first instance through the solid
rock of Penmaen Mawr, a saving of from £25,000 to £30,000 would
have been effected. He also said he had arrived at the conclusion
that in railway works engineers should endeavour as far as possible to avoid the necessity of contending with the sea;* but if he

* The simple fact that in a heavy storm the force of impact of the waves is
from one and a half to two tons per square foot, must necessarily dictate the
greatest possible caution in approaching so formidable an element. Mr R.

were ever again compelled to go within its reach, he would adopt, instead of retaining walls, an open viaduct, placing all the piers edgeways to the force of the sea, and allowing the waves to break upon a natural slope of beach. He was ready enough to admit the errors he had committed in the original design of this work; but he said he had always gained more information from studying the causes of failures and endeavouring to surmount them than he had done from easily won successes. While many of the latter had been forgotten, the former were indelibly fixed in his memory.

But by far the greatest difficulty which Robert Stephenson had to encounter in executing this railway, was in carrying it across the Straits of Menai and the estuary of the Conway, where, like his predecessor Telford when forming his high road through North Wales, he was under the necessity of resorting to new and altogether untried methods of bridge construction. At Menai the waters of the Irish Sea are perpetually vibrating along the precipitous shores of the Strait; rising and falling from 20 to 25 feet at each successive tide; the width and depth of the channel being such as to render it available for navigation by the largest ships. The problem was, to throw a bridge across this wide chasm – a bridge of unusual span and dimensions – of such strength as to be capable of bearing the heaviest loads at high speeds, and at such a uniform height throughout as not in any way to interfere with the navigation of the Strait. From an early period, Mr Stephenson had fixed upon the spot where the Britannia Rock occurs, nearly in the middle of the channel, as the most eligible point for crossing; the water-width from shore to shore at high water there being about 1,100 feet. His first idea was to construct the bridge of two cast iron arches, each of 350 feet span. There was no novelty in this idea; for, as early as the year 1801, Mr Rennie prepared a design of a cast iron bridge across the Strait at the Swilly rocks, the great centre arch of which was to be 450 feet span; and at a later period, in 1810, Telford submitted a design of a similar bridge at Inys-y-Moch, with a single cast iron arch of 500 feet. But the same objections which led to the rejection of Rennie's and Telford's designs, proved fatal to Robert Stephenson's, and his iron-arched railway bridge was rejected by the Admiralty. The navigation of the Strait was under no circumstances to be interfered with; and even the erection of scaffolding from below, to support the bridge

Stevenson (Edinburgh) registered a force of three tons per square foot at Skerryvore, during a gale in the Atlantic, when the waves were supposed to run twenty feet high.

during construction was not to be permitted. The idea of a suspension bridge was dismissed as inapplicable; a degree of rigidity and strength, greater than could be secured by any bridge constructed on the principle of suspension, being considered an indispensable condition of the proposed structure.

Various other plans were suggested; but the whole question remained unsettled even down to the time when the Company went before Parliament, in 1844, for power to construct the proposed bridges. No existing kind of structure seemed to be capable of bearing the fearful extension to which rigid bridges of the necessary spans would be subjected; and some new expedient of engineering therefore became necessary.

Mr Stephenson was then led to reconsider a design which he had made in 1841 for a road bridge over the river Lea at Ware, with a span of 50 feet, the conditions only admitting of a platform 18 or 20 inches thick. For this purpose a wrought iron platform was designed, consisting of a series of simple cells, formed of boiler-plates riveted together with angle-iron. The bridge was not, however, carried out after this design, but was made of separate wrought iron girders composed of riveted plates. Recurring to his first idea of this bridge, Mr Stephenson thought that a stiff platform might be constructed, with sides of strongly trussed framework of wrought iron, braced together at top and bottom with plates of like material riveted together with angle-iron; and that such platform might be suspended by strong chains on either side to give it increased security. 'It was now,' says Mr Stephenson, 'that I came to regard the tubular platform as a beam, and that the chains should be looked upon as auxiliaries.' It appeared, nevertheless, that without a system of diagonal struts inside, which of course would have prevented the passage of trains *through* it, this kind of structure was ill-suited for maintaining its form, and would be very liable to become lozenge-shaped. Besides, the rectangular figure was deemed objectionable, from the large surface which it presented to the wind.

It then occurred to him that circular or elliptical tubes might better answer the intended purpose; and in March 1845, he gave instructions to two of his assistants to prepare drawings of such a structure, the tubes being made with a double thickness of plate at top and bottom. The results of the calculations made as to the strength of such a tube, were considered so satisfactory, that Mr Stephenson says he determined to fall back on a bridge of this

description, on the rejection of his design of the two cast iron
arches by the Parliamentary Committee. Indeed, it became evident
that a tubular wrought iron beam was the only structure which
combined the necessary strength and stability for a railway, with
the conditions deemed essential for the protection of the navigation. 'I stood,' says Mr Stephenson, 'on the verge of a responsibility from which, I confess, I had nearly shrunk. The construction
of a tubular beam of such gigantic dimensions, on a platform
elevated and supported by chains at such a height, did at first
present itself as a difficulty of a very formidable nature. Reflection,
however, satisfied me that the principles upon which the idea was
founded were nothing more than an extension of those daily in use
in the profession of the engineer. The method, moreover, of calculating the strength of the structure which I had adopted, was of
the simplest and most elementary character; and whatever might
be the form of the tube, the principle on which the calculations
were founded was equally applicable, and could not fail to lead to
equally accurate results.'* Mr Stephenson accordingly announced
to the directors of the railway that he was prepared to carry out a
bridge of this general description, and they adopted his views,
though not without considerable misgivings.

While the engineer's mind was still occupied with the subject, an
accident occurred to the *Prince of Wales* iron steamship, at Blackwall, which singularly corroborated his views as to the strength of
wrought iron beams of large dimensions. When this vessel was
being launched, the cleat on the bow gave way, in consequence of
the bolts breaking, and let the vessel down so that the bilge came
in contact with the wharf, and she remained suspended between
the water and the wharf for a length of about 110 feet, but without
any injury to the plates of the ship; satisfactorily proving the
great strength of this form of construction. Thus, Mr Stephenson
became gradually confirmed in his opinion that the most feasible
method of bridging the Strait at Menai and the river at Conway
was by means of a hollow beam of wrought iron. As the time was
approaching for giving evidence before Parliament on the subject,
it was necessary for him to settle some definite plan for submission
to the committee. 'My late revered father,' says he, 'having always
taken a deep interest in the various proposals which had been
considered for carrying a railway across the Menai Straits,

* Robert Stephenson's narrative in Clark's *Britannia and Conway Tubular
Bridges*, vol. i, p. 27.

requested me to explain fully to him the views which led me to suggest the use of a tube, and also the nature of the calculations I had made in reference to it. It was during this personal conference that Mr William Fairbairn accidentally called upon me, to whom I also explained the principles of the structure I had proposed. He at once acquiesced in their truth, and expressed confidence in the feasibility of my project, giving me at the same time some facts relative to the remarkable strength of iron steamships, and invited me to his works at Millwall, to examine the construction of an iron steamship which was then in progress.' The date of this consultation was early in April 1845, and Mr Fairbairn states that, on that occasion, 'Mr Stephenson asked whether such a design was practicable, and whether I could accomplish it: and it was ultimately arranged that the subject should be investigated experimentally, to determine not only the value of Mr Stephenson's original conception (of a circular or egg-shaped wrought iron tube, supported by chains), but that of any other tubular form of bridge which might present itself in the prosecution of my researches. The matter was placed unreservedly in my hands; the entire conduct of the investigation was entrusted to me; and, as an experimenter, I was to be left free to exercise my own discretion in the investigation of whatever forms or conditions of the structure might appear to me best calculated to secure a safe passage across the Straits.'* Mr Fairbairn then proceeded to construct a number of experimental models for the purpose of testing the strength of tubes of different forms. The short period which elapsed, however, before the bill was in committee, did not admit of much progress being made with those experiments; but from the evidence in chief given by Mr Stephenson on the subject, on 5 May following, it appears that the idea which prevailed in his mind was that of a bridge with openings of 450 feet (afterwards increased to 460 feet); with a roadway formed of a hollow wrought iron beam, about 25 feet in diameter, presenting a rigid platform, suspended by chains. At the same time, he expressed the confident opinion that a tube of wrought iron would possess sufficient strength and rigidity to support a railway train running inside of it without the help of the chains.

While the bill was still in progress, Mr Fairbairn proceeded with his experiments. He first tested tubes of a cylindrical form, in consequence of the favourable opinion entertained by Mr Stephenson of the tubes in that shape, extending them subsequently to

* *Account of the Construction of the Britannia and Conway Tubular Bridges*, by W. Fairbairn, C.E., London, 1849.

those of an elliptical form.* He found tubes thus shaped more or less defective, and proceeded to test those of a rectangular kind. After the bill had received the Royal Assent on 30 June 1845, the directors of the company, with great liberality, voted a sum for the purpose of enabling the experiments to be prosecuted, and upwards of £6,000 were thus expended to make the assurance of their engineer doubly sure. Mr Fairbairn's tests were of the most elaborate and eventually conclusive character, bringing to light many new and important facts of great practical value. The due proportions and thicknesses of the top, bottom, and sides of the tubes were arrived at after a vast number of trials; one of the results of the experiments being the adoption of Mr Fairbairn's invention of rectangular hollow cells in the top of the beam for the purpose of giving it the requisite degree of strength. About the end of August it was thought desirable to obtain the assistance of a mathematician, who should prepare a formula by which the strength of a full-sized tube might be calculated from the results of the experiments made with tubes of smaller dimensions. Professor Hodgkinson was accordingly called in, and he proceeded to verify and confirm the experiments which Mr Fairbairn had made, and afterwards reduced them to the required formulae.

Mr Stephenson's time was so much engrossed with his extensive engineering business that he was in a great measure precluded from devoting himself to the consideration of the practical details. The results of the experiments were communicated to him from time to time, and were regarded by him as exceedingly satisfactory. It would appear, however, that while Mr Fairbairn urged the rigidity and strength of the tubes without the aid of chains, Mr Stephenson had not quite made up his mind upon the point. Mr Hodgkinson, also, was strongly inclined to retain them. Mr Fairbairn held that it was quite practicable to make the tubes 'sufficiently strong to sustain not only their own weight, but, in addition to that load, 2,000 tons equally distributed over the surface of the platform, a load ten times greater than they will ever be called upon to support.'

It was thoroughly characteristic of Mr Stephenson, and of the

---

* Mr Stephenson continued to hold that the elliptical tube was the right idea, and that sufficient justice had not been done to it. A year or two before his death Mr Stephenson remarked to the author, that had the same arrangement for stiffening been adopted to which the oblong rectangular tubes owe a great part of their strength, a very different result would have been obtained.

caution with which he proceeded in every step of this great undertaking – probing every inch of the ground before he set down his
foot upon it – that he should, early in 1846, have appointed his
able assistant, Mr Edwin Clark, to scrutinize carefully the results
of every experiment, and subject them to a separate and independent analysis before finally deciding upon the form or dimensions of the structure, or upon the mode of procedure connected
with it. At length Mr Stephenson became satisfied that the use of
auxiliary chains was unnecessary, and that the tubular bridge
might be made of such strength as to be entirely self-supporting.

While these important discussions were in progress, measures
were taken to proceed with the masonry of the bridges simultaneously at Conway and the Menai Straits. The foundation-stone
of the Britannia Bridge was laid on 10 April 1846; and on 12 May
following that of the Conway Bridge was laid. Suitable platforms
and workshops were also erected for proceeding with the punching,
fitting, and riveting of the tubes; and when these operations were
in full progress, the neighbourhood of the Conway and Britannia
Bridges presented scenes of extraordinary bustle and industry.
About 1,500 men were employed on the Britannia Bridge alone,
and they mostly lived upon the ground in wooden cottages erected
for the occasion. The iron plates were brought in shiploads from
Liverpool, Anglesea marble from Penmon, and red sandstone from
Runcorn in Cheshire, as wind and tide, and shipping and convenience, might determine. There was an unremitting clank of
hammers, grinding of machinery, and blasting of rock, going on
from morning till night. In fitting the Britannia tubes together,
not less than 2,000,000 of bolts were riveted, weighing some
900 tons.

The Britannia Bridge consists of two independent continuous
tubular beams, each 1,511 feet in length, and each weighing 4,680
tons, independent of the cast iron frames inserted at their bearings
on the masonry of the towers. These immense beams are supported
at five places, namely, on the abutments and on three towers, the
central of which is known as the Great Britannia Tower, 230 feet
high, built on a rock in the middle of the Strait. The side towers
are 18 feet less in height than the central one, and the abutment
35 feet lower than the side towers. The design of the masonry is
such as to accord with the form of the tubes, being somewhat of an
Egyptian character, massive and gigantic rather than beautiful,
but bearing the unmistakable impress of power.

The bridge has four spans, two of 460 feet over the water, and two of 230 feet over the land. The weight of the larger spans, at the points where the tubes repose on the masonry, is not less than 1,587 tons. On the centre tower the tubes rest solid; but on the land towers and abutments they lie on roller-beds, so as to allow of expansion and contraction. The road within each tube is 15 feet wide, and the height varies from 23 feet at the ends to 30 feet at the centre. To give an idea of the vast size of the tubes by comparison with other structures, it may be mentioned that each length constituting the main spans is twice as long as London Monument is high; and if it could be set on end in St Paul's Churchyard, it would reach nearly 100 feet above the cross.

The Conway Bridge is, in most respects, similar to the Britannia, consisting of two tubes, of 400 feet span, placed side by side, each weighing 1,180 tons. The principle adopted in the construction of the tubes, and the mode of floating and raising them, were nearly the same as at the Britannia Bridge, though the general arrangement of the plates is in many respects different.

It was determined to construct the shorter outer tubes of the Britannia Bridge on scaffoldings in the positions in which they were permanently to remain, and to erect the larger tubes upon wooden platforms at high-water-mark on the Caernarvon shore, from whence they were to be floated in pontoons.

The floating of the tubes on pontoons, from the places where they had been constructed, to the recesses in the masonry of the towers, up which they were to be hoisted to the positions they were permanently to occupy, was an anxious and exciting operation. The first part of this process was performed at Conway, where Mr Stephenson directed it in person, assisted by Captain Claxton, Mr Brunel, and other engineering friends. On 6 March 1848, the pontoons bearing the first great tube of the upline were floated round quietly and majestically into their place between the towers in about twenty minutes. Unfortunately, one of the sets of pontoons had become slightly slewed by the stream, by which the Conway end of the tube was prevented from being brought home; and five anxious days to all concerned intervened before it could be set in its place. In the mean time, the presses and raising machinery had been fitted in the towers above, and the lifting process was begun on 8 April, when the immense mass was raised 8 feet, at the rate of about 2 inches a minute. On the 16th, the tube had been raised and finally lowered into its permanent bed; the rails were laid along it; and, on the 18th, Mr Stephenson passed through with the first locomotive. The second tube was proceeded

with on the removal of the first from the platform, and was completed and floated in seven months. The rapidity with which this
second tube was constructed was in no small degree owing to the
Jacquard punching-machine, contrived for the purpose by Mr
Roberts of Manchester. This tube was finally fixed in its permanent bed on 2 January 1849.

The floating and fixing of the great Britannia tubes was a still
more formidable enterprise, though the experience gained at Conway rendered it easy compared with what it otherwise would have
been. Mr Stephenson superintended the operation of floating the
first in person, giving the arranged signals from the top of the tube
on which he was mounted, the active part of the business being
performed by a numerous corps of sailors, under the immediate
direction of Captain Claxton. Thousands of spectators lined the
shores of the Strait on the evening of 19 June 1849. On the land
attachments being cut, the pontoons began to float off; but one of
the capstans having given way from excessive strain, the tube was
brought home again for the night. By next morning the defective
capstan was restored, and all was in readiness for another trial. At
half past seven in the evening the tube was afloat, and the pontoons swung out into the current like a monster pendulum, held
steady by the shore guide-lines, but increasing in speed to almost
a fearful extent as they neared their destined place between the
piers. 'The success of this operation,' says Mr Clark, 'depended
mainly on properly striking the "butt" beneath the Anglesey
tower, on which, as upon a centre, the tube was to be veered round
into its position across the opening. This position was determined
by a 12-inch line, which was to be paid out to a fixed mark from
the Llanfair capstan. The coils of the rope unfortunately overrode
each other upon this capstan, so that it could not be paid out. In
resisting the motion of the tube, the capstan was bodily dragged
out of the platform by the action of the palls, and the tube was in
imminent danger of being carried away by the steam, or the pontoons crushed upon the rocks. The men at the capstan were all
knocked down, and some of them thrown into the water, though
they made every exertion to arrest the motion of the capstan-bars.
In this dilemma Mr Rolfe, who had charge of the capstan, with
great presence of mind, called the visitors on shore to his assistance; and handing out the spare coil of the 12-inch line into the
field at the back of the capstan, it was carried with great rapidity
up the field, and a crowd of people, men, women, and children,
holding on to this huge cable, arresting the progress of the tube,

which was at length brought safely against the butt and veered round. The Britannia end was then drawn into the recess of the masonry by a chain passing through the tower to a crab on the far side. The violence of the tide abated, though the wind increased, and the Anglesey end was drawn into its place beneath the corbelling in the masonry; and as the tide went down, the pontoons deposited their valuable cargo on the welcome shelf at each end. The successful issue was greeted by cannon from the shore and the hearty cheers of many thousands of spectators, whose sympathy and anxiety were but too clearly indicated by the unbroken silence with which the whole operation had been accompanied.'* By midnight all the pontoons had been got clear of the tube, which now hung suspended over the waters of the Strait by its two ends, which rested upon the edges cut in the rock for the purpose at the base of the Britannia and Anglesey towers respectively, up which the tube had now to be lifted by hydraulic power to its permanent place near the summit. The accuracy with which the gigantic beam had been constructed may be inferred from the fact that, after passing into its place, a clear space remained between the iron plating and the rock outside of it of only about three-quarters of an inch!

Mr Stephenson's anxiety was, of course, very great up to the time of performing this trying operation. When he had got the first tube floated at Conway, and saw all safe, he said to Captain Moorsom, 'Now I shall go to bed.' But the Britannia Bridge was a still more difficult enterprise, and cost him many a sleepless night. Afterwards describing his feelings to his friend Mr Gooch, he said: 'It was a most anxious and harassing time with me. Often at night I would lie tossing about, seeking sleep in vain. The tubes filled my head. I went to bed with them and got up with them. In the grey of the morning, when I looked across the Square,† it seemed an immense distance across to the houses on the opposite side. It was nearly the same length as the span of my tubular bridge!' When the first tube had been floated, a friend observed to him, 'This great work has made you ten years older.' 'I have not slept sound,' he replied, 'for three weeks.' Sir F. Head, however relates, that when he revisited the spot on the following morning, he observed, sitting on a platform overlooking the suspended tube, a gentleman, reclining entirely by himself, smoking a cigar, and gazing, as if

---

* *The Britannia and Conway Tubular Bridges*, by Edwin Clark, vol. II, pp. 683–4.
† No. 34, Gloucester Square, **Hyde Park,** where he lived.

indolently, at the aerial gallery beneath him. It was the engineer himself, contemplating his new-born child. He had strolled down from the neighbouring village, after his first sound and refreshing sleep for weeks, to behold in sunshine and solitude, that which during a weary period of gestation had been either mysteriously moving in his brain, or, like a vision – sometimes of good omen, and sometimes of evil – had, by night as well as by day, been flitting across his mind.

The next process was the lifting of the tube into its place, which was performed very deliberately and cautiously. It was raised by powerful hydraulic presses, only a few feet at a time, and carefully under-built, before being raised to a farther height. When it had been got up by successive stages of this kind to about 24 feet, an extraordinary accident occurred, during Mr Stephenson's absence in London, which he afterwards described to the author in as nearly as possible the following words: 'In a work of such novelty and magnitude, you may readily imagine how anxious I was that every possible contingency should be provided for. Where one chain or rope was required, I provided two. I was not satisfied with "enough": I must have absolute security, as far as that was possible. I knew the consequences of failure would be most disastrous to the Company, and that the wisest economy was to provide for all contingencies at whatever cost. When the first tube at the Britannia had been successfully floated between the piers, ready for being raised, my young engineers were very much elated; and when the hoisting apparatus had been fixed, they wrote to me saying, "We are now all ready for raising her: we could do it in a day, or in two at the most." But my reply was, "No: you must only raise the tube inch by inch, and you must build up under it as you rise. Every inch must be made good. Nothing must be left to chance or good luck." And fortunate it was that I insisted upon this cautious course being pursued; for, one day, while the hydraulic presses were at work, the bottom of one of them burst clean away! The crosshead and the chains, weighing more than 50 tons, descended with a fearful crash upon the press, and the tube itself fell down upon the packing beneath. Though the fall of the tube was not more than nine inches, it crushed solid castings, weighing tons, as if they had been nuts. The tube itself was slightly strained and deflected, though it still remained sufficiently serviceable. But it was a tremendous test to which it was put, for a weight of upwards of 5,000 tons falling even a few inches must be admitted to be a very serious matter. That it stood so well was extraordinary. Clark immediately wrote me an account of the circumstance, in which he said, "Thank God, you have been so obstinate. For if this accident had occurred without a bed for the end of the tube to fall on, the whole would now have been lying across the bottom of the Straits." Five thousand pounds extra expense was caused by this accident, slight though it might seem. But careful provision was made against future failure; a new and improved cylinder was provided: and the work was very soon advancing satisfactorily towards completion.'

When the Queen first visited the Britannia Bridge, on her return from the North in 1852, Robert Stephenson accompanied Her Majesty and Prince Albert over the works, explaining the principles on which the bridge had been built, and the difficulties which had attended its erection. He conducted the Royal party to near the margin of the sea, and, after describing to them the incident of the fall of the tube, and the reason of its preservation, he pointed with pardonable pride to a pile of stones which the workmen had there raised to commemorate the event. While nearly all the other marks of the work during its progress had been obliterated, that cairn had been left standing in commemoration of the caution and foresight of their chief.

The floating and raising of the remaining tubes need not be described in detail. The second was floated on 3 December, and set in its permanent place on 7 January 1850. The others were floated and raised in due course. On 5 March, Mr Stephenson put the last rivet in the last tube, and passed through the completed bridge, accompanied by about a thousand persons, drawn by three locomotives. The bridge was opened for public traffic on 18 March. The cost of the whole work was £234,450.

The Britannia Bridge is one of the most remarkable monuments of the enterprise and skill of the present century. Robert Stephenson was the master spirit of the undertaking. To him belongs the merit of first seizing the ideal conception of the structure best adapted to meet the necessities of the case; and of selecting the best men to work out his idea, himself watching, controlling, and testing every result, by independent check and counter-check. And, finally, he organized and directed, through his assistants, the vast band of skilled workmen and labourers who were for so many years occupied in carrying his magnificent original conception to a successful practical issue. As he himself said of the work, 'The true and accurate calculation of all the conditions and elements essential to the safety of the bridge had been a source not only of mental

but of bodily toil; including, as it did, a combination of abstract
thought and well-considered experiment adequate to the magnitude of the project.'

The Britannia Bridge was the result of a vast combination of
skill and industry. But for the perfection of our tools and the
ability of our mechanics to use them to the greatest advantage;
but for the matured powers of the steam-engine; but for the improvements in the iron manufacture, which enabled blooms to be
puddled of sizes before deemed impracticable, and plates and bars
of immense size to be rolled and forged; but for these, the Britannia
Bridge would have been designed in vain. Thus, it was not the
product of the genius of the railway engineer alone, but of the
collective mechanical genius of the English nation.

CHAPTER XVIII — GEORGE STEPHENSON'S CLOSING YEARS — ILLNESS AND DEATH

IN describing the completion of the series of great works detailed in the preceding chapter, we have somewhat anticipated the closing years of George Stephenson's life. He could not fail to take an anxious interest in the success of his son's designs, and he accordingly paid many visits to Conway and to Menai, during the progress of the works. He was present on the occasion of the floating and raising of the first Conway tube, and there witnessed a clear proof of the soundness of Robert's judgement as to the efficiency and strength of the tubular bridge, of which he had at first expressed some doubts; but before the like test could be applied at the Britannia Bridge, George Stephenson's mortal anxieties were at an end, for he had then ceased from all his labours.

Towards the close of his life, George Stephenson almost entirely withdrew from the active pursuit of his profession. He devoted himself chiefly to his extensive collieries and lime-works, taking a local interest only in such projected railways as were calculated to open up new markets for their products.

At home he lived the life of a country gentleman, enjoying his garden and grounds, and indulging his love of nature, which, through all his busy life, had never left him. It was not until the year 1845 that he took an active interest in horticultural pursuits. Then he began to build new melon-houses, pineries, and vineries, of great extent; and he now seemed as eager to excel all other growers of exotic plants in his neighbourhood, as he had been to surpass the villagers of Killingworth in the production of gigantic cabbages and cauliflowers some thirty years before. He had a pine-house built 68 feet in length and a pinery 140 feet. Workmen were constantly employed in enlarging them, until at length he had no fewer than ten glass forcing-houses, heated with hot water, which he was one of the first in that neighbourhood to make use of for such a purpose. He did not take so much pleasure in flowers as in fruits. At one of the county agricultural meetings, he said that he intended yet to grow pine-apples at Tapton as big as pumpkins. The only man to whom he would 'knock under' was his friend Paxton, the gardener to the Duke of Devonshire; and he was so old in the service, and so skilful, that he could scarcely hope to beat him. Yet his 'Queen' pines did take the first prize at a competition with the Duke, though this was not until shortly after his death, when the plants had become more fully grown. His grapes also took the first prize at Rotherham, at a competition open to all England. He was extremely successful in producing melons, having invented a method of suspending them in baskets of wire gauze, which, by relieving the stalk from tension, allowed nutrition to proceed more freely, and better enabled the fruit to grow and ripen.

He took much pride also in his growth of cucumbers. He raised them very fine and large, but he could not make them grow straight. Place them as he would, notwithstanding all his propping of them, and humouring them by modifying the application of heat and the admission of light for the purpose of effecting his object, they would still insist on growing crooked in their own way. At last he had a number of glass cylinders made at Newcastle, for the purpose of an experiment; into these the growing cucumbers were inserted, and then he succeeded in growing them perfectly straight. Carrying one of the new products into his house one day, and exhibiting it to a party of visitors, he told them of the expedient he had adopted, and added gleefully, 'I think I have bothered them noo!'

Mr Stephenson also carried on farming operations with some success. He experimented on manure, and fed cattle after methods of his own. He was very particular as to breed and build in stock-breeding. 'You see, sir,' he said to one gentleman, 'I like to see the *coo's* back at a gradient something like this' (drawing an imaginary line with his hand), 'and then the ribs or girders will carry more flesh than if they were so – or so.' When he attended the county agricultural meetings, which he frequently did, he was accustomed to take part in the discussions, and he brought the same vigorous practical mind to bear upon questions of tillage, drainage, and farm economy, which he had been accustomed to exercise on mechanical and engineering matters.

All his early affection for birds and animals revived. He had favourite dogs, and cows, and horses; and again he began to keep rabbits, and to pride himself on the beauty of his breed. There was not a bird's nest upon the grounds that he did not know of; and from day to day he went round watching the progress which the birds made with their building, carefully guarding them from injury. No one was more minutely acquainted with the habits of British birds, the result of a long, loving, and close observation of nature.

At Tapton he remembered the failure of his early experiment in hatching birds' eggs by heat, and he now performed it success-fully, being able to secure a proper apparatus for maintaining a uniform temperature. He was also curious about the breeding and fattening of fowls; and when his friend Edward Pease of Darling-ton visited him at Tapton, he explained a method which he had invented for fattening chickens in half the usual time.

Mrs Stephenson tried to keep bees, but found they would not thrive at Tapton. Many hives perished, and there was no case of success. The cause of failure was a puzzle to the engineer; but one day his acute powers of observation enabled him to unravel it. At the foot of the hill on which Tapton House stands, he saw some bees trying to rise up from among the grass, laden with honey and wax. They were already exhausted, as if with long flying; and then it occurred to him that the height at which the house stood above the bees' feeding-ground rendered it difficult for them to reach their hives when heavy laden, and hence they sank exhausted. He after-wards incidentally mentioned the circumstance to Mr Jesse the naturalist, who concurred in his view as to the cause of failure, and was much struck by the keen observation which had led to its solution.

Mr Stephenson had none of the indoor habits of the student. He read very little; for reading is a habit which is generally acquired in youth; and his youth and manhood had been for the most part spent in hard work. Books wearied him, and sent him to sleep. Novels excited his feelings too much, and he avoided them, though he would occasionally read through a philosophical book on a subject in which he felt particularly interested. He wrote very few letters with his own hand; nearly all his letters were dictated, and he avoided even dictation when he could. His greatest pleasure was in conversation, from which he gathered most of his imparted information.

It was his practice, when about to set out on a journey by railway, to walk along the train before it started, and look into the carriages to see if he could find 'a conversable face'. On one of these occasions, at the Euston Station, he discovered in a carriage a very handsome, manly, and intelligent face, which he afterwards found was that of the late Lord Denman. He was on his way down to his seat at Stony Middleton, in Derbyshire. Mr Stephenson entered the carriage, and the two were shortly engaged in interesting conversation. It turned upon chronometry and horology, and the engineer amazed his lordship by the extent of his knowledge on the subject, in which he displayed as much minute information, even down to the latest improvements in watchmaking, as if he had been bred a watchmaker and lived by the trade. Lord Denman was curious to know how a man whose time must have been mainly engrossed by engineering, had gathered so much knowledge on a subject quite out of his own line, and he asked the question, 'I learnt clockmaking and watchmaking,' was the answer, 'while a working man at Killingworth, when I made a little money in my spare hours, by cleaning the pitmen's clocks and watches; and since then I have kept up my information on the subject.' This led to further questions, and then Mr Stephenson told Lord Denman the interesting story of his life, which held him entranced during the remainder of the journey.

Many of his friends readily accepted invitations to Tapton House to enjoy his hospitality, which never failed. With them he would 'fight his battles o'er again', reverting to his battle for the locomotive; and he was never tired of telling, nor were his auditors of listening to, the lively anecdotes with which he was accustomed to illustrate the struggles of his early career. While walking in the woods or through the grounds, he would arrest his friend's attention by allusion to some simple object, such as a leaf, a blade of grass, a bit of bark, a nest of birds, or an ant carrying its eggs across the path, and descant in glowing terms upon the creative power of the Divine Mechanician, whose contrivances were so exhaustless and so wonderful. This was a theme upon which he was often accustomed to dwell in reverential admiration, when in the society of his more intimate friends.

One night, when walking under the stars, and gazing up into the field of suns, each the probable centre of a system, forming the Milky Way, a friend said to him, 'What an insignificant creature is

man in sight of so immense a creation as that!' 'Yes!' was his reply;
'but how wonderful a creature also is man, to be able to think and
reason, and even in some measure to comprehend works so
infinite!'

A microscope, which he had brought down to Tapton, was a
source of immense enjoyment to him; and he was never tired of
contemplating the minute wonders which it revealed. One evening,
when some friends were visiting him, he induced them each to
puncture their skin so as to draw blood, in order that he might
examine the globules through the microscope. One of the gentlemen present was a teetotaller, and Mr Stephenson pronounced his
blood to be the most lively of the whole. He had a theory of his
own about the movement of the globules in the blood, which has
since become familiar. It was, that they were respectively charged
with electricity, positive at one end and negative at the other, and
that thus they attracted and repelled each other, causing a circulation. No sooner did he observe anything new, than he immediately set about devising a reason for it. His training in mechanics,
his practical familiarity with matter in all its forms, and the strong
bent of his mind, led him first of all to seek for a mechanical
explanation. And yet he was ready to admit that there was a
something in the principle of *life* – so mysterious and inexplicable –
which baffled mechanics, and seemed to dominate over and control
them. He did not care much, either, for abstruse mechanics, but
only for the experimental and practical, as is usually the case with
those whose knowledge has been self-acquired.

Even at his advanced age, the spirit of frolic had not left him.
When proceeding from Chesterfield station to Tapton House with
his friends, he would almost invariably challenge them to a race
up the steep path, partly formed of stone steps, along the hillside.
And he would struggle, as of old, to keep the front place, though by
this time his 'wind' had greatly failed. He would occasionally
invite an old friend to take a quiet wrestle with him on the lawn,
to keep up his skill, and perhaps to try some new 'knack' of throwing. In the evening, he would sometimes indulge his visitors by
reciting the old pastoral of 'Damon and Phyllis', or singing his
favourite song of 'John Anderson my Joe'. But his greatest glory
among those with whom he was most intimate, was a 'crowdie!'
'Let's have a crowdie night', he would say; and forthwith a kettle
of boiling water was ordered in, with a basin of oatmeal. Taking a
large bowl, containing a sufficiency of hot water, and placing it
between his knees, he poured in oatmeal with one hand, and stirred

the mixture vigorously with the other. When enough meal had been added, and the stirring was completed, the crowdie was made. It was then supped with new milk, and Stephenson generally pronounced it 'capital!' It was the diet to which he had been accustomed when a working man, and all the dainties with which he had become familiar in recent years had not spoiled his simple tastes. To enjoy crowdie at his age, besides, indicated that he still possessed that quality on which no doubt much of his practical success in life had depended, a strong and healthy digestion.

He would also frequently invite to his house the humbler companions of his early life, and take pleasure in talking over old times with them. He never assumed any of the bearings of a great man on such occasions, but treated the visitors with the same friendliness and respect as if they had been his equals, sending them away pleased with themselves and delighted with him. At other times, needy men who had known him in youth would knock at his door, and they were never refused access. But if he had heard of any misconduct on their part he would rate them soundly. One who knew him intimately in private life has seen him exhorting such backsliders, and denouncing their misconduct and imprudence with the tears streaming down his cheeks. And he would generally conclude by opening his purse, and giving them the help which they needed 'to make a fresh start in the world'.

Mr Stephenson's life at Tapton during his latter years was occasionally diversified with a visit to London. His engineering business having become limited, he generally went there for the purpose of visiting friends, or 'to see what there was fresh going on'. He found a new race of engineers springing up on all hands – men who knew him not; and his London journeys gradually ceased to yield him pleasure. A friend used to take him to the opera, but by the end of the first act, he was generally in a profound slumber. Yet on one occasion he enjoyed a visit to the Haymarket with a party of friends on his birthday, to see T. P. Cooke, in 'Black-eyed Susan' – if that can be called enjoyment which kept him in a state of tears during half the performance. At other times he visited Newcastle, which always gave him great pleasure. He would, on such occasions, go out to Killingworth and seek up old friends, and if the people whom he knew were too retiring, and shrunk into their cottages, he went and sought them there. Striking the floor with his stick, and holding his noble person upright, he would say, in his own kind of way, 'Well, and how's all here to-day?' To the last he had always a warm heart for Newcastle and its neighbourhood.

Sir Robert Peel, on more than one occasion, invited George Stephenson to his mansion at Drayton, where he was accustomed to assemble round him men of the highest distinction in art, science, and legislation, during the intervals of his parliamentary life. The first invitation was respectfully declined. Sir Robert invited him a second time, and a second time he declined: 'I have no great ambition,' he said, 'to mix in fine company, and perhaps should feel out of my element among such high folks.' But Sir Robert a third time pressed him to come down to Tamworth early in January 1845, when he would meet Buckland, Follett, and others well known to both. 'Well, Sir Robert,' said he, 'I feel your kindness very much, and can no longer refuse: I will come down and join your party.'

Mr Stephenson's strong powers of observation, together with his native humour and shrewdness, imparted to his conversation at all times much vigour and originality, and made him, to young and old, a delightful companion. Though mainly an engineer, he was also a profound thinker on many scientific questions: and there was scarcely a subject of speculation, or a department of recondite science, on which he had not employed his faculties in such a way as to have formed large and original views. At Drayton, the conversation usually turned upon such topics, and Mr Stephenson freely joined in it. On one occasion, an animated discussion took place between himself and Dr Buckland on one of his favourite theories as to the formation of coal. But the result was, that Dr Buckland, a much greater master of tongue-fence than Mr Stephenson, completely silenced him. Next morning, before breakfast, when he was walking in the grounds, deeply pondering, Sir William Follett came up and asked what he was thinking about? 'Why, Sir William, I am thinking over that argument I had with Buckland last night; I know I am right, and that if I had only the command of words which he has, I'd have beaten him.' 'Let me know all about it,' said Sir William, 'and I'll see what I can do for you.' The two sat down in an arbour, and the astute lawyer made himself thoroughly acquainted with the points of the case; entering into it with all the zeal of an advocate about to plead the dearest interests of his client. After he had mastered the subject, Sir William rose up, rubbing his hands with glee, and said, 'Now I am ready for him.' Sir Robert Peel was made acquainted with the plot, and adroitly introduced the subject of the controversy after dinner. The result was, that in the argument which followed, the man of science was overcome by the man of law; and Sir William

Follett had at all points the mastery over Dr Buckland. 'What do *you* say, Mr Stephenson?' asked Sir Robert, laughing. 'Why,' said he, 'I will only say this, that of all the powers above and under the earth, there seems to me to be no power so great as the gift of the gab.'*

One Sunday, when the party had just returned from church, they were standing together on the terrace near the Hall, and observed in the distance a railway-train flashing along, tossing behind its long white plume of steam. 'Now Buckland,' said Stephenson, 'I have a poser for you. Can you tell me what is the power that is driving that train?' 'Well,' said the other, 'I suppose it is one of your big engines.' 'But what drives the engine?' 'Oh, very likely a canny Newcastle driver.' 'What do you say to the light of the sun?' 'How can that be?' asked the doctor. 'It is nothing else,' said the engineer, 'it is light bottled up in the earth for tens of thousands of years, light, absorbed by plants and vegetables, being necessary for the condensation of carbon during the process of their growth, if it be not carbon in another form, and now, after being buried in the earth for long ages in fields of coal, that latent light is again brought forth and liberated, made to work as in that locomotive, for great human purposes.'

During the same visit, Mr Stephenson, one evening repeated his experiment with blood drawn from the finger, submitting it to the microscope in order to show the curious circulation of the globules. He set the example by pricking his own thumb; and the other guests, by turns, in like manner, gave up a small portion of their blood for the purpose of ascertaining the comparative liveliness of their circulation. When Sir Robert Peel's turn came, Mr Stephenson said he was curious to know 'how the blood globules of a great politician would conduct themselves'. Sir Robert held forth his finger for the purpose of being pricked; but once, and again, he sensitively shrunk back, and at length the experiment, so far as he was concerned, was abandoned. Sir Robert Peel's sensitiveness to pain was extreme, and yet he was destined, a few years after, to die a death of the most distressing agony.

In 1847, the year before his death, Mr Stephenson was again invited to join a distinguished party at Drayton Manor, and to assist in the ceremony of formally opening the Trent Valley Railway, which had been originally designed and laid out by himself many years before. The first sod of the railway had been cut by the Prime Minister, in November 1845, during the time when Mr

* The above anecdote is given on the authority of Mr Sopwith, F.R.S.

Stephenson was abroad on the business of the Spanish railway. The formal opening took place on 26 June 1847, the line having thus been constructed in less than two years.

What a change had come over the spirit of the landed gentry since the time when George Stephenson had first projected a railway through that district! Then they were up in arms against him, characterizing him as the devastator and spoiler of their estates; now he was hailed as one of the greatest benefactors of the age. Sir Robert Peel, the chief political personage in England, welcomed him as a guest and friend, and spoke of him as the chief among practical philosophers. A dozen Members of Parliament, seven baronets, with all the landed magnates of the district, assembled to celebrate the opening of the railway. The clergy were there to bless the enterprise, and to bid all hail to railway progress, as 'enabling them to carry on with greater facility those operations in connection with religion which were calculated to be so beneficial to the country'. The Army, speaking through the mouth of General A'Court, acknowledged the vast importance of railways, as tending to improve the military defences of the country. And representatives from eight corporations were there to acknowledge the great benefits which railways had conferred upon the merchants, tradesmen, and working classes of their respective towns and cities.

In the spring of 1848 Mr Stephenson was invited to Whittington House, near Chesterfield, the residence of his friend and former pupil, Mr Swanwick, to meet the distinguished American, Emerson. Upon being introduced, they did not immediately engage in conversation; but presently Stephenson jumped up, took Emerson by the collar, and giving him one of his friendly shakes, asked how it was that in England we could always tell an American? This led to an interesting conversation, in the course of which Emerson said how much he had been everywhere struck by the haleness and comeliness of the English men and women; and then they diverged into a further discussion of the influences which air, climate, moisture, soil, and other conditions exercised upon the physical and moral development of a people. The conversation was next directed to the subject of electricity upon which Stephenson launched out enthusiastically, explaining his views by several simple and striking illustrations. From thence it gradually turned to the events of his own life, which he related in so graphic a manner as completely to rivet the attention of the American. Afterwards Emerson said, 'that it was worth crossing the Atlantic to have seen Stephenson alone; he had such native force of character and vigour of intellect'.

The rest of Mr Stephenson's days were spent quietly at Tapton, among his dogs, his rabbits, and his birds. When not engaged about the works connected with his collieries, he was occupied in horticulture and farming. He continued proud of his flowers, his fruits, and his crops; and the old spirit of competition was still strong within him. Although he had for some time been in delicate health, and his hand shook from nervous affection, he appeared to possess a sound constitution. Emerson had observed of him that he had the lives of many men in him. But perhaps the American spoke figuratively, in reference to his vast stores of experience. It appeared that he had never completely recovered from the attack of pleurisy which seized him during his return from Spain. As late, however, as 26 July 1848, he felt himself sufficiently well to be able to attend a meeting of the Institute of Mechanical Engineers at Birmingham, and to read to the members his paper 'On the Fallacies of the Rotatory Engine'. It was his last appearance before them. Shortly after his return to Tapton, he had an attack of intermittent fever, from which he seemed to be recovering, when a sudden effusion of blood from the lungs carried him off, on 12 August 1848, in the sixty-seventh year of his age. When all was over, Robert wrote to Edward Pease, 'With deep pain I inform you, as one of his oldest friends, of the death of my dear father this morning at 12 o'clock, after about ten days' illness from severe fever.' Mr Starbuck, who was also present, wrote, 'The favourable symptoms of yesterday morning were towards evening followed by a serious change for the worse. This continued during the night, and early this morning it became evident that he was sinking. At a few minutes before 12 today he breathed his last. All that the most devoted and unremitting care of Mrs Stephenson* and the skill of medicine could accomplish, has been done, but in vain.'

George Stephenson's remains were followed to the grave by a large body of his workpeople, by whom he was greatly admired and beloved. They remembered him as a kind master, who was ever ready actively to promote all measures for their moral, physical, and mental improvement. The inhabitants of Chesterfield evinced their respect for the deceased by suspending business, closing their shops, and joining in the funeral procession, which

---

* The second Mrs Stephenson having died in 1845, George married a third time in 1848, about six months before his death. The third Mrs Stephenson had for some time been his housekeeper.

was headed by the corporation of the town. Many of the surrounding gentry also attended. The body was interred in Trinity Church, Chesterfield, where a simple tablet marks the great engineer's last resting-place.

The statue of George Stephenson, which the Liverpool and Manchester and Grand Junction Companies had commissioned, was on its way to England when his death occurred; and it served for a monument, though his best monument will always be his works. The statue referred to was placed in St George's Hall, Liverpool. A full-length statue of him, by Bailey, was also erected a few years later, in the noble vestibule of the London and North-Western Station, in Euston Square. A subscription for the purpose was set on foot by the Society of Mechanical Engineers, of which he had been the founder and president. A few advertisements were inserted in the newspapers, inviting subscriptions; and it is a notable fact that the voluntary offerings included an average of two shillings each from 3,150 working men, who embraced this opportunity of doing honour to their distinguished fellow workman.

But unquestionably the finest and most appropriate statue to the memory of George Stephenson is that erected in 1862, after the design of John Lough, at Newcastle-upon-Tyne. It is in the immediate neighbourhood of the Literary and Philosophical Institute, to which both George and his son Robert were so much indebted in their early years; close to the great Stephenson locomotive foundry established by the shrewdness of the father; and in the vicinity of the High Level Bridge, one of the grandest products of the genius of the son. The head of Stephenson, as expressed in this noble work, is massive, characteristic, and faithful; and the attitude of the figure is simple yet manly and energetic. It stands on a pedestal, at the respective corners of which are sculptured the recumbent figures of a pitman, a mechanic, an engine-driver, and a plate-layer. The statue appropriately stands in a very thoroughfare of working men, thousands of whom see it daily as they pass to and from their work; and we can imagine them, as they look up to Stephenson's manly figure, applying to it the words addressed by Robert Nicoll to Robert Burns, with perhaps still greater appropriateness:

> 'Before the proudest of the earth
>   We stand, with an uplifted brow;
> Like us, thou wast a toiling man –
>   And we are noble, now!'

The portrait included in this volume gives a good indication of George Stephenson's shrewd, kind, honest, manly face. His fair, clear countenance was ruddy, and seemingly glowed with health. The forehead was large and high, projecting over the eyes, and there was that massive breadth across the lower part which is usually observed in men of eminent constructive skill. The mouth was firmly marked, and shrewdness and humour lurked there as well as in the keen grey eye. His frame was compact, well-knit, and rather spare. His hair became grey at an early age, and towards the close of his life it was of a pure silky whiteness. He dressed neatly in black, wearing a white neckcloth; and his face, his person, and his deportment at once arrested attention, and marked the Gentleman.

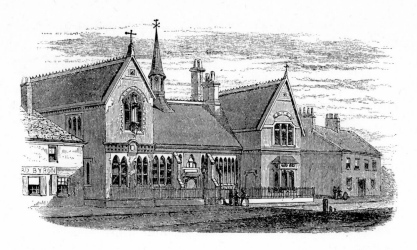

CHAPTER XIX – ROBERT STEPHENSON'S VICTORIA BRIDGE, LOWER CANADA – ILLNESS AND DEATH – STEPHENSON CHARACTERISTICS

GEORGE STEPHENSON bequeathed to his son his valuable collieries, his share in the engine manufactory at Newcastle, and his large accumulation of savings, which, together with the fortune he had himself amassed by railway work, gave Robert the position of an engineer millionaire – the first of his order. He continued, however, to live in a quiet style; and although he bought occasional pictures and statues, and indulged in the luxury of a yacht, he did not live up to his income, which went on rapidly accumulating until his death.

There was no longer the necessity for applying himself to the laborious business of a parliamentary engineer, in which he had now been occupied for some fifteen years. Shortly after his father's death, Edward Pease strongly recommended him to give up the more harassing work of his profession; and his reply (15 June 1850) was as follows: 'The suggestion which your kind note contains is quite in accordance with my own feelings and intentions respecting retirement; but I find it a very difficult matter to bring to a close so complicated a connection in business as that which has been established by twenty-five years of active and arduous professional duty. Comparative retirement is, however, my intention; and I trust that your prayer for the Divine blessing to grant me happiness and quiet comfort will be fulfilled. I cannot but feel deeply grateful to the Great Disposer of events for the success which has

hitherto attended my exertions in life; and I trust that the future
will also be marked by a continuance of His mercies.'

Although Robert Stephenson, in conformity with this expressed
intention, for the most part declined to undertake new business, he
did not altogether lay aside his harness; and he lived to repeat his
tubular bridges both in Lower Canada and in Egypt. The success
of the tubular system, as adopted at Menai and Conway, was such
as to recommend it for adoption wherever great span was required;
and the peculiar circumstances connected with the navigation of
the St Lawrence and the Nile, may be said to have compelled its
adoption in carrying railways across those great rivers.

The Victoria Bridge, of which Robert Stephenson was the
designer and chief engineer, is, without exception, the greatest
work of the kind in the world. For gigantic proportions and vast
length and strength there is nothing to compare with it in ancient
or modern times. The entire bridge, with its approaches, is only
about sixty yards short of *two miles*, being five times longer than
the Britannia across the Menai Straits, seven and a half times
longer than Waterloo Bridge, and more than ten times longer than
the new Chelsea Bridge across the Thames! It has not less than
twenty-four spans of 242 feet each, and one great central span –
itself an immense bridge – of 330 feet. The road is carried within
iron tubes 60 feet above the level of the St Lawrence, which runs
beneath at a speed of about ten miles an hour, and in winter
brings down the ice of two thousand square miles of lakes and
rivers, with their numerous tributaries. The weight of iron in the
tubes is about ten thousand tons, supported on massive piers,
which contain, some six, and others ten thousand tons of solid
masonry.

So gigantic a work, involving so heavy an expenditure – about
£1,300,000 – was not projected without sufficient cause. The Grand
Trunk Railway of Canada, upwards of 1,200 miles in length,
traverses British North America from the shores of the Atlantic to
the rich prairie country of the Far West. It opens up a vast extent
of fertile territory for future immigration, and provides a ready
means for transporting the varied products of the Western States
to the seaboard. So long as the St Lawrence was relied upon, the
inhabitants along the Great Valley were precluded from communication with each other for nearly six months of the year,
during which the navigation was closed by the ice.

The Grand Trunk Railway was designed to furnish a line of
communication through this great district at all seasons; following

the course of the St Lawrence along its north bank, and uniting
the principal towns of Canada. But stopping short on the north
shore, it was still an incomplete work; unconnected, except by a
dangerous and often impracticable ferry, with Montreal, the capital of the province, and shut off from connection with the United
States, as well as with the coast to which the commerce of Canada
naturally tends. Without a bridge at Montreal, therefore, it was
felt that the system of Canadian railway communication would
have been incomplete, and the benefits of the Grand Trunk Railway in a great measure nugatory.

As early as 1846 the construction of a bridge across the St
Lawrence at Montreal was strongly advocated by the local press
for the purpose of directly connecting that city with the then projected Atlantic and St Lawrence Railway. A survey of the bridge
was made, and the scheme was reported to be practicable. A period
of colonial depression, however, intervened, and although the project
was not lost sight of, it was not until 1852, when the Grand Trunk
Railway Company began their operations, that there seemed to be
any reasonable prospect of its being carried out. In that year,
Mr A. M. Ross – who had superintended, under Robert Stephenson, the construction of the tubular bridge over the Conway –
visited Canada, and inspected the site of the proposed bridge,
when he readily arrived at the conclusion that a like structure was
suitable for the crossing of the St Lawrence. He returned to
England to confer with Robert Stephenson on the subject, and the
result was the plan of the Victoria Bridge, of which Robert
Stephenson was the designer, and Mr A. M. Ross the joint and
resident engineer.

The particular kind of structure to be adopted, however, formed
the subject of much preliminary discussion. Even after the design
of a tubular bridge had been adopted, and the piers were commenced, the plan was made the subject of severe criticism, on the
ground of its alleged excessive cost. It therefore became necessary
for Mr Stephenson to vindicate the propriety of his design in a
report to the directors of the railway, in which he satisfactorily
proved that as respected strength, efficiency, and economy, with a
view to permanency, the plan of the Victoria Bridge was un-
impeachable. There were various methods proposed for spanning
the St Lawrence. The suspension bridge, such as that over the
river Niagara, was found inapplicable, for several reasons, but
chiefly because of its defective rigidity, which greatly limited the
speed and weight of the trains, and consequently the amount of

traffic which could be passed over such a bridge. Thus, taking the
length of the Victoria Bridge into account, it was found that not
more than twenty trains could pass within the twenty-four hours,
a number insufficient for the accommodation of the anticipated
traffic. To introduce such an amount of material into the suspension
bridge as would supply increased rigidity, would only be approxi-
mating to the original beam, and neutralizing any advantages in
point of cheapness which might be derivable from this form of
structure, without securing the essential stiffness and strength.
Iron arches were also considered inapplicable, because of the large
headway required for the passage of the ice in winter, and the
necessity which existed for keeping the springing of the arches
clear of the water-line. This would have involved the raising of the
entire road, and a largely increased expenditure on the upper
works. The question was therefore reduced to the consideration of
the kind of *horizontal beam* or *girder* to be employed.

Horizontal girders are of three kinds. The *Tubular* is constructed
of riveted rectangular boiler plates. Where the span is large, the
road passes within the tube; where the span is comparatively
small, the roadway is supported by two or more rectangular beams.
Next there is the *Lattice* girder, borrowed from the loose rough
timber bridges of the American engineers, consisting of a top and
bottom flange connected by a number of flat iron bars, riveted
across each other at a certain angle, the roadway resting on the
top, or being suspended at the bottom between the lattice on either
side. Bridges on the same construction are now extensively used
for crossing the broad rivers of India, and are especially designed
with a view to their easy transport and erection. The *Trellis* or
Warren girder is a modification of the same plan, consisting of a
top and bottom flange, with a connecting web of diagonal flat
bars, forming a complete system of triangulation – hence the name
of 'Triangular girder', by which it is generally known. The merit
of this form consists in its comparative rigidity, strength, lightness,
and economy of material. These bridges are also extensively employed in spanning the rivers of India. One of the best specimens is
the Crumlin viaduct, 200 feet high at one point, which spans the
river and valley of the Ebbw near the village of Crumlin in South
Wales. This viaduct is about a third of a mile long, divided into
two parts by a ridge of hills which runs through the centre of the
valley – each part forming a separate viaduct, the one of seven
equal spans of 150 feet, the other of three spans of the same diameter. The bridge has been very skilfully designed and con-

structed, and, by reason of its great dimensions and novel arrangements, is entitled to be regarded as one of the most remarkable
engineering works of the day.

'In calculating the strength of these different classes of girders,'
Mr Stephenson observed, 'one ruling principle appertains, and is
common to all of them. Primarily and essentially, the ultimate
strength is considered to exist in the top and bottom, the former
being exposed to a compression force by the action of the load, and
the latter to a force of tension; therefore, whatever be the class or
denomination of girders, they must all be alike in amount of
effective material in these members, if their spans and depths are
the same, and they have to sustain the same amount of load.
Hence, the question of comparative merit among the different
classes of construction of beams or girders is really narrowed to the
method of connecting the top and bottom *webs*, so called.' In the
tubular system the connection is effected by continuous boiler
plates riveted together; and in the lattice and trellis bridges by
flat iron bars, more or less numerous, forming a series of struts and
ties. Those engineers who advocate the employment of the latter
form of construction, set forth as its principal advantage the
saving of material which is effected by employing bars instead of
iron plates; whereas Mr Stephenson and his followers urge, that in
point of economy the boiler plate side is equal to the bars, while in
point of effective strength and rigidity it is decidedly superior. To
show the comparative economy of material, he contrasted the
lattice girder bridge over the river Trent, on the Great Northern
Railway near Newark, with the tubes of the Victoria Bridge. In
the former case, where the span is 240½ feet, and the bridge 13 feet
wide, the weight including bearings is 292 tons; in the latter, where
the span is 242 feet, the width of the tube 16 feet, the weight
including bearings is 275 tons, showing a balance in favour of the
Victoria Tube of 17 tons. The comparison between the Newark
Dyke Bridge and the Tubular Bridge over the river Aire is equally
favourable to the latter; and no one can have travelled over the
Great Northern line to York, without noting that, as respects
rigidity under the passing train, the Tubular Bridge is decidedly
superior. It is ascertained that the deflection caused by a passing
load is considerably greater in the former case; and Mr Stephenson
was also of opinion that the sides of all trellis or lattice girders are
useless, except for the purpose of connecting the top and bottom,
and keeping them in their position. They depend upon their connection with the top and bottom webs for their own support; and

since they could not sustain their shape, but would collapse immediately on their being disconnected from their top and bottom members, it is evident that they add to the strain upon them, and consequently to that extent reduce the ultimate strength of the beams. 'I admit,' he added, 'that there is no formula for valuing the *solid* sides for strains, and that at present we only ascribe to them the value or use of connecting the top and bottom; yet we are aware that, from their continuity and solidity, they are of value to resist horizontal and many other strains, independently of the top and bottom, by which they add very much to the stiffness of the beam; and the fact of their containing more material than is necessary to connect the top and bottom webs, has by no means been fairly established.' Another important advantage of the Tubular bridge over the Trellis or Lattice structure, consists in its greater safety in event of a train running off the line, a contingency which has more than once occurred on a tubular bridge without detriment, whereas in event of such an accident occurring on a Trellis or Lattice bridge, it must infallibly be destroyed. Where the proposed bridge is of the unusual length of a mile and a quarter, it is obvious that this consideration must have had no small weight with the directors, who eventually decided on proceeding with the Tubular Bridge according to Mr Stephenson's original design.

From the first projection of the Victoria Bridge, the difficulties of executing such a work across a wide river, down which an avalanche of ice rushes to the sea every spring, were pronounced almost insurmountable by those best acquainted with the locality. The ice of two thousand miles of inland lakes and upper rivers, besides their tributaries, is then poured downstream, and, in the neighbourhood of Montreal especially, it is often piled up to the height of from forty to fifty feet, placing the surrounding country under water, and doing severe damage to the massive stone buildings along the noble river front of the city. To resist so prodigious a pressure, it was necessary that the piers of the proposed bridge should be of the most solid and massive description. Their foundations are placed in the solid rock; for none of the artificial methods of obtaining foundations, suggested by some engineers for cheapness' sake, were found practicable in this case. Where the force exercised against the piers was likely to be so great, it was felt that timber ice-breakers, timber or cast iron piling, or even rubble-work, would have proved but temporary expedients. The two centre piers are eighteen feet wide, and the remaining twenty-two piers fifteen feet; to arrest and break the ice, an inclined plane, composed of great blocks of stone, was added to the upriver side of each pier – each block weighing from seven to ten tons, and the whole were firmly clamped together with iron rivets.

To convey some idea of the immense force which these piers are required to resist, we may briefly describe the breaking up of the ice in March 1858, while the bridge was under construction. Fourteen out of the twenty-four piers were then finished, together with the formidable abutments and approaches to the bridge. The ice in the river began to show signs of weakness on 29 March, but it was not until the 31st that a general movement became observable, which continued for an hour, when it suddenly stopped, and the water rose rapidly. On the following day, at noon, a grand movement commenced; the waters rose about four feet in two minutes, up to a level with many of the Montreal streets. The fields of ice at the same time were suddenly elevated to an incredible height; and so overwhelming were they in appearance, that crowds of the townspeople, who had assembled on the quay to watch the progress of the flood, ran for their lives. This movement lasted about twenty minutes, during which the jammed ice destroyed several portions of the quay-wall, grinding the hardest blocks to atoms. The embanked approaches to the Victoria Bridge had tremendous forces to resist. In the full channel of the stream, the ice in its passage between the piers was broken up by the force of the blow immediately on its coming in contact with the cutwaters. Sometimes thick sheets of ice were seen to rise up and rear on end against the piers, but by the force of the current they were speedily made to roll over into the stream, and in a moment after were out of sight. For the next two days the river was still high, until on 4 April the waters seemed suddenly to give way, and by the following day the river was flowing clear and smooth as a millpond, nothing of winter remaining except the masses of bordage ice which were strewn along the shores of the stream. On examination of the piers of the bridge, it was found that they had admirably resisted the tremendous pressure; and though the timber 'cribwork' erected to facilitate the placing of floating pontoons to form the dams, was found considerably disturbed and in some places seriously damaged, the piers, with the exception of one or two heavy stone blocks, which were still unfinished, escaped uninjured. One heavy block of many tons' weight was carried to a considerable distance, and must have been torn out of its place by sheer force, as several of the broken fragments were found left in the pier.

The works in connection with the Victoria Bridge were begun on 22 July 1854, when the first stone was laid, and continued uninterruptedly during a period of five and a half years, until 17 December 1859, when the bridge was finished and taken off the contractor's hands. It was formally opened for traffic early in 1860; though Robert Stephenson did not live to see its completion.

The tubular system was also applied by the same engineer, in a modified form, in the two bridges across the Nile, near Damietta in Lower Egypt. That near Benha contains eight spans or openings of 80 feet each, and two centre spans, formed by one of the largest swing bridges ever constructed, the total length of the swing-beam being 157 feet, a clear waterway of 60 feet being provided on either side of the centre pier. The only novelty in these bridges consisted in the road being carried *upon* the tubes instead of within them; their erection being carried out in the usual manner, by means of workmen, materials, and plant sent out from England.

During the later years of his life, Mr Stephenson took considerable interest in public affairs and in scientific investigations. In 1847 he entered the House of Commons as member for Whitby; but he does not seem to have been very devoted in his attendance, and only appeared on divisions when there was a 'whip' of the party to which he belonged. He was a member of the Sanitary and Sewage Commissions, and of the Commission which sat on Westminster Bridge. The last occasions on which he addressed the House were on the Suez Canal and the cleansing of the Serpentine. He pronounced the Suez Canal to be an impracticable scheme. 'I have surveyed the line,' said he, 'I have travelled the whole distance on foot, and I declare there is no fall between the two seas. Honourable members talk about a canal. A canal is impossible – the thing would only be a ditch.'

Besides constructing the railway between Alexandria and Cairo, he was consulted, like his father, by the King of Belgium, as to the railways of that country; and he was made Knight of the Order of Leopold because of the improvements which he had made in locomotive engines, so much to the advantage of the Belgian system of inland transit. He was consulted by the King of Sweden as to the railway between Christiana and Lake Miösen, and in consideration of his services was decorated with the Grand Cross of the Order of St Olaf. He also visited Switzerland, Piedmont, and Denmark, to advise as to the system of railway communications best suited for those countries. At the Paris Exhibition of 1855 the Emperor of France decorated him with the Legion of Honour in consideration of his public services; and at home the University of Oxford made him a Doctor of Civil Laws. In 1855 he was elected President of the Institute of Civil Engineers, which office he held with honour and filled with distinguished ability for two years, giving place to his friend Mr Locke at the end of 1857.

Mr Stephenson was frequently called upon to act as arbitrator between contractors and railway companies, or between one company and another, great value being attached to his opinion on account of his weighty judgement, his great experience, and his upright character, and we believe his decisions were invariably stamped by the qualities of impartiality and justice. He was always ready to lend a helping hand to a friend, and no petty jealousy stood between him and his rivals in the engineering world. The author remembers being with Mr Stephenson one evening at his house in Gloucester Square, when a note was put into his hands from his friend Brunel, then engaged in his first fruitless efforts to launch the *Great Eastern*. It was to ask Stephenson to come down to Blackwall early next morning, and give him the benefit of his judgement. Shortly after six next morning Stephenson was in Scott Russell's building-yard, and he remained there until dusk. About midday, while superintending the launching operations, the baulk of timber on which he stood canted up, and he fell up to his middle in the Thames mud. He was dressed as usual, without great-coat (though the day was bitter cold), and with only thin boots upon his feet. He was urged to leave the yard, and change his dress, or at least dry himself; but with his usual disregard of health, he replied, 'Oh, never mind me – I'm quite used to this sort of thing'; and he went paddling about in the mud, smoking his cigar, until almost dark, when the day's work was brought to an end. The result of this exposure was an attack of inflammation of the lungs, which kept him to his bed for a fortnight.

He was habitually careless of his health, and perhaps he indulged in narcotics to a prejudicial extent. Hence he often became 'hipped' and sometimes ill. When Mr Sopwith accompanied him to Egypt in the *Titania*, in 1856, he succeeded in persuading Mr Stephenson to limit his indulgence in cigars and stimulants, and the consequence was that by the end of the voyage he felt himself, as he said, 'quite a new man'. Arrived at Marseilles, he telegraphed from thence a message to Great George Street, prescribing certain stringent and salutary rules for observance in the office there on his return. But he was of a facile, social disposition, and the old associations proved too strong for him. When he sailed for Norway,

in the autumn of 1859, though then ailing in health, he looked a
man who had still plenty of life in him. By the time he returned,
his fatal illness had seized him. He was attacked by congestion of
the liver, which first developed itself in jaundice, and then ran into
dropsy, of which he died on 12 October, in the fifty-sixth year of
his age.* He was buried by the side of Telford in Westminster
Abbey, amidst the departed great men of his country, and was
attended to his resting-place by many of the intimate friends of his
boyhood and his manhood. Among those who assembled round his
grave were some of the greater men of thought and action in
England, who embraced the sad occasion to pay the last mark of
their respect to this illustrious son of one of England's greatest
working men.

It would be out of keeping with the subject thus drawn to a
conclusion, to pronounce any panegyric on the character and
achievements of George and Robert Stephenson. These for the
most part speak for themselves. Both were emphatically true men,
exhibiting in their lives many sterling qualities. No beginning
could have been less promising than that of the elder Stephenson.
Born in a poor condition, yet rich in spirit, he was from the first
compelled to rely upon himself; and every step of advance which
he made was conquered by patient labour. Whether working as a
brakesman or an engineer, his mind was always full of the work in
hand. He gave himself thoroughly up to it. Like the painter, he
might say that he had become great 'by neglecting nothing'. Whatever he was engaged upon, he was as careful of the details as if
each were itself the whole. He did all thoroughly and honestly.
There was no 'scamping' with him. When a workman he put his
brains and labour into his work; and when a master he put his
conscience and character into it. He would have no slop-work
executed merely for the sake of profit. The materials must be as
genuine as the workmanship was skilful. The structures which he
designed and executed were distinguished for their thoroughness
and solidity; his locomotives were famous for their durability and
excellent working qualities. The engines which he sent to the
United States in 1832 are still in good condition; and even the
engines built by him for the Killingworth Colliery, upwards of

* In 1829 Robert Stephenson married Frances, daughter of John Sander-
son, merchant, London; but she died in 1842, without issue, and Mr
Stephenson did not marry again. Until the close of his life, Robert Stephenson was accustomed twice in every year to visit his wife's grave in Hamp-
stead churchyard.

thirty years ago, are working steadily there to this day. All his work was honest, representing the actual character of the man.

He was ready to turn his hand to anything – shoes and clocks, railways and locomotives. He contrived his safety-lamp with the object of saving pitmen's lives, and perilled his own life in testing it. Whatever work was nearest him, he turned to and did it. With him to resolve was to do. Many men knew far more than he; but none were more ready forthwith to apply what he did know to practical purposes. It was while working at Willington as a brakes-man, that he first learnt how best to handle a spade in throwing ballast out of the ships' holds. This casual employment seems to have left upon his mind the strongest impression of what 'hard work' was; and he often used to revert to it, and say to the young men about him, 'Ah, ye lads! there's none o' ye know what *wark* is'. Mr Gooch says he was proud of the dexterity in handling a spade which he had thus acquired, and that he has frequently seen him take the shovel from a labourer in some railway cutting, and show him how to use it more deftly in filling waggons of earth, gravel, or sand. Sir Joshua Walmsley has also informed us, that, when examining the works of the Orleans and Tours Railway, Mr Stephenson, seeing a large number of excavators filling and wheeling sand in a cutting, at a great waste of time and labour, went up to the men and said he would show them how to fill their barrows in half the time. He showed them the proper position in which to stand so as to exercise the greatest amount of power with the least expenditure of strength; and he filled the barrow with comparative ease again and again in their presence, to the great delight of the workmen. When passing through his own workshops, he would point out to his men how to save labour, and to get through their work skilfully and with ease. His energy imparted itself to others, quickening and influencing them as strong charac-ters always do – flowing down into theirs, and bringing out their best powers.

His deportment towards the workmen employed under him was familiar, yet firm and consistent. As he respected their manhood, so did they respect his masterhood. Although he comported him-self towards his men as if they occupied very much the same level as himself, he yet possessed that peculiar capacity for governing which enabled him always to preserve among them the strictest discipline, and to secure their cheerful and hearty services. Mr Ingham, M.P. for South Shields, on going over the workshops at Newcastle, was particularly struck with this quality of the master in his bearing towards his men. 'There was nothing,' said he, 'of undue familiarity in their intercourse, but they spoke to each other as man to man; and nothing seemed to please the master more than to point out illustrations of the ingenuity of his artisans. He took up a rivet, and expatiated on the skill with which it had been fashioned by the workman's hand – its perfectness and truth. He was always proud of his workmen and his pupils; and, while indifferent and careless as to what might be said of himself, he fired up in a moment if disparagement were thrown upon any one whom he had taught or trained.'

In manner, George Stephenson was simple, modest, and un-assuming, but always manly. He was frank and social in spirit. When a humble workman, he had carefully preserved his sense of self-respect. His companions looked up to him, and his example was worth even more to many of them than books or schools. His devoted love of knowledge made his poverty respectable, and adorned his humble calling. When he rose to a more elevated station, and associated with men of the highest position and influence in Britain, he took his place among them with perfect self-possession. They wondered at the quiet ease and simple dignity of his deportment; and men in the best ranks of life have said of him that 'He was one of Nature's gentlemen'.

Probably no military chiefs were ever more beloved by their soldiers than were both father and son by the army of men who, under their guidance, worked at labours of profit, made labours of love by their earnest will and purpose. True leaders of men and lords of industry, they were always ready to recognize and encourage talent in those who worked for and with them. Thus it was pleasant, at the openings of the Stephenson lines, to hear the chief engineers attributing the successful completion of the works to their able assistants; while the assistants, on the other hand, ascribed the glory to their chiefs.

Mr Stephenson, though a thrifty and frugal man, was essentially unsordid. His rugged path in early life made him careful of his resources. He never saved to hoard, but saved for a purpose, such as the maintenance of his parents or the education of his son. In later years he became a prosperous and even a wealthy man; but riches never closed his heart, nor stole away the elasticity of his soul. He enjoyed life cheerfully, because hopefully. When he entered upon a commercial enterprise, whether for others or for himself, he looked carefully at the ways and means. Unless they would 'pay', he held back. 'He would have nothing to do,' he declared, 'with stock-jobbing speculations.' His refusal to sell his name to the schemes of the railway mania – his survey of the Spanish lines without remuneration – his offer to postpone his claim for payment from a poor company until their affairs became more prosperous – are instances of the unsordid spirit in which he acted.

Another marked feature in Mr Stephenson's character was his patience. Notwithstanding the strength of his convictions as to the great uses to which the locomotive might be applied, he waited long and patiently for the opportunity of bringing it into notice; and for years after he had completed an efficient engine he went on quietly devoting himself to the ordinary work of the colliery. He made no noise nor stir about his locomotive, but allowed another to take credit for the experiments on velocity and friction made with it by himself upon the Killingworth railroad.

By patient industry and laborious contrivance, he was enabled, with the powerful help of his son, to do for the locomotive what James Watt had done for the condensing engine. He found it clumsy and inefficient; and he made it powerful, efficient, and useful. Both have been described as the improvers of their respective engines; but, as to all that is admirable in their structure or vast in their utility, they are rather entitled to be described as their Inventors. While the invention of Watt increased the power, and at the same time so regulated the action of the steam-engine, as to make it capable of being applied alike to the hardest work and to the finest manufactures, the invention of Stephenson gave an effective power to the locomotive, which enabled it to perform the work of teams of the most powerful horses, and to outstrip the speed of the fleetest. Watt's invention exercised a wonderfully quickening influence on every branch of industry, and multiplied a thousandfold the amount of manufactured productions; and Stephenson's enabled these to be distributed with an economy and despatch such as had never before been thought possible. They have both tended to increase indefinitely the mass of human comforts and enjoyments, and to render them cheap and accessible to all. But Stephenson's invention, by the influence which it is daily exercising upon the civilization of the world, is even more remarkable than that of Watt, and is calculated to have still more important consequences. In this respect, it is to be regarded as the grandest application of steam-power that has yet been discovered.

The Locomotive, like the condensing engine, exhibits the realization of various capital, but wholly distinct, ideas, promulgated by many ingenious inventors. Stephenson, like Watt, exhibited a power of selection, combination, and invention of his own, by which – while availing himself of all that had been done before him, and superadding the many skilful contrivances devised by himself – he was at length enabled to bring his engine into a condition of marvellous power and efficiency. He gathered together the scattered threads of ingenuity which already existed, and combined them into one firm and complete fabric of his own. He realized the plans which others had imperfectly formed; and was the first to construct, what so many others had unsuccessfully attempted, the practical and economical working locomotive.

Mr Stephenson's close and accurate observation provided him with a fullness of information on many subjects, which often appeared surprising to those who had devoted to them a special study. On one occasion the accuracy of his knowledge of birds came out in a curious way at a convivial meeting of railwaymen in London. The engineers and railway directors present knew each other as railwaymen and nothing more. The talk had been all of railways and railway politics. Mr Stephenson was a great talker on those subjects, and was generally allowed, from the interest of his conversation and the extent of his experience, to take the lead. At length one of the party broke in with – 'Come now, Stephenson, we have had nothing but railways; cannot we have a change and try if we can talk a little about something else?' 'Well,' said Mr Stephenson, 'I'll give you a wide range of subjects; what shall it be about?' 'Say *bird's nests!*' rejoined the other, who prided himself on his special knowledge of this subject. 'Then birds' nests be it.' A long and animated conversation ensued: the bird-nesting of his boyhood, the blackbird's nest which his father had held him up in his arms to look at when a child at Wylam, the hedges in which he had found the thrush's and the linnet's nests, the mossy bank where the robin built, the cleft in the branch of the young tree where the chaffinch had reared its dwelling – all rose up clear in his mind's eye, and led him back to the scenes of his boyhood at Callerton and Dewley Burn. The colour and number of the birds' eggs, the period of their incubation, the materials employed by them for the walls and lining of their nests, were described by him so vividly, and illustrated by such graphic anecdotes, that one of the party remarked that, if George Stephenson had not been the greatest engineer of his day, he might have been one of the greatest naturalists.

His powers of conversation were very great. He was so thoughtful, so original, and so suggestive. There was scarcely a department of science on which he had not formed some novel and sometimes daring theory. Thus Mr Gooch, his pupil, who lived with him when at Liverpool, informs us that when sitting over the fire, he would frequently broach his favourite theory of the sun's light and heat being the original source of the light and heat given forth by the burning coal. 'It fed the plants of which that coal is made,' he would say, 'and has been bottled up in the earth ever since, to be given out again now for the use of man.' His son Robert once said of him, 'My father flashed his bull's eye full upon a subject, and brought it out in its most vivid light in an instant: his strong common sense, and his varied experience operating upon a thoughtful mind, were his most powerful illuminators.'

Mr Stephenson had once a conversation with a watchmaker, whom he astonished by the extent and minuteness of his knowledge as to the parts of a watch. The watchmaker knew him to be an eminent engineer, and asked him how he had acquired so extensive a knowledge of a branch of business so much out of his sphere. 'It is very easy to be explained,' said Mr Stephenson; 'I worked long at watch-cleaning myself, and when I was at a loss, I was never ashamed to ask for information.'

Towards the close of his life he frequently went down to Newcastle, and visited the scenes of his boyhood. 'I have been to Callerton,' said he one day to a friend, 'and seen the fields in which I used to pull turnips at twopence a day; and many a cold finger, I can tell you, I had.'

His hand was open to his former fellow-workmen whom old age had left in poverty. To poor Robert Gray, of Newburn, who acted as his bridesman on his marriage to Fanny Henderson, he left a pension for life. He would slip a five-pound note into the hand of a poor man or a widow in such a way as not to offend their delicacy, but to make them feel as if the obligations were on all his side. When Farmer Paterson, who married a sister of George's first wife, Fanny Henderson, died and left a large young family fatherless, poverty stared them in the face. 'But ye ken,' said our informant, 'George struck in fayther for them.' And perhaps the providential character of the act could not have been more graphically expressed than in these simple words.

On his visit to Newcastle, he would frequently meet the friends of his early days, occupying very nearly the same station, while he had meanwhile risen to almost worldwide fame. But he was no less hearty in his greeting of them than if their relative position had continued the same. Thus, one day, after shaking hands with Mr Brandling on alighting from his carriage, he proceeded to shake hands with his coachman, Anthony Wigham, a still older friend, though he only sat on the box.

Robert Stephenson inherited his father's kindly spirit and benevolent disposition. He almost worshipped his father's memory, and was ever ready to attribute to him the chief merit of his own achievements as an engineer. 'It was his thorough training,' we once heard him say, 'his example, and his character, which made me the man I am.' On a more public occasion he said, 'It is my great pride to remember, that whatever may have been done, and however extensive may have been my own connection with railway development, all I know and all I have done is primarily due to the parent whose memory I cherish and revere.'* To Mr Lough, the sculptor, he said he had never had but two loves – one for his father, the other for his wife.

Like his father, he was eminently practical, and yet always open to the influence and guidance of correct theory. His main consideration in laying out his lines of railway was what would best answer the intended purpose, or, to use his own words, to secure the maximum of result with the minimum of means. He was preeminently a safe man, because cautious, tentative, and experimental; following closely the lines of conduct trodden by his father, and often quoting his maxims.

In society Robert Stephenson was simple, unobtrusive, and modest; but charming and even fascinating in an eminent degree. Sir John Lawrence has said of him that he was, of all others, the man he most delighted to meet in England – he was so manly, yet gentle, and withal so great. While admired and beloved by men of such calibre, he was equally a favourite with women and children. He put himself upon the level of all, and charmed them no less by his inexpressible kindliness of manner than by his simple yet impressive conversation.

His great wealth enabled him to perform many generous acts in a right noble and yet modest manner, not letting his right hand know what his left hand did. Of the numerous kindly acts of his which have been made public, we may mention the graceful manner in which he repaid the obligations which both himself and his father owed to the Newcastle Literary and Philosophical Institute, when working together as humble experimenters in their cottage at Killingworth. The Institute was struggling under a debt of

* Address as President of the Institution of Civil Engineers, January 1856.

£6,200 which seriously impaired its usefulness as an educational agency. Robert Stephenson offered to pay one-half of the sum, provided the local supporters of the Institute would raise the remainder; and conditional also on the annual subscription being reduced from two guineas to one, in order that the usefulness of the institution might be extended. The generous offer was accepted, and the debt extinguished.

Both father and son were offered knighthood, and both declined it. During the summer of 1847, George Stephenson was invited to offer himself as a candidate for the representation of South Shields in Parliament. But his politics were at best of a very undefined sort; indeed his life had been so much occupied with subjects of a practical character, that he had scarcely troubled himself to form any decided opinion on the party political topics of the day; and to stand the cross-fire of the electors on the hustings might have been found an even more distressing ordeal than the cross-questioning of the barristers in the Committees of the House of Commons. 'Politics,' he used to say, 'are all matters of theory – there is no stability in them; they shift about like the sands of the sea: and I should feel quite out of my element among them.' He had accordingly the good sense respectfully to decline the honour of contesting the representation of South Shields.

We have, however, been informed by Sir Joseph Paxton, that although George Stephenson held no strong opinions on political questions generally, there was one question on which he entertained a decided conviction, and that was the question of Free Trade. The words used by him on one occasion to Sir Joseph were very strong. 'England,' said he, 'is, and must be a shopkeeper; and our docks and harbours are only so many wholesale shops, the doors of which should always be kept wide open.' It is curious that his son Robert should have taken precisely the opposite view of this question, and acted throughout with the most rigid party among the protectionists, supporting the Navigation Laws and opposing Free Trade.

But Robert Stephenson will be judged in after times by his achievements as an engineer, rather than by his acts as a politican; and happily these last were far outweighed in value by the immense practical services which he rendered to trade, commerce, and civilization, through the facilities which the railways constructed by him afforded for free intercommunication between men in all parts of the world. Speaking in the midst of his friends at Newcastle, in 1850, he observed:

'It seems to me but as yesterday that I was engaged as an assistant in laying out the Stockton and Darlington Railway. Since then, the Liverpool and Manchester and a hundred other great works have sprung into existence. As I look back upon these stupendous undertakings, accomplished in so short a time, it seems as though we had realized in our generation the fabled powers of the magician's wand. Hills have been cut down and valleys filled up; and when these simple expedients have not sufficed, high and magnificent viaducts have been raised, and if mountains stood in the way, tunnels of unexampled magnitude have pierced them through, bearing their triumphant attestation to the indomitable energy of the nation, and the unrivalled skill of our artisans.'

As respects the immense advantages of railways to mankind, there cannot be two opinions. They exhibit, probably, the grandest organization of capital and labour that the world has yet seen. Although they have unhappily occasioned great loss to many, the loss has been that of individuals; while, as a national system, the gain has already been enormous. As tending to multiply and spread abroad the conveniences of life, opening up new fields of industry, bringing nations nearer to each other, and thus promoting the great ends of civilization, the founding of the railway system by George Stephenson and his son must be regarded as one of the most important events, if not the very greatest, in the first half of this nineteenth century.

Set in 11 point 'Monotype' Modern Extended leaded 1 point
with Scotch Roman for display
and printed by Richard Clay (The Chaucer Press) Ltd,
Bungay, Suffolk
on Fineblade Cartridge paper.
The line blocks made by
V. Siviter Smith & Co. Ltd, Birmingham.
The colour plates printed lithographically
by Alabaster Passmore & Sons Ltd, Maidstone, Kent.
Bound in Red Bridge Bookcloth
by W. & J. Mackay Ltd, Chatham, Kent

Victoria Bridge